D0788326

THE FORGOTTEN
PEOPLE OF
THE PACIFIC

.

PHILIPPE DIOLÉ

THE FORGOTTEN PEOPLE OF THE PACIFIC

Translated from the French
by J. F. Bernard

BARRON'S/WOODBURY, NEW YORK

Les Oubliés Du Pacifique
© Flammarion, 1976

First U.S. Edition

International Standard Book Number: 0-8120-5129-7

Library of Congress Catalog Card Number: 77-6830

Library of Congress Cataloging in Publication Data
Diolé, Philippe.
  The forgotten people of the Pacific.
  Translation of Les oubliés du Pacifique.
  Bibliography: p.
  Includes index.
  1. Ethnology—Melanesia. 2. Melanesia—Description and travel. I. Title.
GN668.D5613 1977 993 77-6830
ISBN 0-8120-5129-7

PRINTED IN FRANCE

CONTENTS

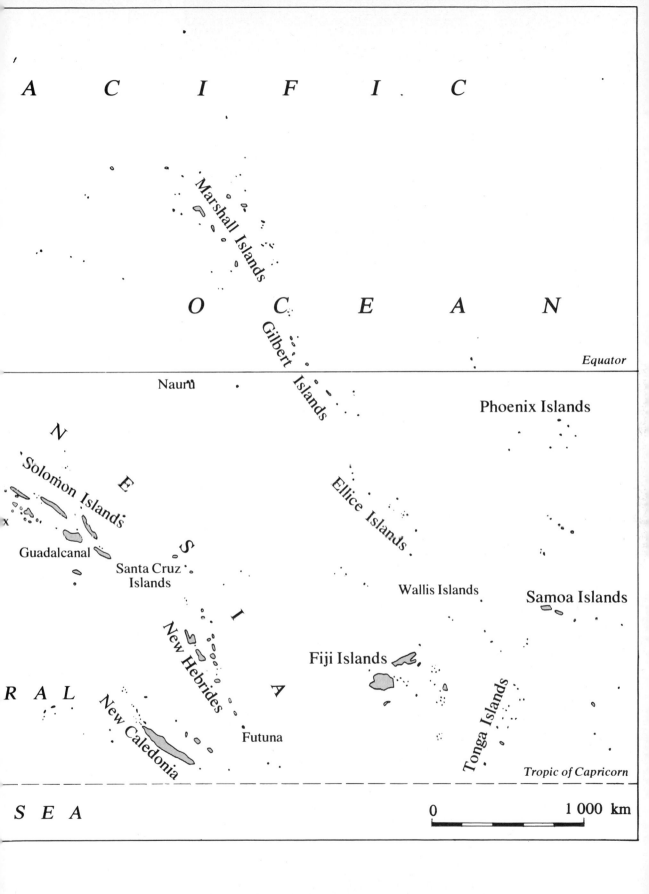

A C I F I C

Marshall Islands

O C E A N

Gilbert Islands

Equator

Nauru

Phoenix Islands

N

E

Solomon Islands

Ellice Islands

S

Guadalcanal

Santa Cruz
Islands

Wallis Islands

Samoa Islands

I

New Hebrides

A

Fiji Islands

Tonga Islands

R A L

New Caledonia

Futuna

Tropic of Capricorn

S E A

0   1 000 km

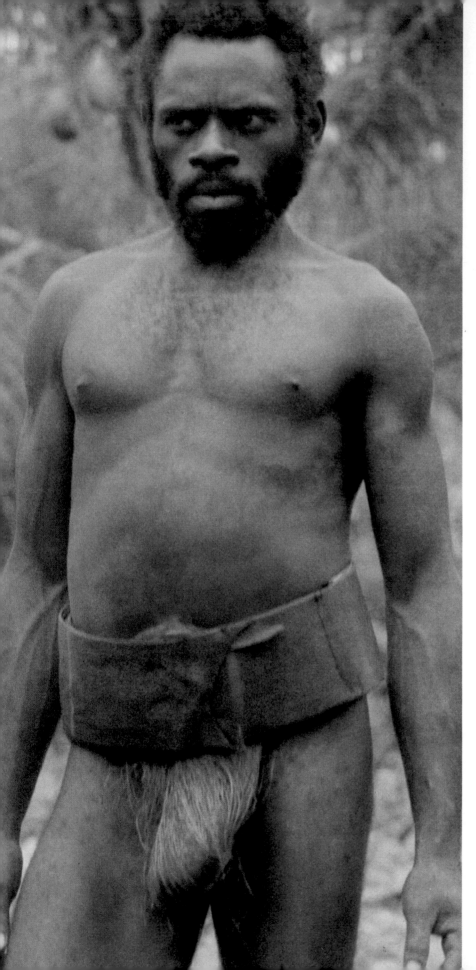

One of the "forgotten men of the Pacific," a Big Nambas of Malikolo Island in the New Hebrides. He is handsome, intelligent—and very cautious. Living in the isolation of the mountains, he is determined not to surrender his nudity or the *namba*, the reddish loincloth made of fiber and held in place by a wide tree-bark belt. The Big Nambas embodies the entire human drama of the South Pacific.

1

the feathered warriors of New Guinea

Every man regards as "barbaric" that which is contrary to his own customs.

MONTAIGNE

The plane turned, sputtered briefly, then, righting itself, began its slow descent. It seemed overheated, torpid, like a horse that has been held at the gallop beyond its strength.

Below, the gray-blue fabric of the sea separated, exhibiting streaks of emerald, the violet tincture of deep water, and the clear, sandy bottom surrounding atolls* and lagoons. The southern seas; the silken iridescence of Oceania. We had finally arrived.

Of the rest of Asia, I had seen practically nothing from the air. Clouds were everywhere, and the flight had been a night comprising several days. Bahrain slept, bright in the flares of its oil wells. Singapore slept, indifferent to the gales that shook its houses. Djakarta slept, lulled by the rain. At times, it seemed that only the plane was alive: a luminous box transporting bits of humanity from one end of the earth to the other, above jungles and deserts, over peaks rising out of the impenetrable darkness.

Three times we had changed crews, and three times we had been welcomed by a new contingent of stewardesses, fresh as flowers in the dawn.

The mysterious Orient; it is no longer easy to find. There are times when I suspect that it no longer exists. It is, in fact, no more than a fragment of savagery, hovering like a fog over the high places of a few islands where naked men still nurse a long memory of the taste of human flesh. That is all that remains; that fragment is what I saw 25,000 feet beneath the plane.

---

*Many terms are explained in the Glossary appearing at the end of the book, where they appear in alphabetical order.

Geographically, the space on which my hopes centered lay between 120° and 170°: from the Makassar Strait, across the Banda Sea, the Arafura Sea, and the Coral Sea to the tiny country of Tonga. Several thousand miles of sea and islands that are still the stuff of which dreams are made. Indeed, it remains mankind's richest preserve of dreams. And it is the subject and the purpose of this book.

The material herein is the result of several voyages and visits to New Guinea, the New Hebrides, the Solomon Islands and the Fiji Islands, as well as to several other archipelagoes of the South Seas. The element common to all these islands, and the basis for relating my observations in a single volume, is that they have all remained on the very fringe of the modern world. Not even World War II, which fell upon them like a hurricane of fire and steel, was able to tear them from the past.

There is another common point: all the islands are the home of headhunters and artists, of farmers rather than of fishermen. One would expect that a people who live literally surrounded by the sea would, quite naturally, be solely a fishing folk. Paradoxically, that is not the case. Everything seems ordered by nature to enable men to live—as they do in Polynesia—from the sea and in the sea. The shores and banks are broad and easily accessible; the waters are warm; fishes and mollusks abound. Yet, the Melanesians seem deliberately to have rejected this proferred abundance. They have turned their backs on the sea and withdrawn onto the mountains and into the jungles, where everything seems designed to reject mankind.

The intense religiosity of the people of the islands is also a common factor. These are lands characterized by magical practices, by a supernatural approach to agriculture, by communication with the hereafter, and by intimacy with the dead.

The largest by far of these isles of mystery is New Guinea which, within its narrow valleys, shelters the treasured skulls of ancestors hidden in cathedrals of tree bark. It is on New Guinea that Oceanic art has achieved its apex. It is an art that has found its inspiration in magic, in agriculture, and in the slaughter of humans; an art of ritualistic cannibalism, practiced by inhabitants of the jungles, far from the lagoons. Even today, the Papuans of New Guinea have not lost their creativity. They are still capable of weaving myths and of devising religious systems such as the extraordinary "cargo cult," which is at once a political statement, a religious expression, and a social creation.

The islands of the South Seas lie in that tropic zone that circles the earth like a belt woven of jungles, heat, and rain. It is a land of impenetrable greenery, of mango trees and gigantic banyans and orchids, of corals, of coconut palms swaying in the sand, of sharks preying in crystal waters. These are the aspects of it that one sees in deodorant commercials and travel films, where even the sharks from the Gulf of Tadjoura to the island of Maupiti are indistinguishable one from the other. This is the "terrestrial paradise" of myth and legend. The reality is far from paradise. The exuberance of tropical growth, the unending rains, the absence of metals, and the scarcity of both wild and domestic animals make human life difficult at best. A great ethnographer, Bronislaw Malinowski, has noted "the apparent futility of the human effort expended in an effort to control the overwhelming power of tropical vegetation," and of the impenetrable density of the undergrowth and the vines of the tropics.

The climate itself is no less an unsuperable obstacle to human well-being. It is, in fact, more reminiscent of Hades than of Eden, with its unbearable combination of heat and humidity. Then there are the waterspouts, the hurricanes, the tornadoes—and even the rain, which transforms paths into rivers of mud and streams into impassable torrents.

Louis-Antoine de Bougainville, one of the great explorers of the Pacific islands, spent only ten days on the island of Tahiti. But that short span was sufficient to awaken such illusions in the Western mind as to make us renounce, forever, this sort of vicarious, duty-free exoticism. It was mere chance that in a few instances—the island kingdom of Queen Pomare, for example—fact was even stranger than the fictions that grew out of Bougainville's expedition to Tahiti, to say nothing of the other visits he made during his trek westward across the Pacific. One of these ports of call was an archipelago that Bougainville christened "the Grand Cyclades," which was also visited later by Captain James Cook and by Count de La Pérouse. Cook, when he stopped there, gave a new name to the islands: the New Hebrides.

Strangely enough, there was no follow-up to these discoveries. There were no colonists dispatched from France or England. There was no upheaval in the life of the inhabitants of these islands. The only trace of the explorers that remained was a name (and not a very euphonic one) that came to be applied to this area of the Pacific: *Melanesia*, meaning the country of black men, the peoples whom Jean Guiart has called the "unloved tribes of the Pacific." It would perhaps be more accurate to call them the forgotten tribes of the Pacific; tribes placed in quarantine because of their rather terrifying reputation in Europe. If it is true that eighteenth-century Europe had fallen under the spell of Jean Jacques Rousseau's "noble savage," it is equally true that, in the nineteenth century, Europeans came to regard "savages" as evil—as dark-skinned barbarians who feasted on the flesh of missionaries and slaughtered brave pioneers.

It was an injustice—but a felicitous injustice. The result of this quarantine was that Melanesia survived intact. It remained a world unto itself, hedged in between two other worlds; a blank space in the geography of exoticism. Between New Guinea and the immensity of the Polynesian Pacific, Melanesia, the home of terrible savages, was able to preserve its elaborate secret societies, its magical rites, its genital sheaths, and an art which challenges the best that the Western world has produced. The Polynesians[1] can no longer lay claim to being the world's only interesting savages. And the purpose of my visit to Melanesia was to see whether these Papuans, the last habitually nude people on the face of the earth, a race of former headhunters and cannibals, still deserve their reputation.

Port Moresby

The first thing I did, as soon as the plane landed, was to dive into the waters off Port Moresby. I wanted to wash off the dust of Europe and Asia. And I also

---

[1]The Polynesians, in fact, were every bit as cannibalistic as the Melanesians and took equal delight in the flesh of the "long pig," as the white man was called.

wanted to attain that state of self-renewal that always comes when I experience the freshness of the sea's landscape from behind a diver's mask. It mattered little that the water was rough; the coral, blackish and moribund; the bottom, muddy.

Port Moresby is a place of considerable size. It stretches along the shore of a bay. There are usually women in the water, throwing their nets—sometimes in water up to their necks. There are a few old motor barges in deeper water, and, of course, the ubiquitous pirogues (a type of canoe). It was late in the morning, and the heat was already stifling in its dampness. There was no relief anywhere; not even in the shade of the filao trees which sheltered a few ice-cream vendors and several large American cars. My skin dried as soon as I got out of the water, and then almost immediately was covered with perspiration. Another world, another climate. I would have to learn to live with it.

A man passed carrying a spear, on his way to fish from a pile of rocks that I saw further along the shore. I decided to follow him. Near the rocks, the water was clearer. There were sharks here, the fisherman warned me.

Crocodiles, and specifically marine crocodiles, are a part of my childhood memories. I knew them from having read the books of Reverend André Dupeyrat, *Twenty Years Among the Papuans* and *The Beast and the Papuans*. Father Dupeyrat, obviously, had not spent those twenty years at Port Moresby, but along the same coast of New Guinea, and also to the west on Yule Island and Port Leon. At Port Leon, I was told, there were still man-eating crocodiles, some of them twenty-five feet long. Dupeyrat's tales of his encounters with these monsters are one of the vivid recollections of my youth.

There are very few islands the coasts of which are guarded by marine crocodiles. These enormous reptiles generally lie in wait at the mouths of rivers and streams flowing out from the thick growths of mangrove. The redundancy of nature is sometimes astounding. It is not as though sharks, poisonous fishes, and stingrays were inadequate to defend these tiny islands from intruders.

My fisherman friend did not succeed in flushing out a crocodile; but he did turn up an octopus of respectable size. With this specimen impaled upon his spear, he and I returned to the city, walking along the beach side by side, barefoot. On the other side of the trees which lined the main avenue of Port Moresby, I could hear the sounds of traffic, the roar of bus engines, the horns of automobiles. I reflected that, while the body of water at our side, glistening in the noonday sun, might be called the Gulf of Papua, this was not the place to find Papuans. There was not a sign of the Papuans that I wanted to see. In the city, they dress like everyone else, in shorts and Japanese-made T-shirts.

Papua

The adjective *Papuan*—a word which once triggered youthful dreams of adventure in exotic lands—is applied indiscriminately to most of the natives of New Guinea. It derives from a Malaysian word, *papuwah*, which means, simply, "friz-

The islands of the Pacific do not all have the same geological formation. Some islands are coral and some, of volcanic origin. The upper photograph is a view of the Vaté lagoon in the New Hebrides. The lower shows the volcano on Tanna Island, also in the New Hebrides.

zy'' or ''kinky.'' As to where the Papuans originated and who they are precisely, nothing definite is known, and there are many opinions.

There are today between 800,000 and 1,000,000 Papuans, all of whom are land-dwellers and none of whom, paradoxically, are seafaring people. Despite the fact that they speak some 360 distinct dialects[1], modern-day Papuans are a cohesive political force in New Guinea and, they are a force with which the islands' newly established government must reckon.

Papua, in a political sense, comprises only the southeastern part of New Guinea, including the Fly Valley. In 1906, it became an Australian protectorate. After World War I, the League of Nations also turned over to Australia the former German colony of East New Guinea.

New Guinea attained independence on September 16, 1975. Australian influence, however, remains paramount; unfortunately, the Australian dollar is still the decisive factor in the internal affairs of the new nation.

"The restricted area"

For a traveler like myself, the golden rule in New Guinea is to flee the cities and to go into the bush, the latter being not only more instructive but also much less expensive. My hotel in Port Moresby, for instance, was indistinguishable from any in Sydney or Melbourne. It was full of well-fed Australians arguing loudly over business lunches.

Port Moresby, to me, was nothing more than a gateway to the real world of New Guinea. I could hardly wait to launch out into the interior of the island, into that awesome, mountainous mass, with its perilous jungles and its hidden tribes of former headhunters and reformed cannibals whose reputation had so long been the terror of the west.

Until 1960, a large part of the interior of New Guinea was classified as ''restricted,'' uncontrolled by the Australian authorities, forbidden to travelers. It was in that restricted area that Pierre D. Gaisseau encountered naked tribesmen who had never before laid eyes on a white man. What, I wondered, would I find there now? A country spoiled by tourists? Tribesmen reformed—which is to say, deformed—by governmental restrictions and missionaries?

At dawn, I left Port Moresby behind, with its incredibly costly taxis, its interminable avenues, and its prosperous Australians.

The Asaro valley

The flight to Goroka, in the heart of the highlands, took two hours. We flew over valleys of unbelievable greenness and over hills whose vegetation ended sharply at landslides of ochre earth. The skies were as diverse as the landscape

---

[1]"We know what a culture is," writes anthropologist Claude Levi-Strauss, "but we do not know what a race is." We might even question whether we indeed know what a culture is.

below: black clouds gathered over the mountains, hiding them momentarily and then separating to give passage to the sun. It was a tornado sky over an equatorial jungle. On the crests of the hills I could distinguish a clearing, like a wound in the dense greenery. A few moments later, I could see huts in the clearing.

I thought of Africa.

My neighbor on the plane turned to me. "Looks like Switzerland, doesn't it?" he commented.

Dear God, I prayed, please don't let it be like Switzerland. . . .

The mountain chain grew more dense, more formidable. Some of the peaks of New Guinea are over 12,000 feet high and are covered with eternal snow. Our small aircraft, bucking and snorting, rose valiantly above the clouds. . . .

One can only imagine what an obstacle the topography of New Guinea is to the white man. It is not surprising that the "restricted area" survived until recently—or that, in fact, there are still vast tracts where the white man has never set foot.

It was not until 1914, at the beginning of World War I, that the Germans began to penetrate into the interior of their colony of East New Guinea; and it was not until 1927, under Australian sponsorship, that a link was established between the valley of the Fly River and that of the Sepik, thereby establishing communication for the first time with the inhabitants of the highlands. For these highlands are the central bastion of New Guinea, the home of tribes which until recently, were untouched by the outside world.

The solitude of the highlanders was violated, as so often happens both in fact and in fiction, by the search for gold. In 1933, Australian prospectors penetrated the mountains and discovered a succession of valleys, some of them empty, but others populated by tribes existing in a state of continual guerrilla warfare. These first explorers were struck by the uniforms of these Papuan warriors: their feathered headdresses, which varied from tribe to tribe. They were also struck by the fact that, whatever time was not spent in warfare was spent in organizing dances, ceremonies, and feasts. And, finally, they observed that the Papuans were devoted and enthusiastic cannibals. After this initial contact, the highlands remained isolated and virtually unknown until shortly after World War II.

The plane plunged downward suddenly toward a wide, grass-carpeted valley studded with clumps of trees. I saw Goroka ahead.

The town, until quite recently, was hardly more than an outpost of progress; an administrative and commercial headquarters manned by a half-dozen Europeans, situated in a spot of breath-taking beauty in the valley of the Asaro River, at an altitude of some 6,000 feet.

Despite Goroka's recent development, it is still more or less inaccessible by road; so much so that almost everything in the town—tools, furniture, and even machinery—is brought in by air. The other settlements in the area, such as Kainantu, Chimbu, and Okapa, remain nothing more than outposts in the brush, lacking virtually all the amenities of life.

One of the reasons for the slow development of this region is that it is closed to prospectors. There is some gold here (a few comparatively modest veins) but their exploitation is reserved for the local inhabitants.

The warriors of Papua New Guinea would never think of being seen in public without their bows and arrows.

This lady lives in the vicinity of Port Moresby. She is in holiday attire.

Civilized savages

I had come thousands of miles in order to see the "forgotten men of the Pacific." And I had come to the right place. But my dreams were inadequate as preparation for reality. I stood there, marveling like a child.

It is true that the Papuans wear the tusk of a boar in the membrane that separates their nostrils. It is true that they are more or less naked. It is true that in their bushy hair, they wear hibiscus flowers, or the tail feathers of a sacred bird, the bird of paradise.

There were so many of them, all equally gorgeous in their finery, that it occurred to me (although only for a moment), that it was a spectacle organized solely in order to attract tourists, except that no Chamber of Commerce could ever have conceived such a display.

Yet, I soon discovered that, far from being costumed actors, the Papuans were simply being themselves. The arrival of the white man, the advent of "civilization"—these things, to the Papuans, were not events that substantially affected their lives. This is not to say, however, that the Papuans are not astonished by the white invasion. It occurred to me that their surprise is not unlike that of the Pompeiians who looked up one day and saw the ashes of Mount Vesuvius falling upon their city—and with much the same effect. We can observe Pompei today very much as it was two thousand years ago. Similarly, we can observe the Papuans virtually as they were before the first European set foot on New Guinea. Or can we?

They stand there, between Goroka's gasoline station and its drugstore, smiling vaguely as though to say, "Being a real savage is the easiest thing in the world."

One of these splendid creatures held out a stone axe. I took it, looked at it carefully. The head of it was a sharp stone, attached by a length of vine to a wooden handle. It was something from the Stone Age, except that it had probably been made only a few weeks before. Was it truly so easy to be a "real" savage? I was beginning to have my doubts. It is difficult to say at what point a man ceases being "wild" and becomes domesticated. There is no doubt, however, that the process of domestication has begun in New Guinea. At practically every step of my venture into the highlands, I saw evidence of it.

The Wahgi, for example, a warrior race of the valley, still are beplumed and caparisoned in dazzling colors, and they still perform the ceremonial dances that have been part of their culture for uncounted centuries. Yet now they dance them for the edification of visitors, after endless haggling over price, terms, and conditions with tourist guides. Every tourist office has its own favorite tribe of headhunters; and every busload of forty or fifty tourists is treated, by prearrangement, to a dance.

Australians are formidable businessmen. They know how to mount a spectacle for the benefit of visitors and how to turn a profit from the spectacle. But, one wonders, do they also know how to share the profit with those who perform in the spectacle?

A good part of the fascination of these "shows" lies in the elaborate dress of the participants. We cannot call them "costumes." Here is an excerpt from my notes on the importance of dress among the Papuans:

"Here, everything demonstrates that dress is a very serious matter indeed. I've witnessed the same phenomenon in Mexico, in Brazil, in Africa. But what splendor there is here in that demonstration! Every one of these magnificent warriors seems to have, as his sole aim, to stress the human value of decoration.

"Among the cannibals, we meet models of courtesy who comb and decorate themselves as naturally as they walk or talk. A houseboy would not think of sweeping the house in the morning before he had picked a fresh hibiscus and arranged it in his hair. The bus driver would feel indecent without a plume on his head. One particular ornament seems to play a particularly important role. It is a large crescent-shaped piece of mother-of-pearl, highly polished, which is worn either around the neck or around the chin, like a surrogate beard. It is held in place by links attached to the earlobes; surely a most uncomfortable arrangement. This crescent is the *kuna,* and it is worn even by children. It serves both as an ornament and as money; and it achieves its most striking effect when one sees it worn in combination with the red-banded cape of the local guard corps.

"To the casual observer, none of this is anything more than elaborate costuming, ideal for photographs to show the folks back home. Actually, far from being actors' costumes, the *kuna* and feathers and headdresses and paints are all part of a well-defined rite. They symbolize and express a tradition. They serve to demonstrate the link that binds one man to another, to his tribe, and to his ancestors. The plumes and feathers have a religious significance not unlike that of priestly vestments. The earrings, the bones, and other objects worn in the nose are signs and symbols. The entire dress and ornamentation of a tribesman is an art, a religious art. It is also part and parcel of man's preoccupation with becoming someone other than himself while at the same time affirming his membership in the human community. It is therefore obvious that, if ever the Wahgi are forced to give up their paints and their feathered crowns, the delicate balance of their lives will be in serious jeopardy.

"The effort to attain personal elegance seems to absorb all the artistic creativity of the inhabitants of the highlands. Here, we find none of the works of art that are so in abundance elsewhere on the island. Yet, we must admit that painting and decorating one's own body with such ingenuity is, in itself, a mode of expression not unlike sculpture or painting. It is all the more so since the appearance of each of these dazzling warriors is the result of personal creativity."

The warrior virgins

Once the tourist buses have departed, the life of the tribes goes on pretty much as it always has. Watching the dancers, I yearned to know what they were like when left to themselves. This feathered warrior was probably a father who

Double page following: In Makehuku, a village in the Asaro valley, the menfolk smear their bodies with mud and wear bizarre masks as they dance in the dim light of the jungle.

A mask from the valley of the Keram River, which is a tributary of the Sepik. (Collection Philippe Diolé)

played games with his children. And this handsome and graceful dancer—was he the beau of the tribe? The ambiguity of what I saw, I confess, disturbed me greatly.

The area around Goroka is inhabited by numerous tribesmen who are, to all appearances, quite content with their lives. Their handsome houses, round with pointed roofs, are usually arranged around a village square. Occasionally, one sees a hangarlike building containing an altar surrounded by bones (the jawbones of swine) and various enigmatic symbols.

I was surprised at the number of women encountered on the road. They were as sumptuously attired as the menfolk, with feathers, collars, necklaces, bracelets, and belts. Their large breasts protruded firmly between their mother-of-pearl necklaces and their high belts. Like the men, they wore bones through their noses; they all carried bows and arrows. These were the unmarried women of the tribe, the "virgin warriors," who, once married, would put aside their feathers and jewels and become more conservative in their dress.

Even the young women, I noted, were of sturdy build, well muscled and without any discernible "figure" in the Occidental meaning of that term. Nor were they frivolous and giggling as we passed them on the road, but instead serious (and perhaps even sullen) in demeanor. These were, to all appearances, women not given to weakness or submission. In the highlands, women are regarded as being of great value—as much as the pigs themselves, who are said to be in direct communication with the spirits of the dead.

At every stop in the road, a number of warriors were waiting. They were never quite sure, however, whether or not our car was the one for which they had been paid to perform. In cases of doubt, they charged one Australian dollar to have their picture taken.

The language barrier proved to be no barrier at all. The Papuans managed to make themselves perfectly well understood in the universal language of the region, pidgin English, which is a mixture of Malaysian and English words. At the present time, there is a pidgin-English crisis in New Guinea. The natives of the island feel that it is a demeaning language, scarcely more than baby talk. (It is not hard to sympathize with them. In pidgin English, for example, *laundry* is "wash-wash.") Still, in a land of countless dialects, it does serve a useful purpose until something better comes along.

The mud-men

The main attraction around Goroka is the dance of the mud-men. It is like a regularly scheduled movie and takes place at Makehuku, a village in the brush of the Asaro valley.

The dance ceremony is deliberate and impressive. It begins when the dancers appear, one by one, from among the trees. Their bodies are smeared with white clay, and their heads are totally covered by a mask. The expression of the mask is invariably tragic; pigs' teeth are used to frame the mouth of the mask.

The dancers advance silently into the clearing with slow, measured steps, shaking the leafed branches in their hands. In the dim light of the jungle, their

The dance of the mudmen probably commemorates an event in the tribe's history, but it is intended above all to celebrate the achievements of the tribe's ancestors.

bodies are grayish rather than white, and they are as supple and insubstantial as ghosts.

Another troop of dancers, also masked and covered with clay, makes its appearance, carrying bows and arrows. The two groups advance toward one another silently. They mingle and begin to move slowly, rhythmically. Gradually, the tempo increases, the mime becomes more frantic, until the climax is reached. Then, in utter stillness, the dancers, still brandishing their bows and arrows and branches, vanish into the trees.

Opinions vary as to the significance of this dance. One school has it that the ceremony commemorates and re-enacts a great victory over the enemies of the tribe which was won by the ruse of lying in ambush overnight in a swamp, covered by mud. Another interpretation is that the gray-white forms of the dancers symbolize the souls of departed ancestors. Actually, these two interpretations are not necessarily contradictory. There is no reason why the ceremony cannot simultaneously commemorate a victory and represent the souls of those who won the victory.

A singular wet-nurse

The road between Goroka and Chimbu leads to the summit of a steep hill from which one looks down upon a seemingly limitless vista of jungle. The tree-tops billow in unending waves of greenery until they are lost in the mists of the horizon. Around us, there were mountain spurs so steep as to appear impassable, some of them 12,000 feet high. As impressive as the mountains were, however, it is the density and continuity of the jungle that truly gives one pause. I could only try to imagine how hostile it must be to human life, and how precarious must be the existence of those who live here. Yet, there are tribes who not only survive in this vastness, but survive in apparent contentment. The primitive road leads through villages of respectable size, built in clearings cut out from the incredible vegetation. The inhabitants' huts are, as usual, placed in a circle around the clearing. I could see well-tended gardens everywhere, carefully fenced.

Every village along the road seemed to be celebrating a holiday of some kind, and all the warriors were wearing long, black cassowary feathers on their heads. The cassowary, a large flightless bird, has been domesticated by some tribes, and, along with the cuscus (a variety of opossum) and the pig, is one of the few fairly common animals (either domestic or wild) found in New Guinea.

I observed a small family group walking alongside the road. The woman was carrying a piglet in her arms. In this area, women nurse their piglets on one breast and their infants on the other. I asked her to let me photograph her, and she agreed willingly. The entire family grouped themselves around her for the occasion. The photograph, quite naturally, included the piglet. Pigs are very highly regarded among the Papuans: they are considered sacred. In fact, they are treated as members of the family, showered with affection, and cared for with great tenderness. When a pig dies, it is mourned as genuinely as a close relative.

The son of a chief

Here is an extract from my diary:

"At noon, we stopped in a clearing for a bite to eat. I picked this particular spot because, as we were coming up the road, I noticed a gathering of some sort which seemed somehow different from the groups I had seen before. What it turned out to be was a rehearsal for a dance. I watched as the dancers put the finishing touches to their make-up and their attire. There was a good deal of running around, shouting, and trying out of some particularly intricate steps. Not very different from a dress rehearsal anywhere. Finally, everyone was ready and in place. The dancers moved forward, waving their branches and bows. . . .

"Their dress was, to say the least, eye-catching. They were wearing gigantic black hats that reminded me of nothing so much as those monstrous turn-of-the-century creations which were so fashionable in Edwardian times, weighted down with fringes and flowers and surmounted by a red plume. The hats were worn on the rear of the head, slanted rakishly to the right, framing the face of the dancers with their cheeks set off by vermillion noses. The features were stiff, immobile, deadly serious. It was bizarre—"creepy," I should say—like seeing a Mafia hit-man masquerading as a clown.

"The dancers' naked bodies were painted with large reddish patches or studded with smaller patches. Some of them had smeared their bodies with a glistening unguent of some kind (probably oil and soot) which gave a tawny cast to their black skin. The unguent caught and reflected every ray of sunlight that filtered through the trees as though the dancers were clothed in polished steel.

"The performers were richly decorated with jewelry. In addition to the usual mother-of-pearl crescent around their chins, one man wore a necklace with a string of pig's teeth hanging down to his waist. At the end of this string were attached several cirular shells that, whenever the dancer moved, tinkled like cymbals.

"There was one exception: a muscular giant who wore neither jewelry nor hat. His chest was covered with black mud, as was his long tree-bark skirt, and he carried a large club that he occasionally shifted from one shoulder to the other. I can only guess what the function was of this formidable personage. Was he a sergeant-at-arms of some kind who was supposed to keep order among the dancers? Or did he represent a mythical character—perhaps the Papuan equivalent of Hercules?

"Occasionally, the dancers took a break from their strenuous rehearsal and stretched out on the ground to rest. When they did, they each placed a wooden support under their necks so as not to disturb or soil their elaborate headdresses. This ingenious device appears to be a necessary accessory, since the arrangement of hats and hair is undoubtedly a lengthy and painstaking process.

"At the beginning of the rehearsal, I had noticed a small boy, perhaps ten or eleven years of age, standing to one side on a rock. His expression, like those of the dancers, was cold, unflinchingly serious; and his eyes seemed to be looking far off into the distance. He held a small spear in his hand. He was wearing a black

This young lady, wearing her very best, is sitting in the marketplace at Chimbu. Her fur piece is of cuscus, a cousin of the opossum.

A young virgin warrior of the Wahgi Valley. She and her male companion are both in full dress. Their headdresses are made of black cassowary feathers.

feathered headdress, and his face was touched with red and white. My impression was that his function was to observe the ceremony but not participate in it. From his demeanor, one might even conclude that the entire rehearsal was staged for his benefit. It occurred to me that he might be the son of a particular dancer who stood out from the others because of his size and the impression of nobility that he gave. And, in fact, when the rehearsal was over, this man took the child by the hand and led him away. Was he the son of the chief, being educated to succeed his father? If so, no doubt the mastery of the ceremonial dance, as well as of the dancers' attire, required a long apprenticeship. I could not help but think of Joash, child-king of the ancient Hebrews, and of Louis XIV, at the same age as this Papuan child, dictating from his throne to the Parliament of Paris.

"The final impression left with me was of the intense seriousness with which this rehearsal was regarded by the Papuans. No doubt, the finished performance is intended for the entertainment of a busload of tourists. Yet, the dancers themselves view the dance with great respect, and it is obvious that, in their eyes, it is far more than an "exhibition" for strangers. Also, the presence of that self-possessed child is as intriguing as it is mysterious. But then, there is so much about the place of children in Papuan society that remains to be explained."

Modeling, New Guinea style

I reached Chimbu at the same time as the inevitable evening monsoon. The warm rain beat densely on the brush for a while, then quite suddenly stopped. The pink light of sunset broke through the clouds, and the entire valley seemed bathed in lavender steam.

The next morning, I went early to the marketplace. In Chimbu, unlike Port Moresby and Goroka, there is little to suggest the presence of the tourist industry. The marketplace itself is protected from sun and rain by a stretch of drooping canvas, under which are crowded both merchants and buyers—the latter having come mostly from the surrounding area down the paths leading from the mountains. Some of the women are completely nude; others wear the ridiculous "mission dress" with its equally ridiculous fringed jacket. Their purchases are carried in a net that hangs down their backs and which is supported by a band on their foreheads. The *billum,* as this net is called, also is used to carry children too young to walk.

The unmarried girls still wear the traditional dress of Papua, which consists of a curtain (one cannot really call it a skirt) of fibers, or a narrow panel of cords, that hangs from the waist to slightly below the knees. In a practical sense, it is more an ornament than a covering, for it moves with every movement of the wearer and conceals little or, in most cases, nothing. Papuans seem to place little

Opposite, upper: A group of dancers wearing ceremonial hats. Their bodies are smeared with mud.

Opposite, lower left: This serious young man seems to be presiding over the dance of the adults. Children are initiated at an early age into the ceremonies of their people.

Opposite, lower right: This dancer is resting. He uses a sturdy forked stick to support his head, so as not to disturb his hat or his coiffure.

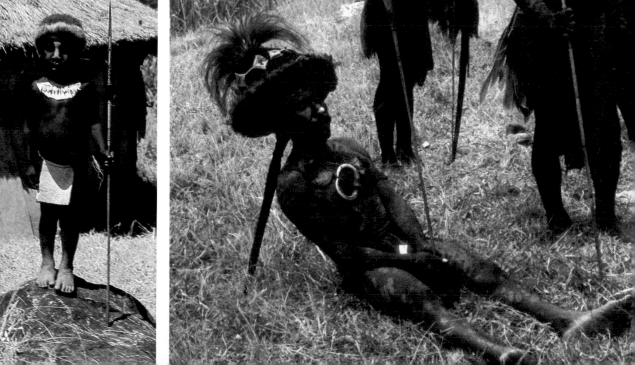

value on premarital chastity, and it is generally believed that unmarried girls participate freely in the sexual life of the community. In any event, their large, well-formed breasts are uniformly bare, and the girls carry themselves in such a way as to display to best advantage what nature has so generously bestowed.

Most of the girls wear around their necks a fur piece of cuscus—the cuscus being an animal similar to and a cousin of the American and Australian opossum—which is peculiar to New Guinea. This fur piece, obviously, is not intended to protect the wearer from the cold. It is worn by almost everyone, men as well as women, and it seems to serve as a status symbol among these people who take great pride in embellishing their bodies without covering themselves.

One of the young women graciously consented to pose for me. Seated on the grass, one leg folded under her, her head slightly to one side, she tried pose after pose with all the professional poise of a model. Even the black and red paint on her face, which gave her a clown's nose and a chimneysweep's cheeks, could not diminish the beauty of her smile.

There were many warriors in the marketplace also. Some of them were there to allow themselves to be seen and admired. Others, like middle-class husbands everywhere, were simply shopping with their wives. Even in their everyday, non-ceremonial decorations, they were like walking shrines. I have no doubt that Papuan men take more time and trouble with their appearance than the vainest of Western women.

Their body makeup is very sophisticated, and it is never quite the same for any two men. It consists chiefly of red, yellow, or black designs outlined in brown. Often, the eyes are circled in white. Astonishingly enough, this extraordinary use of makeup does not, at least in the case of these well-muscled athletes of New Guinea, appear ridiculous in the slightest degree.

The men wear a long netlike skirt secured by a belt, which seems to serve the purpose neither of modesty nor of protection from the elements. Like the skirts of the young women, those of the men constantly expose the wearer, from the muscular, well-articulated thighs to the hips. The feathered headdresses are not worn in the marketplace, but are reserved for ceremonial occasions. The same cannot be said for jewelry. No Papuan male would leave the house without his ornaments. The most striking of these is the nose ornament—a large feather, or a pig's tooth, or a shell—that is passed through the membrane separating the nostrils. Sometimes all three of these objects are worn simultaneously; how they are all held in place is one of the mysteries of the East.

The Papuan's axe is like his jewelry. He is never without it. Until recently, these tools were always of polished stone. Today, they are often of steel and, instead of being made at home, are bought in a village shop. In either case, the axe is suspended from the belt.

When he dresses up, a Papuan warrior attaches mother-of-pearl patches to his belt, which tinkle when he walks. To complete the picture, he adds a tuft of leaves to the small of his back, bracelets on his arms, and a garter above the thigh. When it comes to self-adornment, Papuans are not inclined to resist progress. Necklaces and bracelets of plastic and colored beads made into ornaments of various kinds have been adopted enthusiastically.

The cuscus is a marsupial. It is easily tamed and is a favorite pet among the Papuans.

This young woman is breast-feeding a piglet. Pigs play a major role in Papuan family life. They are believed to be in direct communication with the spirits of the family's ancestors.

Above: Papuan girls are very flirtatious and, until they marry, they are free to live as they wish.
Opposite: The gorgeous headdress of this Wahgi warrior is made of the feathers of birds of paradise.

Captive birds of paradise

I left Chimbu's marketplace (and then only with regret) when the last of the families had departed to return to their mountain villages. Then I left for Nondugl, with the intention of seeing the famous birds of paradise of New Guinea.

The torturous road followed along the Wahgi valley where the population, despite the Chimbu and the Hagen tribes around them, have managed to retain their own peculiar customs and cultures. They are an agricultural people, and they raise excellent yams. They are comparatively prosperous. And they share the craze of their neighbors for personal adornment. One of their practices is to cover their bodies with grease. This serves not only to enhance the appearance of their muscles, but also to protect them from the cold. (In the mountains, the temperature sometimes dips below freezing at night.)

The bird sanctuary at Nondugl is a strange kind of preserve, established to meet a particular need. Its purpose is not to preserve a species of bird, but to exhibit it. The Papuans are vegetarians, and they eat meat very rarely—and then only pork, on great occasions. So, it was not for the sake of the Papuans, or of the birds, that the sanctuary was established, but for that of the tourists.

New Guinea's birds of paradise are extraordinarily beautiful and, like the warrior-dancers, are a great tourist attraction. The tourist industry discovered, however, that the birds were not as docile as the dancers and not nearly so easy to exhibit. Often, the only chance a tourist had to see their gorgeous plumage was on the heads of the dancers.

So that the birds might be readily accessible, they have been caged. Nondugl,

therefore, far from being a "sanctuary," is a zoo. There are forty-five padlocked cages, each one containing a single species of bird of paradise. When tourists arrive, an Australian keeper, rattling a ring of keys like a jailer, opens a cage, enters, and begins waving his massive, red-haired arms. A marvelous form, seemingly composed of all the colors of the dawn, adorned with incredible plummage, rises into the air, flies frantically around the narrow confines of the case, striking itself violently against the wire. This gruesome display continues until the poor bird, exhausted, manages to take shelter in some dark corner of its prison.

The tourists move to the next cage, where the scene is repeated. Forty-five cages: forty-five "exhibits." Hindered by the wire and by the massive form of the keeper, the tourists snap madly away with their cameras. "There it is! Quick, shoot! . . . Make it fly again, please. . . . Use the 135 this time! . . . Hell, I should have used the 500 ASA. . . ."

Such is the relationship today between man and animal on a distant island that is still regarded as half "wild" and partly unexplored.

New Guinea has about 1,000 distinct species of birds; this represents the major part of the island's very limited number of animals. The fauna here is related to that of Australia. There was once a land-bridge connecting New Guinea and Australia, where the Torres Strait is now located. That is why New Guinea has a few representatives of the families of strange animals peculiar to Australia: for example, the echidna and the marsupials. Among the latter, the cuscus (*Phalanger orientalis*), is especially noteworthy. Its fur, so prized by the Papuans, is yellowish-white; its unusually large round eyes convey an expression of simultaneous astonishment and shyness that gives the animal an air of great gentleness—which is probably why it is so popular as a pet in New Guinea. The diet of the cuscus consists exclusively of insects and fruit, and it is primarily a nocturnal animal.

The sing-sing

Mount Hagen today is a town of considerable size; in fact, almost a city. It has retained its ancient role as a gathering place for all the warrior tribes of the region—a sort of prehistoric Papuan capital. It alternates with Goroka as the location of the annual *sing-sing*, which attracts thousands of gorgeously attired warriors who assemble to dance and celebrate in keeping with a centuries-old Papuan tradition. In the course of these festivities, there is much buying and selling and bartering of ornaments.

As one can well imagine, the plummage of the birds of paradise native to New Guinea is a most spectacular decoration and, for that reason, the subject of extraordinarily passionate haggling. (Happily, these transactions take place only among the natives of the island, since the export of plummage is now forbidden.) Bargaining is not restricted to birds of paradise, however. At Mount Hagen, anything that can be used to embellish the human body is the object of the most heated disputes between buyers and sellers. It is true that the most striking ornament is generally regarded as the great black feathers of the cassowary, which are used chiefly in headdresses. But parrot feathers, in tones of pink and yellow, are also in great demand, as are the feathers of the eagle. Even the talons of the eagle are sometimes used as nose-ornaments.

All of these items are more or less readily available in the area, and it is not hard to understand why. They are prized among a people who love self-decoration. Mother-of-pearl, however, which is held in equally high regard, is a different situation. These people inhabit a narrow valley enclosed by mountains and situated far from the coast. How, then, can one explain the fact that, long before the white man opened up even the primitive routes that exist today, the highlanders were passionate collectors of mother-of-pearl? There had never been any means of access to the coast; and the highlanders, of course, had never been a seafaring people. The only plausible explanation appears to be that, despite incessant warfare among the tribes, there was some kind of commercial contact between the highlands and the coast. Probably it was in the nature of a slow passing, from village to village, of the mother-of-pearl that eventually worked its way into the remotest parts of the interior. Even today, when access to the coast is relatively easier, mother-of-pearl has retained its value both as a medium of exchange and as an ornamental item.

Different values are attached to different kinds of mother-of-pearl. This system of valuation is quite well defined, although the gradations are so subtle as to elude the Occidental mind. As far as I was able to make out, the value of a particular piece depends upon such factors as its thickness, the regularity of its surface, and the degree of its brilliance. The true connoisseurs of the Wahgi valley regard certain individual pieces as worth a small fortune. Some of these pieces are quite well known and have histories, as do some famous gems in the West, such as the Koh-i-noor diamond or the Regent. The added value of such pieces is a supernatural one; they are linked to the memory of an ancestor (that is a spirit) . . . another instance in which the connection between attire and the supernatural is evident.

Before leaving the highlands, I made an effort to order my thoughts on what I had seen, particularly with respect to the whole question of dress and ornamentation. There is obviously a status factor involved: the more elaborate the feathers, shells, and makeup of a Papuan, the greater the local rank and importance of the wearer. But it is quite obvious that there is more to it than that. The competition in self-decoration, I have come to believe, is essentially a way for a warrior to distinguish himself now that it is no longer possible for him to be a hero on the battlefield. We do not have to look far for analogies in the West. It was not until the aristocrats of Europe lost their primary function—which was to wage war on behalf of their sovereign—that they turned their attention to silks, jewels, and exotic plumes. If princes and dukes glittered at Versailles, it was because they were no longer allowed to glitter on the battlefield. The splendor of one's dress can be, and quite often is, a substitute for the splendor of one's courage. Decorative attire has a places in warfare. It reflects and memorializes the battlefield; and, in fact, it is the uniform of the latter.

2

the Sepik valley

*The inhabitants of Oceania are the
only people in the world who have
made of aesthetics the most important factor in their lives. This is not
the result of a conscious decision,
or of a rarified culture; for the people of the Sepik, while they are
magnificent artists, live in a state of
savagery. They, however, illustrate
the fact that artistic beauty is experienced before it is conceptual-
ized; that it exists even at the most
primitive level of human life.*
MAURICE LEENHARDT

    It is only forty-five minutes by air from Mount Hagen to the Sepik valley. I
spent every one of those minutes glued to the window of the plane. The mountainous landscape of the area, with its redoubtable peaks and deep, dark valleys, is of
a savage grandeur that defies description.

    Coming down through the saddle of the mountains, we seemed to skim the
treetops. Then, flying between two stretches of dark jungle below, we entered a
cloud-covered valley.

    Flying above one of the slopes, I saw a village directly under one of our
wings. It was so close that I could distinguish gardens among the brush, a few fires
burning, and women looking up at the sky. It was an oasis of humanity in a sea of
jungle green. I could not see a single road or path connecting the village with the
outside world. The growth of vegetation, I thought, was so thick that perhaps
there were trails not visible from the air.

    Suddenly, the mountains separated and the horizon opened. Below us was a

The Sepik is an extraordinarily beautiful river. Like the Nile, it nurtures a population of artists along its
banks.

network of muddy rivers stretching into the brush and the forests. How, I wondered, could there be room for man in such dense growth?

The aircraft began to descend. Ahead, I saw a long course of yellowish water following a limitless maze through the greenery. My eye followed it until the river was lost in the clouds of the distant horizon. The majestic Sepik—a royal river, 750 miles long and 4,500 feet wide.

The Sepik deserves a place among the great historic rivers of the world. Like the Nile, it is one of the artistic highways of the planet. Like the Nile, it nourishes along its banks a race of men who, for centuries, have created both gods and artistic masterpieces. And, like the Nile, the Sepik River carries an enormous alluvial burden to its mouth at the Bismarck Sea—enormous trees and entire floating islands.

The Sepik flows through mountains, jungles, plains, and swamps supporting, along its banks, a population hardened to existence in a hostile environment. The tropical heat, the rains, the crocodiles, and the mosquitoes—nothing has lessened the determination of the hundred tribes populating this inhospitable land to survive.

The Sepik has always been, and is still, the only roadway and only means of communication for the entire region. There is hardly a time when one does not see motorboats, rafts, and hundreds of pirogues plying its waters. The river's course twists and turns like a great yellow serpent; at almost every turn, there is a village, its houses built on pilings. Each tributary contains, within the narrow walls of its valley, a community with its own particular customs. Sometimes, this community has its own language. And, always, it has its own art.

The Asaro valley, from which I had just come, may be described as the Valley of Feathered Warriors. The Sepik, however, is the Valley of Artists, which is not to say that these river-dwellers have not also been, in the past, enthusiastic headhunters.

Today, the region has been pacified. Boats go unmolested up and down and across the river, sometimes skirting, or even passing through, large rose-colored patches of vegetation: *pit pit*—a variety of wild sugarcane. Occasionally, the passage of the boats causes a cloud of birds to rise from among the trees—herons, geese, ducks, and egrets.

The villages that I saw from the air were attractive and neat. The river, while not generous to the point of abundance, does confer a modicum of well-being, simply because it is an opening in the jungle, an opportunity for light to reach the ground and for humans to exist. Below, I could see women in pirogues, either alone or with young children, fishing. In the sterns of these frail canoes, there were small fires, their yellowish smoke rising above the water as the women moved silently to lower or raise their nets. The menfolk were fishing also, but their game was larger fish and, occasionally, crocodiles. They were not using nets, but harpoons. There was a time when the Sepik was infested with crocodiles; but so many have been killed that one never sees them nowadays—except sculpted on the village's drums. The advent of the motorboat and of the rifle marked the end of the crocodiles' domination of the river.

The Iatmül used to carve the bows of their boats in the form of a crocodile's head. They no longer do so; but the reptile still has some religious significance among this tribe, as is apparent particularly in the ceremony by which youths are initiated into manhood.

I could see children splashing in the water, playing among the tufts of *pit-pit*. They would soon know the agony of this initiation. For many of these children living on the banks of the Sepik, the crocodile is the lord of the world of adults; he is the gatekeeper of that world. When the time comes, the child will be placed in a pirogue on the river and will spend the night there, alone. Symbolically, he will be devoured by crocodiles; but, at dawn, he will be reborn—terrified, no doubt, but with proof that he has attained manhood.

Household hooks

The first village I visited was a pleasant place. The square houses, mounted on pilings, were shaded by tall coconut trees bending gently toward the water.

Everything was quiet. It was the time of day when everyone was fishing on the life-giving river. In the entire village, there were only two old men and an old woman, who gladly acted as my guides.

I have never seen in New Guinea a village as neat and clean as this one. The houses were immaculate and every household article was in its place. Hanging from the ceilings were hooks, which serve to keep food out of the reach of children, dogs, and cats. Everywhere along the Sepik, the basic foodstuff is sago, the pulp of a species of palm tree that is God's gift to the region and which grows in the swamps. With flour made from this pulp, one can make a soup or little fried cakes, which are eaten with fried fish. The leaves of the sago tree make excellent roofing material.

Occasionally, one finds the family treasures all together in a net hanging from one of the beams of a house: various shells, a bamboo knife, a dagger made of cassowary bone.

The hooks are raised and lowered by means of a system of pulleys and cords, the latter made of vines. Woven disks, painted red, are strung onto the cords to prevent rats from reaching the food.

These household hooks, practical as they are, also have a religious character in that they watch over and protect the home. In time past, they were used to hang heads. The older hooks are carved in the shape of a human face or of a human or animal body. Today, it would be extremely difficult to find a hook in the village that would qualify as a genuine work of art. Everything has been carried off by traders and merchants. The best pieces however, are displayed in the great museums of the world.

It was at the end of the nineteenth century, when the artists of the West were dividing themselves into cubists, surrealists, and fauvists, that the art of the Sepik peoples was first discovered. It may be said that Oceanic art, even more than African art, introduced into the West what Europeans generally regarded as artistic challenge. The first pieces were hailed, not without some justification, as representative of the best of Oceanic art. This, however, was in an era when very little was known of the extraordinary variety of forms and material familiar to the artists of Oceania: wooden funeral statues, carved house beams, masks, decorated

Fashion dictates that this young belle of the Sepik valley paint her nose red.

Opposite: This inhabitant of the Sepik valley is an artist as well as a planter.

pottery, bark painting, etc. Even so, as a number of experts have pointed out, Africa's art and her civilizations were relatively homogenous when compared to those of Oceania. From the pygmies of the Telefolmin valley, on the frontier between Papua and Irian, to the banks of the Middle Sepik where live the players of the sacred flute, to the Lower Sepik valley inhabited by the headhunting Mundugumor, the tribes of the river had developed distinctive cultures and styles that shared a fundamental unity because of a common religious character.

Here, along the Sepik, far from the concepts and means familiar to the Western world, tribes about which we knew practically nothing had elaborated an astonishingly rich system of thought and repertory of expression. Their concern was with life and death. They forged a concept of another world, of the sacred, which is at once the basis and the justification of their art.

Headhunters

Coming from Europe, as soon as one passes through the Strait of Malacca, one enters a world preoccupied with death: the world of the headhunters. It takes a while to become accustomed to seeing skulls: whole baskets of skulls hanging in the "long houses" of the Dayaks of Borneo and piles of ancestral skulls in the caves of the Toradja of Celebes.[1] And, of course, there are the innumerable skulls of New Guinea. I saw some in the villages along the Sepik, hanging from the woven walls of the House of Men or the House of Tambaran[2] on the river bank. One of the old men allowed me to examine them. He himself seemed ready to join his ancestors, and it occurred to me that this was the cause of his serenity (or was it indifference?) in the presence of the skulls. Once dead, the old man will become a personage to be reckoned with among the villagers. Now, he is merely a feeble scarecrow, good for nothing but to keep watch while the others are fishing. I could not help thinking that his skull, bald and shrunken, was not very different from those hanging from the walls of the House of Tambaran.

Occidental man's horror, or uneasiness, in the presence of human remains is of comparatively recent origin. There was a time when he was as interested in bones as the people of the Sepik are today. I am not referring to the age when good monks meditated on the sight of a human skull to rimind them of their mortality. Rather, I am thinking of the pre-Hellenistic and pre-Roman days of what is now France, when the Gauls were as concerned with skulls as the inhabitants of New Guinea. We have, I think, been so enchanted with our Gallo-Roman history that we have neglected our Ligurian and Celtic origins. If we inspect the Roquepertuse porticle, with its skulls stored in niches and its enigmatic bird, or the skulls at Entremont, we will realize that the habits of our ancestors were not very far removed form those of the Papuans.

The importance of skulls is of religious origin. The peoples of New Guinea do not believe that the human soul is, of itself, immortal. The dead can survive only

---

[1] See Chapter Four.

[2] *Tambaran*, or *Tamboran*, is a difficult word to define, since its origin is unknown. The plural is *waremas*, the suffix of which applies generally to mixed groups. It seems to be used to designate one or more supernatural beings who inhabit a house made of bark. However, the supernatural being is considered to be unique, so as better to convey the idea of the sacred and the fear of it. It is said that the Tambaran arrives in a village, takes up residence in his house, speaks through the sacred flutes, and makes a practice of terrorizing children. The arrival of the Tambaran is the greatest religious ceremony of the year, and is also the occasion for which the bones of the dead are exhumed and divided among the families. The House of Tambaran is so called because it is the dwelling place of this spirit or spirits. It is known alternately as the House of Men because it is the gathering place of the men of the village and is taboo to women.

Human-headed wooden statues are used as household hooks in villages along the Sepik. They hang from the rafters of the houses, and serve to keep food above floor level and away from the animals. In the past, they were primarily religious objects and were used to display the heads of enemies defeated in combat. (Photograph by J. Oster. Collection Musée de l'Homme)

The people along the banks of the Sepik depend on the river for part of their livelihood. The woman above is setting out in her pirogue with her children for a day's fishing.

Opposite: The elaborate carving on the bow of this pirogue represents the heads of ancestors.

Practically every bend of the Sepik is the site of a village. The houses are built on pilings. (Collection Musée de l'Homme)

to the extent that their memory is preserved on earth. It is therefore the task of their descendants to preserve them from extinction.

This belief is the basis for the ancestor cult that entails a constant exchange between the living and the remains of the dead, and of the religion that is based largely upon the preservation of skulls. Thus, one finds the skull of an ancestor, preserved and decorated, placed upon a carved wooden socle which represents the dead man's body. Along the northern coast of New Guinea, this representation is known as a *Korwar*. It is a symbol of higher forces, an expression of super-human powers.

The most important part of this representation is the head. It must be dispro-portionately large, since it is the seat of supernatural and sacred power. This is true, even if the skull is not that of an ancestor. The skull of a man killed in com-bat confers on the living additional life and supernatural powers. Moreover, it is believed that when one member of a tribe receives these benefits, the entire tribe shares in them. It is not difficult to understand, then, why so many of the tribes of New Guinea were formidable headhunters.

The way of the masks

It is one of the paradoxes of anthropology that the less clothing people wear, the more determined they are to cover their faces. Thus it is that the tribes in which total nudity prevails are those that are the great creators of masks.

The paradox resolves itself, to some extent, when we realize that it is all a matter of perspective. One tends to cover—that is, to protect— that part of the body that is regarded as most important. The mask therefore is a protective de-vice. It is also a means of metamorphosis; it enables an individual to become someone else, to escape from his own limitations. A mask, in that sense, is not a means of deception; rather, it is a means of rising above reality. In the Pacific, a masked man identifies with the supernatural being whose image he wears—usual-ly with the ancestor who is represented by the mask. The mask is therefore part of the cult of the dead—a liturgical element animated by the wearer. It is a link be-tween the living and the dead, between the here-and-now and the hereafter. It is the door through which the supernatural enters this world and takes possession of the masked man and of the spectators.

The mask, to be efficacious, must bear as little resemblance to a human being as possible; but, at the same time, it cannot be altogether unrecognizable. The more completely it fulfills these two conditions and achieves this balance, the more effective it is thought to be. The human visage, therefore, is the point of de-parture for uncounted metamorphoses, for deformations that are extensions of the skull-cult. And this is what Claude Levi-Strauss refers to as "the way of the masks." We see masks with impossibly long noses (a symbol of virility); the

Opposite, upper: A series of heads depicting enemies killed in combat is carved and painted on the fa-çade of the House of Spirits.

Lower: This cathedral of tree bark is about 65 feet high at its peak and is a masterful combination of solidity and lightness of construction. (Photo Bernard Sonneville)

tongue hangs out of the mouth; the eyes leap from the head as though they were the tips of antennae. All these elements have cryptic meanings and they demonstrate that the exalted and frenzied wearer of the mask achieves his emotional peak through use of the bizarre. At that point, there is no longer a mask and a wearer of the mask. The symbol becomes the reality. The mask is the ancestor; and that is why it must be so awesome and terrible.

The use of costumes and of paint on the face and body is a form of masking, a means of becoming someone else. The dancers of the Wahgi tribe put feathers in their hair as a way of rising above themselves. Those of the Sepik valley tie a strip of opossum hide around their heads and crown it with the black feathers of the cassowary. But, in the case of the latter, the transfiguration of humans is achieved principally by the use of masks. A man must carve wood and weave straw in order to stir his faith, to calm his anguish, to awaken his hope.

The Orator's Stool

I mentioned earlier in this chapter that I had inspected the House of Tambaran in the first Sepik village I visited. The fact is that, today, the villages have absolutely no objection to anyone—even tourists—entering the domicile of the spirits and viewing the masks, the sculptures, and the skulls lying around in the dust.

My first impression was that this tolerance was based on religious indifference; on a gradual abandonment of ancestral beliefs. Later, however, I came to believe that those beliefs are still thriving, and that the presence of strangers is simply a matter of no importance to the Papuans. In the view of the natives, we Occidentals are a matter of no consequence. We are without spiritual power. We have no connection with their families, living or dead. The traditional taboos, however, apply to Westerners as well. For example, women would not be allowed to enter the House of Tambaran because it is open only to men. The same applies to the music which was born and evolved along the banks of the Sepik. Music is regarded as a religious art, as a sacred symphony achieved through bamboo flutes and hourglass drums, with the voices of supernatural beings speaking through the sounds of those instruments. All musical activity, therefore, is restricted to men. Women are not even allowed to see the flutes, which are kept in the House of Spirits.

The most important article stored in the House is an object known as the "Orator's Stool." That term may be misleading. The piece of sacred furniture to which it refers is used as an altar and as an offertory table as well as a liturgical seat. Theoretically, each tribe should have its own Orator's Stool. In practice, however, they are difficult to find nowadays. The best of them have been sold.

The Orator's Stool is of wood, carved with such infinite complexity, with a maze of symbols and an overlapping of signs, that it virtually defies analysis by the Western mind. Physically, it has the form of a high chair, with the backrest occasionally reaching a height of five feet. Usually it resembles a human silhouette, with the face having a particularly dramatic or sorrowful expression—the image of an ancestor. The most outstanding characteristic of the chair is that, from its base to its apex, it offers a combination of forms—usually of animals, such as a fish with the head of a crocodile. Generally, the overall work shows a disconcertingly different view when seen from the front and from the back.

It is possible that the disappearance of this liturgical piece from the villages coincides with the historical evolution of the area. The chairs were particularly necessary during major ceremonies, when they were used by the speaker to express the opinion of the tribe; that is, to act as the interpreter both of the ancestors and of those who inhabited the village. In this sense, the chair was also an example of the social function of art in Oceania—a function that Maurice Leenhardt referred to as the "element of coherence and of cohesion in Oceanic society."

The art of the skeleton

Once one has seen the household hooks and the Orator's Stools of the Sepik valley—and, above all, the artistic masterpieces on exhibit in the Port Moresby Museum—it is impossible to forget them. They linger ineradicably, not only because of their haunting beauty, but also because of the ingenuity of the minds that conceived them and the hands that fashioned them. For the artists of the Sepik had little to work with, either in materials or in inspiration. They had no stones, no bronze, and hardly any clay. They could use only the most primitive materials: wood, straw, tree bark, bamboo. And, as far as spiritual resources, they had no religious epic, no legendary hero, from which to draw inspiration. There was, in Oceania, no Buddha and no *Ramayana*. In their physical poverty and spiritual isolation, they turned to all that they had: the human body. It was the only masterpiece available as a model, and it was the sole victim available to torture and dissect until the artists arrived at an artistic expression which, in its sheer tension, was without equal. It is a religious art without a god; an art in which man, physical man, is constantly offered in sacrifice[1]; a rigorously anonymous art.

The cuts, slashes, and strokes that carved out the human form burst the thoracic cage in order to place the ribs in a single rank below the head. The nose is elongated until it reaches the sexual organs. Everything works to heighten and raise the artistic expression toward a tension, toward a level of anguish and horror, which becomes almost impossible to bear as soon as one perceives it. It is an art that flays the human body, a method of sculpture that is redolent of dissection—and which is at once the complement and the illustration of a cult of skulls

---

[1] In the religious art of the West, the image of the crucified Christ is also the symbol of the human body offered in sacrifice.

Double page following: A monumental frieze, painted across the entire façade of the House of Spirits, reproduces the faces of the tribe's ancestors. (Photo Bernard Sonneville)

These two decorated skulls are hanging from an ornamented household hook.

and bones. These works of art are masterpieces produced by a cannibal culture. The mental universe of the Papuan people is still inhabited by corpses which their forebears eviscerated, dismembered, and stripped of their flesh. Nowhere in Papuan art does one see the curve of a shoulder or the articulation of a thigh. There are only bones; and even these are assembled in an order alien to the human body: fleshless silhouettes and sightless skulls with empty sockets. This art form, which occupies so humble a portion of space, rises to dizzying heights because of its total lack of formal density, because of the very ease with which it becomes the subject of contemplation.

Its fascination lies in the fact that it stimulates our emotions by means that are foreign to us. It is "realistic" art, certainly. Its themes are figurative, but their arrangement defies reason and awakens a sense of dread and subtle horror. We sigh—but from an agony that we have never experienced. There is nothing here to evoke memories of the macabre masterpieces of our Middle Ages, those images of dancing skeletons and depictions of the Last Judgment. Here, there are no souls to save. We see nothing before us but the remains of a meal: the skulls, the bones.

Oceanic art, as one can see, is not soothing to the sensibilities of Occidental man. The reason is that it runs contrary to our centuries-old respect for the human body. From the time of the Greeks, we have been taught to accept an aesthetic of the flesh. From Phidias to Rodin, our sculpture is an art of curves and volumes, a method in which the human form is wrapped in flesh. Now, Oceanic art comes to put an end to this glorification of the flesh. The skeleton is stripped of its covering. The bones protrude, like bleak, leafless branches. It is difficult to determine if the bones arching out from the vertebrae are truly bones—or boughs. In this work of stripping the human form, Oceanic art has gone further than African art. The latter inclines to serenity and good humor. Sepik art, however, is the art of implacability.

Since headhunting is no longer practiced on the banks of the Sepik, what has become of the creative force that brought about so many masterpieces? It is possible that, in renouncing murder, the people of the Sepik valley have also given up the source of their genius. Slaughter, the trophies of combat, and sculpture were inextricably linked. Formerly, headhunting was regarded as a moral undertaking superior to all others. It was that undertaking which enabled the tribe to grow in spiritual strength. It appears, in fact, that the most elaborate artistic works, those in which the force of expression is most intense, were the work of those tribes that were most determinedly cannibalistic.[1]

---

[1] Margaret Mead, in her study of morals and sexuality in Oceania, points out that the Mundugumor (who live along the banks of the Yuat, a tributary of the Sepik), when they gave up headhunting and cannibalism, lost completely their zest for life. The life of the tribe came to a total halt, "like a watch whose mainspring has broken." Nonetheless, Dr. Mead observes, the memory of their former mode of life, which the Mundugumor had abandoned with great regret, was still vivid in their minds. Even the children had taken part in feasts of human flesh.

The beginnings of a search

The Sepik village, charming and hospitable as it was, did not hold me long. It was necessary for me to leave the river and to travel along the tributaries of the Sepik, if I was to rediscover whatever had been spared by civilization of the original and still-living art of Oceania.

From the Sepik, I flew to the seaside city of Wewak, which is the communications center of the entire region and is connected to Port Moresby and to several larger communities along the river, such as Angoram and Ambuti (Ambunti).

The entire coast of this area was once a battlefield. The Japanese landed here in 1942, and they remained until the Allied offensive in 1945. Nine thousand Japanese were killed before the Japanese retreated to the south of Wewak and along the Sepik. It was their intention to hold out to the last man and to wage guerrilla warfare. After the atomic blast at Hiroshima, however, they were ordered to lay down their arms. Early in September, the Japanese commander, Lieutenant General Adachi, formally surrendered at Cape Wom, near Wewak. The Australians marked the site by a monument which, today, consists of rusting cannons and mortars. Inland, the debris of war is plentiful. I saw a great deal of it in the Maprik area. But it is gradually being swallowed up by the roots and vines of the jungle. How paradoxical, I thought, that all this rusting metal, which once killed thousands of men, now seems so useless and futile compared to a single piece of carved wood representing an ancestor. Only art can attain pathos.

Cathedrals of bark

Despite obvious differences between the art of the Maprik mountains and that of the Sepik valley, there is a similarity between the two. Maprik architecture is exceptionally striking, and the painting—or, at least colored forms—is more usual than wood sculpture.

Access to the Maprik mountains is difficult but the traveler's pains are well rewarded, for there one finds the celebrated "cathedrals of bark," as the Houses of Tambaran are called.

The first of these cathedrals that I saw was the largest, but perhaps not the most impressive. It is too open, too flowery, too *soigné*. It rises from a flat stretch of land, and it lies at the end of an esplanade bordered by rows of hibiscus. Despite one's reservations, the sight of the cathedral evokes a gasp of admiration. The façade rises in a single triangle toward the heavens. The pinnacle rounds into a dome, from which hangs a woven chain. The arris, which, on the façade, rises to a height of sixty-five feet, then slopes sharply toward the rear to within six feet of the ground. The structure's length is about 125 feet. Overall, the impression is one of majesty and style—like that of a cathedral.

One stands in awe before these edifices—so high, so fragile, so monumental, and apparently so much at the mercy of a strong wind. Yet these Houses of Tam-

The numerous villages along the Sepik River are invariably clean, with solidly built houses.

baran, thatched and covered with dried leaves and with walls of woven straw, are surprisingly solid. In the interior, the whitewashed beams and joists, with calculated subtlety, serve to maintain the balance of the entire structure.

The roofing is constructed to protect the paintings within from the tropical rains. These paintings are of considerable importance. They have been compared to the stained glass windows of European cathedrals. Those on the facade are the first ones visible: long, oval faces—stylized, elongated—some 15 feet high and interconnected by means of an intricately woven arabesque traced in red and black. These are all identical faces; they represent the *Ngwaldnu*—the spirits. The artists are not ignorant of portraiture. The paintings are identical so as to give to these images of the dead an air of eternity, to raise them above their human forms. A vine hangs from the mouth of each of the images, representing the human tongue—a symbol of knowledge and wisdom.[1] Below these visages is a row of heads, which are smaller than those of the enemies whose skulls were piled in the House of Tambaran. The entire surfaces of the walls are painted in interlaced ribbons, symbols, and festoons. Yet, the walls of braided bark retain a feeling of openness and lightness, as though a single breath of wind might bring the whole edifice tumbling down.

Access to the cathedral itself is through a narrow, low tunnel on the right side of the façade, which forces a visitor to enter the House of Tambaran in a stooped posture. Once inside, the appellation of "cathedral" seems justified. There is an impressive nave, empty except for several masks and a few sculptures hanging from or leaning against the walls. Off to one side are the drums and sacred flutes. The painted statues, over six feet in height, are images of ancestors. The sculpting is rather crude; but what is important here are the colors and the exaggerated representation of the sexual organs. The ceremonies for which these figures are intended are those of a fertility cult; fertility, obviously, has much to do with ancestors. It is a complex cult, and one that covers fertility of many kinds, from that of women to that of gardens.

The fertility cult of the Abelam (the inhabitants of the Maprik mountains), is more or less identified with that of the Chinese yam, the supremely nourishing plant of the region. The most beautiful specimens of the yam are decorated with flowers and carried on litters; for the Abelam regard the Chinese yam as a human being. If a yam does not germinate, for example, it is regarded as dead and is buried with the same rites as a human. Since it is a male plant and owes its fertility to its ancestors, it is taboo to women. Women, for that matter, are systematically and categorically excluded from participation in the religious life of the tribe. They can have no part in the worship of ancestors or in artistic activity, for these two elements are indissolubly linked.

As I have already mentioned, under no circumstances are women allowed to enter the House of Tambaran. However, the Houses of the Maprik mountains, unlike those of the Sepik valley, are not intended primarily as meeting halls for the men of the tribe. They are truly religious edifices and are used for religious ceremonies—notably for the rites of initiation into manhood. In former times, the warriors of the tribe brought the freshly cut heads of their enemies to this sanctuary. The link between fertility is quite clear. The Chinese yam and cannibalism are but opposite sides of the same coin—in New Guinea and in the New Hebrides.

The readiness with which these tribes allow foreign visitors to enter their Houses of Tambaran is surprising. It is not unlikely that the Houses have lost much of their air of horror since headhunting is no longer practiced as a means of reinforcing the vital powers of the tribe. These structures were erected and created in suffering, violence, and slaughter. In the past, the ground on which a House was to be built was soaked with the blood of an enemy. Today, the House seems to do little more than evoke nostalgia for the good old days of cannibalism.

---

[1] Maurice Leenhardt has noted, "The tongue, because it is the muscle by means of which humans communicate their thoughts and form their words, is a manifestation of man's personality, wisdom, and action. This is a highly sophisticated symbolism."

Compared to the granite and obsidian gods of the ancient Egyptians, or to the marbles of the Greeks and the bronzes of the Romans, the masterpieces of the Sepik are weightless, airy. They are made of perishable wood, of woven straw, of bamboo. The temples themselves are of dried leaves. Yet, it is an art that rivals that of Egypt and Greece and Rome. For what counts in art is not the material of which a masterpiece is made, but what the artist has wrought of that material.

3

the land of naked men

Magic is, above all, a means of de-
nying the absurdity of the world.
ANDRÉ DEVYVER

Thus far, I had seen only the more developed and accessible part of New Guinea, that which was under Australian control for more than half a century. I was
eager to get to the western part of the island, once a Dutch colony, but now part of
the Republic of Indonesia. It is now known as Irian Jaya. Once, however, it was
called Irian Barat: Land of the Naked Men.

The airplane landed first at a city that used to be called Hollandia, a name understandably abhorrent to the Indonesians, who changed it to Jayapura, meaning
"city of victory." It is a city with nothing to distinguish it, and I left as quickly as
possible for Lake Sentani.

The children's lake

The lake is situated in the midst of green hills, which are a bit too bare of trees
because of countless brush fires. The morning sun glistened on the water, which
seemed to stretch far into the distance.

I visited two of the many villages lining the shores of the lake. Both were
alive with the sounds of pigs, chickens, and dogs, all scratching and digging
among the peelings and other garbage under and around the houses. The villages,
though dirty by Western standards, seemed rather prosperous.

The lake is the special domain of the children of the villages. It is said—and
one can believe it—that they swim before they walk. I watched them as they float-
ed around the water in their tiny pirogues, naked, completely at ease under the

In a village near Wamena, a N'Dani has just climbed up onto the roof of his house to fetch a colocynth (a
species related to the watermelon) for me. Colocynths are used to make the penile sheaths worn in the
region around Wamena.

blazing sun. They were obviously at home on the water, and that was as it should have been. An early familiarity with the lake is a form of education, for it prepares them to earn their livelihood from the water, as their parents do.

The appearance of Lake Sentani, after the high mountains and narrow valleys, after the majestic basin of the Sepik River, served to emphasize the size and diversity of New Guinea. Here, everything seemed motionless, peaceable, like a world unto itself. The local population, the Asmat people, enjoy a life-style and activities different from those of other Papuans. Their appearance, however, is the same as that of their fellow islanders: the men are nude or semi-nude, and self-embellishment is of great importance. Here, as elsewhere, the *kuna,* or crescent mother-of-pearl pendant, is held in high regard. The women wear the skirt of red-dyed fibers that is fashionable throughout almost all of Oceania.

Lake Sentani was once a center of artistic creativity, and it even originated a particular style of which some museums in the United States have remarkable examples—notably, wooden platters carved in a frog motif. The creative tradition now seems extinct among the lake dwellers.[1]

A social obligation

The next stop was Wamena which, though hardly even a village, offers a unique spectacle unmatched by any of the great tourist centers of the world. Everywhere—around the landing field, in the village's only store, under the trees—groups of naked men were standing, their only attire a penile or genital sheath.[2] These sheaths, mostly golden yellow in color, were of every size and shape. Some were straight, others were curved, and some were spiral. A few were so long that they touched the wearer's chin and had to be held in place by a ribbon attached to a belt.

Other than the sheath itself, the men wore nothing. There were no feathers or plumes like those of the Wahgi of the highlands. No paint on the face or body. Nothing but their highly visible and no doubt serviceable sheath.

In Wamena, which is regarded as a "civilized center," the men were competely at ease as they promenaded in the street and stood chatting under the trees. They were quite willing to accommodate anyone who wanted to photograph them—and they did not even ask for a "tip." It is usually the photographer rather than the subject who is embarrassed. When I began snapping photos of one strapping fellow, I smiled apologetically; and I received in return a smile in which it was easy to read both irony and indulgence.

The penile sheaths did not come as a surprise to me. I had expected to see them, and I knew that I would see many more elsewhere in Oceania. Even now, however, I confess that I do not know quite what to think of them. The ethnolo-

---

[1]Quite recently, a number of art objects were fished out of the waters of the lake, where they had been thrown many years before at the urging of Christian missionaries. No one in the area knew what became of those objects once they were recovered.
[2]See Appendix III.

gists have had little to say about them, and what they have said is not especially illuminating. About all that one can know with certainty is that the significance of the penile sheath is not clear, and that it apparently serves more than one purpose. It may be an affirmation of the wearer's virility. It may be an amulet of sorts against evil spirits. It may be simply an item of clothing dictated by a not-very-exacting sense of modesty. It is very likely that it is all those things, and more. The wearing of the penile sheath has its origins in a social and religious sytem with which the rationalism of the Western mind has yet to come to grips successfully.

One factor that strikes even the casual observer is that the penile sheath is a social obligation, regardless of whether the sheath is used to diminish or magnify the male sex organ, to hide it, or to give it prominence by decorating it. The making and wearing of the sheath is governed by strict rules, for its use is dictated by an overriding concern for the dignity of the wearer. (If this seems strange to us, let us recall that the natives of New Guinea regard our own attitude toward our genital organs as both ridiculous and grossly indecent.) A native would never consent to remove his sheath in the presence of a stranger—as Western doctors and nurses have discovered.

To this concern for dignity is added a desire to protect the sex organ against danger. These dangers, apparently, are less those of the jungle than those presented by evil spirits, the dead, and sometimes the living. "The symbolism attached to the sexual organs," writes Robert Lantier, an expert in prehistory, "seems to constitute man's first, tentative step into the realm of metaphysics." Be that as it may, it is worth noting that nowhere in the world does there exist such a thing as habitual and total nudity or absolute indifference to sexual organs. There is always something used to "dress," or at least to support, the organ. (In some instances—I have observed this in Africa—the male genitals are pulled backward and tied between the legs in such a way as to become invisible.) This preoccupation with covering or decorating the male genital, however, seems a matter of social usage, of "education," rather than of modesty.

A peculiar practice

The marketplace at Wamena would be enough to drive an ethnologist mad. It is a collection of the populations of twenty different villages, all of them belonging to the people known as N'Dani. The womenfolk, all wearing grass skirts, were seated on the ground. They were neither pretty nor ugly. Their large, pear-shaped breasts seemed full and firm, at least among the younger women. Their skin was dark brown, with touches of copper. Even when seated, they wore the *billum*, or net, on their backs. It could not have been very comfortable, since the net, which is used to carry everything from groceries to firewood to babies, is supported by a strap around the forehead.

It appeared that the women spend all of their time talking in groups of three or four, and made not the slightest effort to sell their fruits and vegetables. As they talked, they smoked twists of tobacco that resembled straws. Thin wisps of lavender smoke rose into the air everywhere.

I stood watching them for a few minutes before I was struck by something strange. The fingers of one of the women—I could see them clearly as she raised her tobacco twist—were only stubs. The tips had been amputated.

I knew of the old custom, one of the least edifying traditions of New Guinea, that required that a woman cut off, with a bamboo knife, the tip of a finger every time one of her children died and every time a pig died that she had nursed at her breast. But I was under the impression that the custom had been abolished, and that the practice was forbidden. Yet, this woman seemed to be quite young, and it is young indeed in a country where women age very quickly. She was probably in her early twenties, certainly not more than twenty-nine or thirty. She saw me staring at her hands, and she smiled at me. No doubt, if I had had the bad manners to ask her about her fingers, she would have expressed pride in her self-mutilation. I looked at the hands of the other women in the marketplace. There were hardly any whose fingertips were intact. Traditions and customs, even those as horrible as self-mutilation, die hard in New Guinea.

An excursion into local politics

I set out on foot from Wamena, across country to a nearby village where, I was told, an important ceremony was to take place. After an hour and a half of

Opposite. The women of Wamena wear nets on their backs. These nets are arranged so that the weight of the contents—food, mostly, and occasionally an infant—is supported by the woman's head.

Above: The women at the marketplace seem more concerned with chatting and smoking than with selling their produce.

Below: It is an ancient custom for a woman to cut off the tip of a finger when one of her children, or a pig that she has raised, dies. The left hand of the woman in the photograph is a record of four such deaths.

walking on a kind of dirt levee through the marshland, I reached the village. It was a place of fair size, located on the bank of a river. And indeed there was a ceremony in progress, although it was hardly what I had expected. There were no fantastic costumes, no painted faces or bodies, no waving of bows and arrows. In fact, there was nothing more than a gathering of a large number of men in everyday clothes; that is, naked, except for their penile sheaths.

I had sworn beforehand that, under no circumstances, would I show the slightest surprise or curiosity concerning the sheaths. After all, I was a guest in this village, and the last thing I wanted was to offend or embarrass my hosts, who were the most courteous and considerate of people. Still, it was very difficult to keep my promise. I had never seen so many sheaths in so many sizes and shapes. I could not help staring, and comparing: That's the biggest one I've ever seen . . . I wonder why that one is worn at that peculiar angle. . . .

I was furious at myself for being so childish. Yet, when I saw one man carefully re-arranging one of his testicles which had slipped out of the sheath, I could not repress a regrettably foolish grin.

The ceremony in progress actually had nothing to do with penile sheaths, despite my fascination with them on this occasion. In fact, it was not a "ceremony" so much as a thoroughly modern phenomenon, very similar to what we know as a municipal election.

A uniformed man—no doubt an Indonesian official—was seated behind a white wooden table that had been set up between the pigpen and the yam-drying racks. A soldier stood guard next to him, ostentatiously holding a large rifle. The assembled villagers were seated around this official on the ground next to the river. Standing to one side, apart from the others, were five men. These were the candidates for public office.

The first of the five candidates spoke. A man from the audience rose to his feet and interrupted the speaker. From the sound and tone of his voice, I gathered that he was saying some rather unpeasant things to the candidate. When he had finished, the man left the line of candidates. "Aha," I said to myself, "that's the end of him."

The next candidate spoke, and was cross-examined by the audience with the same vigor as the first one. Then he too left the line.

The same thing happened to the remaining three candidates, one after the other. I could only conclude that the electorate had rejected all of the candidates. Yet, as soon as the speeches and questions were over, the five candidates formed a line once more. This time, it was a reception line. The villagers filed past them, shaking hands with each one and smiling amiably. Finally, everyone, electors and candidates alike, broke into groups and performed a few dance steps together. I smiled as I watched the dancers, their sheaths jiggling in rhythm with their movements.

The mud

Some of the most interesting things I saw were discovered when I traveled on foot along the paths of New Guinea, crossing over rivers and swamps on the trunks of fallen trees.

This work is typical of the art of Korwar: the stand, or reliquary, represents a human form holding a shield and is surmounted by a human skull. (Photograph Pasquino, Collection Musée de l'Homme)

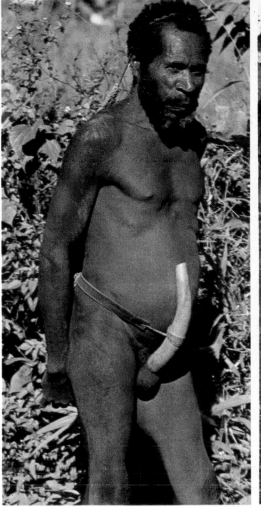

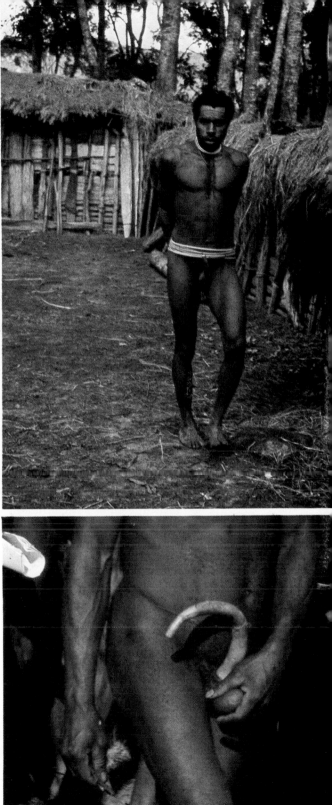

Penile sheaths play an extremely important role in village life. There is a great diversity in the shapes and sizes of the sheaths. Some of them are straight; some curve forward or backward, or to the side. There are even spiral sheaths. As can be seen in these photographs, the sheaths are usually held in position by a belt or strap worn around the waist.

On one particular occasion, I left at dawn. It was rather cold, and there was a light fog hanging over the trees. The trail that the guide and I were following was impassable in any kind of vehicle. It ran along the the side of a mountain, down into the valley, and seemed to finish in the middle of a marsh. We continued on, over branches and slippery tree trunks until, inevitably, I fell off into the mud and sank to mid-thigh. My guide, with some difficulty, pulled me out. My cameras and equipment, fortunately, were in watertight cases. The rest of me was a mess. By the time the guide got me out of the marsh, I was covered with mud, literally from head to foot.

My guide seemed hardly more comfortable than I did. His penile sheath, which he stopped to adjust periodically as we hurried along, obviously bothered him. It is hardly a convenient accessory to wear in the brush, even for one who is accustomed both to sheaths and to brush. Some scholars maintain that man's behavior and his dress are dictated by his environment and climate. That certainly does not seem to be the case in New Guinea. Elaborate penile sheaths are not made for walking in jungles, marshes, swamps, and undergrowth. Nor is nudity ideal either for those activities or for the climate of the island. As we were walking along a field, we saw a group of men coming toward us. They were nude, except for the inevitable sheath and for necklaces of dogs' teeth mounted on a leather thong, and they were suffering miserably from the cold. They were hugging their chests, in the universal gesture of men trying to warm themselves. From my own observation, I would say that New Guineans spend a good part of their time in that position. Certainly nudity among these people is not the result of poverty, nor does it exist because the climate makes clothing unnecessary. Its significance, very likely, is social or ritualistic. It may be, after all, that nudity, along with the penile sheath, is simply an affirmation of the virility of the male.

The mummy

We reached our destination at mid-morning. It was a village, several miles away from Wamena. This particular village was surrounded by a fence, as were the fields around it. There was a single gate into the village, low and narrow. The lower part of it had been boarded, no doubt to keep the pigs from running loose. The houses were built side by side, their sides touching, around a large interior courtyard or square, with the rear of the houses toward the jungle.

There were women and nude children in the square, all of them shivering in the cold. They seemed to be trying to warm themselves in the pale sunlight that was just beginning to dissipate the fog.

Several men came out of the houses, crawling on all fours. The entrances to the houses were quite low, hardly more than holes in the base of the walls. The reason for this became obvious when I visited one of the houses. Inside, the temperature was many degrees above the outside temperature. It was also quite damp, and there was a rather strong smell—no doubt due to lack of ventilation, since the houses are designed to retain warmth. There were embers still glowing among the ashes of a primitive fireplace.

In honor of my visit, one of the elders of the village brought out a mummy. It was the corpse of a man who had, long ago, been the undisputed chief of the entire valley. The elder placed the mummy on the ground, on a blanket of banana leaves, where I could inspect it. It was hardly more than a skeleton, its black skin, lovingly anointed with oil, stretched tight over the bones.

Once more I was struck by that intimacy with death which is the rule in New Guinea. In this village, however, the people do not rely solely on skulls, as in the Sepik valley and in *Korwar* art; they have skeletons, and even corpses, as part of their daily lives. Despite the proximity of these constant reminders of death, which appear at almost every turn, the people here do not seem to develop the instinctive and irrational fear of death that is characteristic of so much of human society throughout the world. On the contrary, it seems to relieve them of a great deal of anguish concerning death.

The explanation of death in this area is quite simple: death is a mistake. There was a time when humans could choose, of their own free will, to disappear and then reappear, following the cyle of the moon. Or, if they wished, they could reappear as serpents.

At the risk of adding fuel to the much-misunderstood myth of the "noble savage," I must add that, while in this village, I could not help but notice the almost tangible atmosphere of peace that prevailed everywhere. It was as though everything there was in perfect balance; everything had a reason; everything was "normal." Perhaps the isolation of the village had something to do with this peculiar feeling. The village was surrounded by thick, virtually impenetrable jungle the silence of which was broken only by the sounds of birds and insects. This wall of greenery was reinforced by a belt of marshes and swamps. We were a day's walk away from Wamena and a plane trip (with three changeovers) from Port Moresby. The sense of isolation here was constant, heavy, like the walls of a prison. Yet, I did not feel particularly out of place. Nothing appeared unexpected or alien. The logic of the way of life in the village seemed clear, inevitable, once I was able to overcome my rather naive Western prejudices and view it objectively.

If one reflects for a moment, even the more bizarre aspects of village life here are not truly more astonishing than some of our practices in the West. Is the mummy, gruesome as it may be, really more horrifying than, say, our relics of the saints? Certainly, as the product of a culture that has produced the tasteless bronze effigies of a place like Père Lachaise Cemetery in Paris, I will not be the one to throw the first stone.

And would it make sense to people to wear clothing in New Guinea, where they are constantly exposed to heavy tropical rains? The clothes would never dry—while their exposed bodies dry very quickly. In fact, when the missionaries insisted that their converts clothe themselves with Christian modesty, the poor converts quickly developed all sorts of pulmonary diseases because their clothing never dried.

Double page following: In this village near Wamena, all the houses are built to face a central square. The doorways of the houses are so low that the residents (and the visitors) have to crawl in and out.

Still, one wonders if everything is really for the best in this manner of doing things. It was noon in the village before the sun had warmed the air sufficiently for human comfort. Until then, women and children huddled together in the court-yard, shivering and shifting their bodies to catch every ray of sun.

We Westerners have things to learn from the people of New Guinea, and one of those things is hospitality. These ex-cannibals and former headhunters are true models of courtesy and consideration. Everyone is perfectly willing, even eager, to satisfy the insatiable curiosity of white visitors. They answer all questions as best they can. To express an interest in some everyday object often results in the object being offered as a gift. (One of the men of the village climbed up on the roof of a house to get a dried colocynth—a type of fruit related to the watermelon—for me. Dried colocynths are used to make penile sheaths. I was now fully equipped for life in New Guinea.

Treetop burials

The government of Indonesia has interfered in some aspects of the life-styles of the various ethnic groups of the island. One of the areas they have left un-touched, however, has been the disposal of corpses. Certainly, they are more indifferent to hygiene than the Australian authorities were. In the interior of the island, in the remote and narrow valleys of Irian Jaya, human remains are no more than half-hidden in the brush. I have seen bodies only a few feet off trails and paths. Sometimes they are simply carried up to the top of a hill and exposed there. Some tribes—among them, the Wahgi of the highlands—place their corpses in tree trunks or hang them from branches. Often the body of a dead man is simply placed on a small wooden platform and, to all appearances, abandoned there.

I was told that a treetop burial had taken place recently in the neighborhood of Wamena, and I expressed an interest in seeing this phenomenon. The site, nat-urally, was accessible only on foot; there was no road, only trails which, as usual, led through swamps, where the only foothold was over slippery, fallen trees. This time, I fell twice into the soft, black mud. The most alarming thing about these swamps is that once you feel yourself sinking into the mud, you are never quite sure when (or if) you will stop sinking. . . .

It took half a day to reach the small village where the treetop burial was sup-posed to have taken place. Once I was there, however, the people of the village were not markedly eager to allow me to see the corpse. In fact, they did every-thing they could to discourage me. First my guide led me up the face of a nearly vertical cliff of clay. Then, when I had reached the top and was gasping for breath, the guide told me casually that this was not the place after all; that what I wanted to see was "down there"—he pointed vaguely to a spot at the bottom of the cliff. We climbed down again and walked to the spot. It was nothing more than a small platform, supported by four posts, on which were two moss-covered skulls star-ing at us out of black eye sockets. As a reward for my exhaustion, I learned a val-uable lesson: not to chase after morbid tourist attractions in New Guinea.

Actually, the bodies of the dead that are exposed in the jungle, on hilltops, and in trees are not abandoned by the bereaved. What usually happens is that, after being exposed for a certain length of time, the corpse is gathered up in preparation for a second funeral ceremony which will serve as the final leave-taking for the family and friends. The interval of exposure is designed to purge the dead body of any ability or will to harm the living. The rain and heat, to say nothing of the birds and insects, quickly reduce the corpse to a skeleton. At that point, it is regarded as "safe." A skeleton or a skull is less frightening, apparently, than a ghost.

Everything having to do with attitudes toward death in New Guinea is so complex and variable that confusion is almost inevitable. I think that the basic distinction to be made is that between the cult of the dead and the cult of ancestors. Apparently, the purpose of the cult of the dead is to elevate a dead man to the rank of an ancestor—or at least to assure the deceased of a position in the heareafter so satisfactory that he will not become a danger to the living. But, as I have pointed out, the frontier between the cult of the dead and ancestor-worship is seldom obvious, and there exists an infinity of variations and exceptions.

Corydon

I was eager to reach Enaratoli, on the shore of Lake Wissel (Paniai). There was, however, no direct route. First, I had to take a plane to Nabire; from there, I was told, the only transportation would be a decrepit old cargo plane that was used to carry supplies to missionaries and geologists in the brush. (Geologists are rather numerous in New Guinea, as might be expected from the abundance of mineral resources. They are particularly avid in the search for gold, copper, and uranium.)

I was greeted bya troop of warrior-dancers on the landing strip at Enaratoli. These New Guineans showed not the slightest curiosity about the aircraft. The days are long gone when, as soon as a plane landed, the natives crawled under the tail of the "great bird from the sky" so as to determine its sex.

There were about a dozen men, marking time in cadence with their feet, carrying bows and arrows. They wore necklaces and bracelets, and their cheeks were painted red and blue. The warriors at Wamena, I noted, used more subdued colors than these; alas, they seemed to move more smoothly than the dancers of Anaratoli. Here, as at Wamena, however, the dancers all wore penile sheaths of considerable size.

I should not say "all." There was one exception: a strapping, muscular warrior who wore a black brassiere and, instead of a sheath, a woman's straw skirt. Like a woman, he wore the universal net, hanging down his back and covering his head. Other than his dress, there was nothing feminine about him. He danced and sang like the others. There was not a trace of femininity in the way he moved or carried himself.

It is no secret that homosexuality is common, and even ritualistic, in New Guinea. Yet, the sight of this strapping warrior, with his enormous square shoulders and glistening muscles, decked out in brassiere and grass skirt, was, I con-

Above: The chief of this village brought out his
ancestor's mummy in order to welcome me.
The ancestor at one time ruled over all the villages of the valley.

Opposite: Pigs are raised very carefully and
cared for by the womenfolk. These animals
are the only wealth of the village.

Left: Despite the frequent cold and the humidity, both men and women spend their lives virtually naked. These young women are trying
to keep warm by wrapping their arms around
their necks.

fess, something of a surprise. Perhaps the most surprising thing of all was the perfect naturalness with which he handled the situation. Other than for the obvious difference in dress, he was, in all respects, a warrior among warriors. Indeed, unless I had been aware of the significance of the grass skirt and of the brassiere (which, since it was black, was quite inconspicuous), it would have been impossible to discern anything unusual about the man.

The mission

Enaratoli is merely a hamlet on the shore of the lake. It has no hotel or rooming house. A stranger, if he intends to stay overnight, must rely upon the hospitality either of the local chief or of the Catholic mission, which was founded by the Dutch. This is not an extraordinary situation in Irian Jaya, which is under Indonesian control. In Papua New Guinea, there are comfortable inns and hotels. Here, there are few such amenities; when they exist, they are generally uncomfortable. To my mind, this was a favorable omen. It meant that the people here had probably not yet been spoiled by contact with tourists.

Lake Wissel, surrounded by stately trees, lies in a circle of high mountains reminiscent of certain areas of Europe—the Tyrol, for example. Because of the altitude, the climate is deliciously cool.

The surface of the lake was alive with pirogues. Here, as elsewhere, women do the fishing, standing in their little boats and wielding oval-shaped nets mounted on frames of curved wood. These lake-dwellers have not lost the art of carving a pirogue out of a single tree trunk. I watched the carpenters at work, their penile sheaths moving at the same cadence and with the same vigor as the tools which they handled with such dexterity.

I was received with cordiality at the mission, which housed a young Franciscan priest and several nuns, all of Dutch nationality. There was nothing in their dress to distinguish them from any other Westerner living in New Guinea, but everything in their attitude: their only concern was for the health and welfare of the local populace. That, of course, is a full-time concern. The Papuans are particularly susceptible to a disease known as trichinosis, brought about by eating pork that is not sufficiently cooked. A wormlike parasite enters the body and eventually reaches the brain, causing damage to the nervous system and, sometimes, death. The victims frequently lose consciousness and fall into the fires that they keep burning in their houses. Two injections usually suffice to arrest the progress of trichinosis. The most difficult task of the hospital administered by the priest and the nuns is to care for the burns of the victims.

The missionaries spoke with simplicity of the use of penile sheaths.

"It is very important to them," the priest remarked. "It is a custom, a tradition; and we respect it."

I wanted to know more. "What is the sheath's real significance?" I asked. "Is it a protective device—against the dangers of the jungle or against evil spirits?"

"It may be," the man replied. "I think that, in any case, it's regarded as a sign of virility. That is why the sheath is so important to them."

"I think there's an element of modesty also," one of the nuns added. "At the hospital, they simply will not let us remove their sheaths, even when they're very sick."

"Yes," I responded, "but don't you think that, underneath it all, there's a religious factor? Isn't it basically the manifestation of a fertility cult that is somehow related to ancestor worship? It seems to me that you really can't separate one element from the others . . . ."

The missionaries did not agree. As we talked, I soon understood why. It would have been hard for them to admit that a rival religion could manifest itself in dried colocynths and phalluses.

In truth, these hard-working, concerned emissaries of the Church were concerned with matters more important than what the people wore or why they wore it. One of the recurring problems with which they had to deal was that of the status of women. Women here are looked down on, treated harshly, and regarded not only as less valuable than a pig (which is, after all, a very valuable animal) but even as being of less account than a dog. Whenever a male expresses an interest in becoming a Catholic, the missionaries insist that he promise to treat his wives as human beings.

The fact that a prospective convert has more than one wife presents another problem. Even the Catholics among the population have several of them. Papuans are a polygamous people. It is an ancient institution, dictated by the economic and social realities of life on the island. To forbid it would compromise any missionary activity. Therefore, an arrangement or, rather, a concession has been worked out. The missionaries reason that Abraham and the prophets were polygamous, and yet they were holy men, saints. Therefore, one can have several wives and, at the same time, still serve God. It is, as was pointed out to me, in the Bible.

I left Enaratoli the following day. The welcoming committee of dancers, which had greeted me on arrival, were at the landing strip to bid me farewell with a spirited dance. This time, I counted three transvestites among them, their grass skirts moving to the same beat as the penile sheaths of the other warriors. Only one of them was wearing a black brassiere: the same strapping athlete that I had seen the previous day.

I changed planes at Nabire for Biak Island. It was a short flight. As we approached the island, I saw, in the jungle below, what appeared to be several enormously long clearings in the greenery, like highways to nowhere in this remote place. I was told that these were landing strips made by bulldozers during World War II. They were not the only reminders of civilization's intrusion into the jungle. As soon as the plane landed, I went for a swim in Geelvink Bay to wash off the dust of travel. It was one of the least enjoyable experiences of my visit to New

Double page following: These are the dancing warriors of Enaratoli. Notice the warrior to the left. He is wearing a black brassiere, a woman's skirt, and a woman's net over his head.

Guinea. The bay bottom was a moonscape of dead coral, empty bottles, and rusted cans.

A contemporary mythology

The island of Biak is the stage of a peculiar drama. In 1886, the Biakai somehow gained possession of a European ship and plundered its cargo. They had no idea where the ship had come from or why it was there. All they knew was that it carried many priceless objects that had never been available to them before—objects like those for which they had always helplessly envied the white man. It was assumed that the ship, and its cargo, was a gift from the spirits.

Eleven years later, in 1897, a prophet arose among the people and foretold the arrival of a great ship. Its cargo, he announced, would be precious indeed: guns, cooking utensils of copper, and fabrics. The captain of this fabled ship was to be Jesus.

Thus was born the cargo cult.

In the past several hundred years, the Biakai have seen a succession of white men arrive on their island: Portuguese, Spaniards, Dutch, Englishmen, Germans, Australians, Japanese, Indonesians. They have heard many languages. They have been exposed to many religions. They watched each succeeding wave of whites disembark with the reaction common to most primitive peoples: they thought that these pale visitors were gods, come from a mysterious place, bringing with them unknown and marvelous objects.

They watched in astonishment as these strangers unloaded basins, kettles, bicycles, furniture, guns, variegated cloth, clocks, and other wondrous items onto their pristine beaches. Yet, they never saw a single white man actually make any of these things; they concluded that they were gifts from the god of the white men. They therefore began praying intently to that god, as the missionaries had been asking them to do all along. And they waited for the great god of the West to send them a cargo ship laden with his gifts.

They are waiting still.

On Biak Island, conditions were particularly favorable for the birth of a myth which fostered belief in a messiah and prepared the populace for supernatural intervention in their lives. Two religions were already represented on the island, Islam and Christianity, both of which added fuel to the fire of religious instinct. Indonesians from the Moluccas, who had converted to Christianity some three hundred years earlier, had spread belief in Jesus. And Islam was there, equally strong, and equally preaching the coming of the *Mahdi*. In addition, a very ancient local tradition taught of the imminent return to Biak of Manggundi, a hero of Herculean stature who would teach men the secret of resurrection from the dead and give them inexhaustible wealth. There were therefore three sources to feed the most extravagant mythology that has ever swept the Pacific isles.

The penile sheaths at Enaratoli are almost as large as the ones I saw at Wamena.

Above: The women use large round nets for fishing at Lake Wissel.

Opposite: A bowman of Enaratoli.

By 1914, the natives were tired of waiting for the cargo ship that never came. If their prayers had gone unanswered, they reasoned, it was because they had not accepted the religion of the white man. Whereupon, they converted to Christianity, in the not wholly absurd belief that they would now, surely, partake of the wealth of the cargo ships.

It was a strange wedding of Christian ritual and native belief. The religious mentality of the Papuan tribesmen is completely innocent of any notion of spirituality. Their own traditional rites and taboos have but a single purpose: to assure their material well-being. Their newly acquired Christianity was therefore transformed very quickly to conform to these values. The native (pidgin English) word for Christianity tells all: *Rot Bilong Kako* (Route Belong Cargo—or the route of the cargo ship).

The teachings of the missionaries were just as quickly interpreted by the natives in accordance with their own preoccupations. Thus, the Biblical account of the Garden of Eden, in its Papuan version is somewhat changed. God created Adam and Eve and placed them on a cargo ship. When they sinned, he made them get off the ship. God did this while living in heaven; that is, in Sydney, Australia.

Still no cargo ships arrived for the Papuans, although they were now "Christians." The fault, obviously, was that of the missionaries, who wanted to keep the secret of the cargo for themselves and refused to teach the converts the true prayers and words that would summon the treasure ships. The Papuans then abandoned the missions and established their own religion, which combines remnants of Christianity with sacrifices to ancestors, extravagant dances, and invocations to the spirits. It was not until shortly before the beginning of World War II that Europeans became even vaguely aware of what was happening.

The war and the messiah

In 1936, a prophet on Biak Island—and an especially inspired prophet at that—foretold a great war between the Japanese and the white man; at the same time, he announced the impending return of the local messiah, Manggundi. When Japanese troops landed on Madang in December 1942, and the Dutch departed, the first part of the prophesy was regarded as fulfilled. (The Japanese tried to pass themselves off as the spirits of ancestors, but they were not believed.)

In April 1944, American and Australian troops recaptured Madang. In the course of the battle, Allied aircraft launched thousands of flares; and this rain of stars was accepted, by believers in Manggundi, as a sign that the coming of the messiah was indeed imminent. Then, hundreds of ships were seen to drop anchor off the island of Meok Wundi, one of the sacred places of the Manggundi myth. The Americans landed, "chasing away the strangers," as had been foretold. The newcomers also distributed, with prodigal abandon, alcohol, cigarettes, and chocolate. The long-awaited Age of Abundance had arrived, and the Americans were declared to be ambassadors of Manggundi—as was proved by the presence among them of soldiers with black skins.

These celestial envoys, unfortunately, did not stay long. They were soon replaced by Dutch colonial officers, who re-established Holland's control over the western half of New Guinea. The sturdy, hard-working Dutch did not attempt to pass themselves off either as ancestors or as surrogate messiahs. Also, they were notably less generous with their goods than the Americans.

The cargo cult, rather than dying out at this reversal, broke out with new virulence. The faithful now placed all their hope in the arrival of a heavenly ship, manned by Americans and loaded with limitless wealth. This belief was made all the more credible by the presence, on Biak, of numerous landing strips, capable of accommodating the largest aircraft.

In the early 1950s, the prophets of the cargo cult made new predictions: shortly, there would be a great change on the earth. The masters would become servants, and the servants would become masters. The black men would become white, and the white men would become black. The fishes would live on land, and the animals would live in the sea.

In the eastern part of New Guinea, a group of natives, armed with military equipment abandoned by the fleeing Japanese, rose in rebellion against the Europeans—in the name of the cargo cult. It became necessary for the white men to organize an expeditionary force in order to put down a large group of Papuans, armed with Japanese grenades, who were preparing to launch an attack on Madang.[1]

---

[1]For details of the cargo cult, see *The Religions of the Pacific and of Australia*, by P. Nevermann, *et al.*

A somber future

I have spent enough time in New Guinea to have at least an approximate idea of the present condition of the island. It is clear that the future of the coastal areas is considerably brighter than that of the highlands; that half of the island that once belonged to Australia, and is now independent, is better off than the half controlled by the Republic of Indonesia.[1]

Yet, it is difficult to foresee the future. After a year of independence, Papua New Guinea is in serious financial difficulty and looks to Australia for help. The Australians, however, are in a sulk over the loss of their half of New Guinea, and have refused all aid. This economic impasse could very easily lead to political crises and social upheavals.

The fact of independence and of the economic straits in which the new country finds itself have had an impact even on the cargo cult. Among many adherents, it has taken the form of a desire for a higher standard of living, now that they are free and masters of their own destiny. But this enlightened attitude is not shared by all. Independence, it is whispered, is merely a new trick of the whites to deprive the black man of the treasures of the cargo ship.

Actually, it is too late for the credulous inhabitants of the brush to revolt against white domination. Revolution may come; but if it does, it will be in the form of a struggle against the more "civilized" inhabitants of Port Moresby and of Jayapura, who are determined to force New Guinea, willy nilly, into the modern world

[1] Irian Jaya, with its 980,000 inhabitants, "having asked, in 1969, by a free act of will, to remain Indonesian," is now a province of the republic.

4

the isle of buffalo

The water buffalo was sunk up to his snout in the mud of the rice paddy. I could see only his forehead marked with pink and white, the crescent-shaped horns sloping sharply backward, the two large ears, and the dark eyes, glazed in their utter placidity.

It took a great deal of shouting and arm-waving before the buffalo could be coaxed from the cool mud into the heat of the day. Finally, he lumbered onto solid bottom, and I could see his great reddish black body. He stood there, pawing the tender new growth in the shallow water, framed against the blazing sky.

This imposing animal seemed strangely in harmony with its man-made surroundings. For everything within sight—the terraced hills, the clumps of bamboo waving like ostrich plumes, the fertile valleys amply wooded but not overgrown—it is all the handiwork of man. Man has created these imposing terraces, rising like some fantastic staircase curving into the heavens, and irrigated them in order to grow his crop of rice. I should say rather that man and the buffalo have created these things, for the buffalo's strength is indispensable in moving the fertile earth—the volcanic mud which I saw arabesqued against the slopes of the hills.

This is Toradja country, on Celebes Island, now known as Sulawesi. The is-

This chief's house, on Celebes, is decorated with many pairs of buffalo horns. Each pair of horns represents ten sacrificed buffalo.

land has a peculiar shape, not unlike that of a spider or a crab. It is neither primitive nor wild. Tropical islands are not always so charming; indeed, they are often unbearable because of the heat and the overwhelming vegetation. Celebes Island, however, is hospitable. It has been totally transformed by agriculture, and there are few tropical islands so beguiling in appearance. At this altitude, the tropics are pleasant and cool. Celebes is a mountanous place—Rantekombola, for instance, has an altitude of 11,000 feet—and a glance at the map explains the exceptional mildness of its climate despite its proximity to the Equator.

The great buffalo, having condescended to show himself briefly, now returned to the paddy and sank blissfully into the mud once more. It is impossible to stand near an unfamiliar animal of such size and strength without experiencing a touch of fear. Yet, the buffalo is known for the gentleness of its disposition and for its utter docility. These traits are the end result of the thousands of years of training, breeding, and domestication which were begun, somewhere in Asia, by a people unknown to us. Thanks to their efforts, there was born what we might call a "buffalo civilization," which is a necessary concommitant of the rice civilization.

The spice smugglers

Celebes Island was long the crossroads of the Asiatic spice trade. The Arabs were there several centuries before Islam arrived. Their hegemony was contested successively by Hindus, Malayans, Khmers, and Chinese. From the South China Sea to the Banda Sea, every religious faith won adherents; then came Islam, like a tidal wave against which only New Guinea in its wildness stood firm.

Today, the island can still lay claim to its rank as a crossroads of commerce. Menado (50,000 population) in the north and Ujung Pandang (Makassar) (100,000 population) in the south are ports bustling with Indonesian trade. The history of the latter city, particularly, is a romantic one. It was a celebrated port during the era of the spice trade and of the East India Company. It was one of the first export centers for nutmeg and clove. At one point in its long history, the Dutch were so determined to retain their monopoly in the spice trade, that they took steps to eliminate all competition—by, among other means, burning all plants over which they could not exercise constant surveillance. Whereupon (and predictably), the smuggling of these precious commodities became a thriving business in the area, particularly among the Arabs and the Malayans; and Makassar was one of the principal centers of contraband goods. Today, the city boasts of an impressive port and an airport. It regards itself as destined to become the Singapore of the Indonesian archipelago; time will probably justify this claim.

Rantepao

It is relatively simple today to travel from Makassar to the Toradja region. The road, however, is long and quite bad. One must count on at least a day's journey by automobile to reach Rantepao. The trip is not unpleasant. The scenery is beautiful. The native pubs are inviting. The people are warm and friendly—particularly since they have given up headhunting.

Rantepao is situated at the very heart of the island, on a mountainous site surrounded by rivers and waterfalls. It is, in truth, little more than the end of the line for the tiny buses that serve the surrounding countryside. The use of these vehicles demonstrates that the inhabitants of the island, although retired from the active list of cannibals, have lost none of their courage. It requires a stout heart indeed to endure a trip on one of these swaying, fragile buses, packed among portly matrons, dogs, and flocks of chickens.

The village of Rantepao has only one street deserving of that name, which is lined by the stores of Chinese shopkeepers. There is little here to attract the tourist, except the inhabitants themselves. I watched them with interest: two peasants, each carrying an end of a pole from which a large, black hog was suspended; a man literally sinking under the weight of his burden of bamboo (except that it was not solely bamboo, for lengths of bamboo are used to tranport *tuak*—a fermented juice which must be drunk while it is still fresh or else it turns into poison).

I was surprised to see several handsome storehouses for rice standing among the shops and houses on the street. They were quite empty, as I discovered. It is considered fashionable in Rantepaoan society to buy these small structures in the countryside, disassemble them, and then have them reconstructed in one's front yard. They serve no purpose except that of conspicuous consumption—and that, perhaps, of preserving some of the best specimens of Toradja architecture.

The marketplace of Rantepao holds unexpected interest for the traveler. At first glance, I saw what appeared to be a sea of small golden roofs, some pointed and some round, arranged in no discernible order, swaying slightly as though moved by an invisible breeze. These "roofs" are the hats of the women of the market, moving in rhythm to their chatter. They are quite large, and are woven of rice straw which shimmers in shades of gold and tan in the sunlight.

Under the shade of an umbrella-hat, the face of the wearer disappears into the shadow. I could see only the bright red of the tomatoes at her feet, or the green of peppers, or the bright pink meat of a watermelon. Then there was an exclamation, a laugh, and the hat was raised to reveal a tiny brown nose, large shining eyes, sparkling teeth, the perfect curve of an ear. A truly handsome race.

Architectural masterpieces

The "road" from Rantepao is, in fact, hardly more than a trail, and it is negotiable only by jeep. We bounced along, across the width of the valley, scaling hills that would have given pause to the most inveterate hiker. Among the fields, large gray rocks rose sharply from the slopes. I caught sight of a steep cliff rising in the distance. As we drew nearer, it seemed less formidable. Along its base were clumps of trees and grass in almost gardenlike order. On the wall of the cliff itself, I could see what appeared to be decorations—ornamental panels of wood, arranged at different heights. A closer inspection revealed that these panels were

The water buffalo is the main actor in the processions and festivals that are so popular among the inhabitants of Celebes.

Opposite: The façades of Toradja houses are decorated with beautiful paintings. Traditionally, one of the ornaments is a sculpted and painted water buffalo head.

The water buffalo is indispensable in cultivating rice paddies. It is such a docile animal that even a child can manage it.

painted with the stylized resemblance of a water buffalo, the crescent horns, the eyes, ears, and muzzle all harmonizing in a sophisticated composition. There was not one panel that was exactly like any other, but all showed a remarkable sense of restraint and balance in their somber hues of dark red and sepia. These panels are tombstones or, rather, the doors of tombs dug into the face of the cliff. Some of the tombs are framed by immense horns, carved out of the rock.

I stopped at all the villages on the slopes. They were all similar, at least superficially: ten or twelve wooden houses, built on pilings. Their roofs rose from among the banana and cassava trees like majestic ships; for the villagers build their houses with enormously high peaks in the front and rear. The roofs, which slope gently between the two peaks, are made of interwoven bamboo and leaves, and are sturdy enough to be proof against the heaviest tropical downpour and even against hurricanes. Under the bowlike front peaks of the houses is usually hung a carving of a buffalo head. The central supporting beam of one chief's house was covered entirely with buffalo horns. The walls of the houses are made of numerous panels of woven straw, strikingly painted.

The storehouses for rice are of lighter construction, but have the same roof-line as the houses and are even more elaborately decorated.

In every village along the way, the inhabitants were friendly, smiling, eager to welcome visitors. The Toradja are a race of dancers and musicians, and they possess a natural dignity, an innate elgance, enhanced by delicate features and that particular looseness of movement associated with some of the peoples of Asiatic stock.

In one village square, I was able to observe a celebration that was played out against a backdrop of bow-roofed houses and storehouses. The spectacle opened with a procession: a majestic water buffalo, its horns wreathed with flowers, preceded and followed by tribesmen. The buffalo's escort, all of them males, wore tunics of red silk flecked with gold. On their heads, they wore a kind of helmet on which a pair of gilded horns had been mounted. It was a procession to the taste of the Toradja; that is, a combination of tawdriness and utter charm. The gold of the tunics is often nothing more than bits of paper, and the swords and shields of the men are of wood. Yet, the flowers are real and very fragrant, and, most striking of all, every color is an absolute harmony with the whole. There is not one clashing hue, not one false note.

The buffalo procession entered the square. The dancers, clad in pink and sky blue, took their places and began moving their arms in rhythm with that eerie Oriental music that never ceases to astound Western ears. The spectators—all Toradja except for myself—were attentive and respectful. Here, a spectacle such as this is one of life's greatest pleasures.

I cannot truly say that I found the Toradja to be a people characterized by gaiety. They are artists, if in that broad term we are willing to include those who, while lacking creative genius, have an unerring sense of what is fitting in decoration. Their celebrations are rarely joyous in nature; more often they are funereal. Their sobriety is part of their way of life and of their culture—a culture about which very little is known. Today, the Toradja are attempting to retain that cul-

This is one of the cliff tombs in Toradja country. Note the water buffalo horns around the entrance to the tomb.

Double page following: The sway back roofs of Toradja architecture harmonize beautifully with the landscape and with the clumps of bamboo around the rice paddies.

This Toradja tomb is decorated with a stylized painting of a buffalo's head.

ture in the face of an invasion of tourists, and perhaps even in the face of the incursions of the Indonesian government.

The cult of the dead

I have already mentioned that the cliffs in this area are used as cemeteries. I was taken to another part of the island where there are deep caves. In these caves are preserved the skulls of the ancestors of the Toradja, and their hats—the enormous hats of straw which are considered the most precious relic of departed forebears. The more important personages among the Toradja are not relegated to the caves. Instead, funeral chambers are excavated high up in the cliffs of Lemo or Londa; these are the tombs, marked by painted wooden panels, that I had seen upon my arrival.

Images of the dead are also exposed on the cliffs, on small balconies of wood attached precariously to the vertical drop. From there, the dolls seem to contemplate the land of the living, their hands fixed forever in the ritual gesture of prayer. These dolls are known as *tau tau*. Every year, in the month of August, the men of the villages, using flimsy bamboo ladders, climb the face of the cliff to fetch the dolls. They are brought down, dressed by the family in new clothes, and then returned to their balconies.

The coffin in which a dead man is carried to his burial place is a miniature of the houses and the rice storehouses. The two ends are raised and pointed, like the bow and the stern of a boat. One may speculate that this peculiar shape is used to commemorate the boats that first brought the Toradja from their country of origin to Celebes Island, and that it is now being used to carry the soul of the departed into the afterlife.

That is a somewhat romantic thought. It is just as possible that the crescent-roofed houses, storehouses, and coffins are shaped in the likeness of the horns of the water buffalo. Indeed, much of what is believed about the Toradja is little more than romantic speculation. All that is known of their origins, for example, is that the remote ancestors of today's 500,000 Toradja probably came from the mainland of Asia. It is said that they are of the same stock as the Batak of Sumatra and the Dayak of Borneo. It is probable that they were a maritime people—which is evidence in favor of the boat theory of the crescent roofs. It is obvious that the Toradja brought with them the secret of growing rice, as well as the one animal indispensable to the cultivation of that commodity: the water buffalo. This indicates that the Toradja may well have come from India or the Indochinese peninsula.

The Indian water buffalo, or *arni* (known in Indonesia as *kerabau*) is classified by zoologists in a genus all to itself. In India, it was already a domestic animal five thousand years ago. The geographic spread of the buffalo has always corresponded to that of irrigated rice paddies, for the reason that the water buffalo is the only domestic animal capable of working in water. It is therefore the providential animal *par excellence* among the nations that have adopted it. It is a tireless worker, a source of milk, of fine meat, and of unusually weather resistant leather.

The blood of sacrifice

The Toradja, like many other peoples, regard their destiny as linked to that of a beneficial and sacred animal. According to their belief, the world is supported on the back of a water buffalo. This symbolism illustrates their dependence on the buffalo for their survival.

It is almost inevitable that a domestic animal as precious as the buffalo will take on a religious character. And, indeed, the sacrifice of a buffalo is a central religious ceremony in several Asian cultures (in Nepal, for example). What could be more fitting as a sacrifice than the immolation of a great beast of high value? Indeed, the mountain-dwellers of central Vietnam raise water buffalo expressly for the purpose of offering them in sacrifice.[1]

Among the Toradja, water buffalo are immolated in great numbers in commemoration of the dead. The funeral services of a noble, a *puang,* continue for months after the individual's death—and sometimes for years. The greater the number of buffalo that are sacrificed, the greater the honor done to the family of the deceased. For every ten buffalo slaughtered, the family will be entitled to mount one horn on the exterior beam of their house. In some villages, I have seen beams covered with horns from bottom to top. The value of the sacrificial buffalo, however, varies according to the color of its hide. Generally, the lighter the color, the more valuable the animal. The most precious animals of all—that is, the lightest in color—are called *bonga.*

The funerals of important persons are often attended by thousands of mourners, and special dwellings are constructed (and elaborately decorated) to house the visitors. The friends and relatives of the deceased are expected to offer a buffalo or a pig at the ceremony, thus satisfying any debts owed to the dead man.

---

[1] The noted French anthropologist, George Condaminas has written of the buffalo, ". . . there is a certain equation between an original human sacrifice and the sacrifice of a buffalo. The buffalo is sacrificed in place of the former victim: man. In a sense, this substitution corresponds to something real. The sacrifice of the buffalo is a high point in the life of the community; it is a feast in the full meaning of that term, and it allows the community to renew and to express its cohesion."

Storehouses for rice are among the successes of Toradja architecture. The line of the roof, with its peaks fore and aft, may commemorate the boats in which the ancestors of the present population came from the North.

The funeral festivities

The lengthy funeral rites are highlighted by procession and displays, for the Toradja have an inborn sense of appropriate and elegant staging. It is difficult to tell the spectators from the dancers, for everyone is dressed as thought they might be called upon to take an active part in the ceremonies. A crown of red paper, a few touches of gold, a hibiscus flower in her hair, and any young woman here could convincingly portray a reigning queen.

There are other, less entrancing sights. A group of men arrive, carrying baskets on their heads. These are the owners of fighting cocks, in stately procession. Then come the sacrificial swine, carried on poles resting on the shoulders of two men. The water buffalo follow the swine. The throats of the animals are cut, and the blood runs scarlet down their dark, quivering flanks.

The Toradja are vegetarians. They eat meat only on great occasions. Now, they will gorge themselves for several days on the sacrificial animals.

They are a gentle people, almost frail in appearance. Yet, they thrive on blood and on combat. Less than a hundred years ago, their ancestors were still hunting heads. The Toradja of today have not lost their taste for violence; rather,

The houses in Toradja villages are arranged in a straight line. Great care is taken in the decoration of the raised peaks. The houses are built on pilings and usually have a front porch.

they have converted it into an enthusiasm for cockfights and, above all, for buffalo fights.

Buffalo, being very placid animals, require a great deal of prodding before they will consent to fight. When a pair of them has been sufficiently stimulated, however, they charge one another with great violence, smashing their great horned heads together with an impact that is like a clap of thunder. It is an encounter that makes no pretense to art or skill. Instead, it is senseless, brutal. Yet, only rarely is a buffalo seriously injured in these encounters. Most often, one of them slips while backing away, then turns and flees.

The Megaliths

The Toradja were probably a seafaring people at one time; otherwise they would never have reached Celebes Island. Why, then, did they withdraw to the interior and completely abandon the sea? The explanation is simple: they were

The Toradja people all preserve reverently the memory of the dead, although the rites of the cult vary from one region to the next. At Londa (above), the skulls and bones of the departed are preserved in caves, along with their hats. The latter are considered to be precious relics. On another cliff (below), wooden balconies, attached to the vertical wall of the cliff, are used to display dolls. The dolls, suitably attired, represent the dead who are buried in a neighboring cave.

pushed back into the hinterlands, along the Sadang valley, by other peoples: the Makassar and the Boughi, Malayans who were the best navigators of the archipelago. They were Moslems, the only maritime inhabitants of Celebes, and, for many years, skilled pirates. It is likely that they had landed on the Australian continent long before the arrival on those shores of Captain James Cook in 1770. (Their graceful sailing craft, with sloping masts, are still seen in the port of Makassar (now Ujung Pandang); but they are gradually being replaced by Japanese, Australian, and American cargo ships.)

It is certain that another race preceded the Toradja to the interior of Celebes Island. I have seen, in the midst of the bamboos, a grassy knoll around which stood a circle of stones. Around these were other stones, some in the shape of phalluses and some hollowed out into giant cups. Nothing is known of the megalithic civilization that erected these stones, or of the significance of the stones themselves.[1]

The price of progress

Celebes Island has a very special and peculiar position in this part of the world, both geographically and otherwise. On a map of the world, Wallace's Line, which passes between the islands of Bali and Lombok and between Borneo and Celebes, was originally accepted as the boundary between the Oriental and Australasian faunal regions. There is another boundary, Weber's Line, which modifies the former and lies between Celebes and the Moluccas.

Celebes Island is situated between these two lines, in a transitional zone known to geographers as "Wallaces." The island is therefore the last outpost of Asia and, at the same time, the first outpost of Oceania. This, no doubt, accounts for the exceptional character of the island. It has all the marks of a sophisticated civilization brought from the Asiatic mainland; and yet, its heart its Toradja soul—remains virtually intact. Only the fringes of Toradja culture have been affected, thus far, by Japanese tourists, English businessmen, or Australian prospectors.

The island's situation as the frontier between Asia and Oceania renders its fu-

---

[1] The ethnic complexity of Celebes Island remains to be unraveled by the ethnographers. Yet, I should point out that a people other than the Toradja are ancient rice-growing inhabitants of the island. They are the Foala, whose origins are as mysterious as those of the Toradja.

Double page following: In a cliff at Lomo, images of the dead are kept in a sort of rectangular grotto cut out of the rock. Once a year, the inhabitants of the area bring the dolls down from the grotto and dress them in new clothing.

Celebes was once the home of a mysterious megalithic civilization. The photograph shows part of a field of megaliths still standing in the middle of the bush.

ture somewhat doubtful. It has more economic potential than the Moluccas; it is more developed than New Guinea; and it is making its entry into the modern world under the political authority of the Indonesian government. Yet, there is virtually no ethnic affinity among the inhabitants of Java, the Toradja of Celebes Island, or New Guinea. In fact, there are some 200 distinct ethnic groups in the 6,000 islands that comprise the Republic of Indonesia.

The case of Celebes is complicated by religious considerations. The Boughi of the south are Moslems; the Alfours of the Manado area are Christians; and the Toradja worship their ancestors.

It is inevitable, I suppose, that the civilization of the twentieth century will make short work of my friends at Rantepao, whose chief concern in life is to honor their dead and to decorate their houses. As luck would have it, the Western world has suddenly become aware of the mineral wealth of Celebes Island. The land of rice and the water buffalo, it seems, is rich in gold in the north, in nickel in the south, and, everywhere else, in bauxite, sulphur, phosphates, manganese, and other resources which the world eyes with cupidity. For once, it is not only the Japanese, the Americans, and the Dutch who are eager to exploit this treasure. France, too, is offering to build plants for the refining of these minerals.

Will the painters, sculptors, and architects of Celebes Island be able to withstand the onslaught of prospectors and engineers? Or will the dancers of Toradja be transformed into miners?

Here, as elsewhere in Asia, every political, technical, and economic step forward is less a measure of progress than a human drama. Dozens of islands, dozens of peoples see their life-styles destroyed, their psychological equilibrium compromised, their arts and their beliefs set aside. The inhabitants of these islands are free men. We may ask whether they must truly pay so high a price to enter the modern world.

the garden of the argonauts

He stood there, lounging around the door, detached, calm, at ease, exhibiting that combination of self-confidence and good breeding which respectable Melanesians adopt on such occasions.
BRONISLAW MALINOWSKI

"Bad weather," the Australian pilot mumbled through his beard.

It was an understatement. Ever since leaving Port Moresby on the flight to the Trobriand Islands, we had been tossed about by winds and rain. The aircraft itself, a dilapidated DC3 dating from World War II, did little to put me at ease. At Port Moresby, it had taken three tries before we even got off the ground. . . .

Finally, I saw the islands below us—mountainous, black, rising out of the sea, their peaks lost in the lowering clouds. It took a while for the pilot to locate the airport. Eventually, we put down on a grassy strip at sea level.

The name "Trobriand" is one that is significant to students of Pacific exploration. The man after whom the islands were named was an officer under Admiral Bruni d'Entrecasteaux, the discoverer of the Trobriand Islands during his fruitless search for Count de La Pérouse. Since d'Entrecasteaux had already exhausted his own resources by giving his name to a group of islands southwest of New Guinea, he selected Trobriand for the honor of standing as godfather, so to speak, for the islands. D'Entrecasteaux, in fact, broke with tradition in this respect. Previously, it had been customary to name newly discovered lands and islands after princes, kings, and saints. The year, however, was 1792; and the great revolution was in full swing in France. Crowned heads were falling, and saints, along with the Church, were in disrepute. Prominent political figures came and went with

Fashionable young women in the Trobriand Islands do not cover their breasts. Their grass skirts have three layers of fiber.

such frequency that even their names were not safe. The Admiral, therefore, found a simple solution to the problem: he named his discoveries after members of his staff. Huon Island was named after Huon de Kermadec, captain of the *Espérance*. Rossel Island was christened in honor of d'Entrecasteaux's flag captain. And the Beaupré Islands were so called after the engineer-hydrographer of the expedition, Lieutenant Beautemps-Beaupré.

The forgotten islands

The rain was falling in torrents on the landing strip, on the little thatched hut that served as an airport, and on the jungle surrounding both. I darted into the hut and saw my first Trobrianders: women with flowers in their hair and naked men. I breathed a sigh of relief. I had been eager to reach these islands; and, at the same time, I had been apprehensive about what I would find. I had heard that the Trobrianders were unspoiled; but I had heard that before about other Pacific islands. and I had sometimes been disappointed. At first glance, I decided, these islanders at least looked unspoiled.

We are often guilty of thinking of small, remote Pacific archipelagoes as being without a past of their own and without a history, as though they suddenly sprang into existence when the first ship of European explorers sailed into the area. The fact is that, although we may be ignorant of much of their past, the islands have not only a history but, in the case of the Trobriands, a pre-history as well. Only recently, a group of burial caves was discovered in the Trobriand Islands, the walls of which are decorated with rupestral paintings.[1] It is thought that these paintings are the result of an ancient Polynesian migration to the islands. And, of course, there are the megaliths that have been discovered on several islands.

The present-day inhabitants of the Trobriands are a crossbreed of Polynesian and Melanesian stock. It is perhaps this mixture that is responsible for the individual aspects of Trobriander culture, and for the fact that the natives are both an agricultural and a seafaring people. They are mariners and fishermen as well as farmers.

The Trobrianders, who inhabit one large island, two smaller ones, and a sprinkling of islets, lived for centuries in absolute isolation from the rest of the world. It was not until the nineteenth century that the first missionary set foot on the Trobriands. In the footsteps of the missionaries came adventurers in search of a Trobriander commodity: pearls. From time immemorial, the natives had had, as their principal edible shellfish, a small mollusk which they called *lapi.* Many of these shellfish contained large, round pearls—which the Trobrianders gave to their children as toys.

The Trobriand Islands became famous in the first part of the twentieth century, through the efforts of a celebrated ethnographer, Bronislaw Malinowski. Malinowski was of Polish extraction, an Austrian subject who emigrated to England

---

[1]It is interesting to note that, in one of these caves, the human figures in the paintings have mutilated hands similar to the prehistoric paintings found in European and Australian caves.

and married an Australian. He held the chair of anthropology at the University of London. Eventually, he emigrated to the United States where, until his death in 1942, he taught at Yale University. He has been called "the wet blanket of anthropology" because he applied the methods of psychological analysis to the study of primitive societies. He was undoubtedly a controversial personality, although it is generally admitted that his field work was not only inspired but touched with genius. A two-year study of the Trobriand archipelago resulted in two works of lasting value: *The Argonauts of the Western Pacific*, and *The Coral Gardens*. Anything that I knew of the Trobriands before visiting them, I owed to those two works.

Malinowski had already completed his study of the islands and published his findings when the Trobriands were engulfed by World War II. The Trobriands, which had been occupied by General Douglas MacArthur in July 1943, served as the assembly point for the American counterattack against the Japanese. Some 60,000 American and Australian troops gathered there prior to their assault on the Solomon Islands.

One can only imagine what an upheaval this caused in the life of the Trobriand Islanders, and what permanent damage to native culture might have resulted. The islanders were driven from their homes so that airstrips and roads might be built. They were deprived of their gardens. Indeed, they were stripped of everything that was familiar and precious to them. Under such conditions, it seemed likely that the Trobriand Islanders—who, until then, were untouched by the modern world would lose forever their traditions and their social structures.

Yet, the improbable happened. In 1945, with the end of the war in the Pacific, the Americans and Australians embarked on their ships and disappeared over the horizon as though by magic. Suddenly, the Trobrianders were alone again, free to go back to their former way of life. By all reports, they did precisely that. The sole lasting effect of World War II, it appeared, was a pronounced distaste among the islanders for any further contact with the white man. My purpose in visiting the Trobriand Islands was to see if that were true.

On the lagoon

From the first primitive airstrip I flew to Losuia, the "capital city" of the islands. Happily, the sky had cleared by then, and the ancient DC3 reached its destination with a minimum of shuddering and groaning.

Even in the Trobriander capital, the airport building was nothing more than a large mud hut. Several citizens lounged around the building, smiling, obviously curious. Nudity, I gathered, was *de rigueur*. Only a few of the men wore anything at all, and their concession to modesty was a rudimentary loincloth of dried leaves.

I had expected to find a hotel in Losuia. There was none. I was told that there had been one, presided over by a Chinese gentleman; but it had burned down. I was then driven—in a taxi, the doors of which were held shut by pieces of wire and through the roof of which I caught glimpses of the sky—to a guest house, of sorts, at the edge of the lagoon.

I was struck by the omnipresence of the jungle. Humanity seemed represented

Above: Trobriand villages are quite attractive and much attention is given to architectural detail. The tall building to the left is a storehouse for yams. The latticelike sides are designed to allow the yams to be admired by passers-by.

Opposite: The chief's house and his personal yam storehouse are elaborately decorated and painted.

by nothing more than a few small clearings in the dense greenery. The airport building had been nothing more than a hut hedged in by trees; and the narrow landing strip, an alleyway dwarfed by looming green walls. The sea itself was not safe from this vegetal invasion, for the mangrove trees and the screwpine grew in the water.

I was assigned a small comfortless cabin at the guest house. Its doorway was virtually covered by the broad leaves of a plant which, serpentlike, seemed determined to engulf the structure.

Just outside of my cabin, at the edge of the lagoon, I saw a fisherman arranging his net in a pirogue. I surmised that he was ready to head out for an evening's fishing.

The first question to be resolved, obviously, was this: are the Trobrianders primarily an agricultural or a fishing folk?

The pirogue moved slowly away from the bank. I gestured frantically, and no doubt incomprehensibly, toward the fisherman. He looked at me curiously, smiled, and somehow understood. The pirogue returned to shore.

We conversed at length using gestures and a few common words of pidgin English. Finally, he agreed to abandon his plans and, instead, to take me out in his boat, among the coral reefs and mangrove trees.

We made our way out into the great lagoon, following a sinuous network of canals with which my guide seemed thoroughly familiar. Seen from a distance, I noted, the jungle was less overwhelming, less impenetrable. Above the thick belt of mangroves along the water's edge, I could distinguish the smooth trunks of palm trees and several large clumps of dracaena. There were mango trees, with shiny green leaves, and, of course, banyan trees. Different species grew close together, their branches intertwining; many were covered by vines. Malinowski observed, quite aptly, that the vertical lines of the palm trees rising in the jungle are reminiscent of "pillars supporting a medieval vault."

The water was smooth, and we glided over it without a sound. Occasionally, a curious bird would swoop down to observe us, and then fly away squawking. I could hear the distant sound of breakers on the reef. Here, on the lagoon, there was not a ripple. It was dusk, and I was spellbound by the soft evening air and the beauty of the sun's last reflection on the water.

We saw a group of pirogues approaching us. The fishermen of the village were returning with their catch. We turned and followed the procession to a point along the shore where the jungle receded from the water and gave way to a small beach almost invisible under the trees. There were women and children in the water, bathing and shouting happily.

It was almost dark by the time we dragged our pirogue up onto the beach alongside those of the fishermen. I inspected the boats briefly, but saw none of those carved bows the form of which is supposedly dictated by tradition. Two of the pirogues were noticeably larger than the others; but they were otherwise distinguished only by the large nylon nets which they contained.

The fishermen, I learned, belonged to the same village as my guide. Their wives and children had come down to the beach to wait for the menfolk and to carry back their day's catch. The village itself was situated only a hundred yards from the shore, and was reached by a winding trail hacked through the underbrush. We reached a clearing. This was the village: a number of huts, the odor of wood fires kindled to cook the evening meal—and a storehouse for Chinese yams. At first I had thought that the village lived exclusively from the sea. It was not so. Even here, at the shore, the people were both fishermen and farmers.

The storehouse was immediately recognizable from the innumerable photographs that I had seen. And it was as elegant as I had expected. High and narrow, raised above the ground on five-foot pilings, its peaked roof sloping gracefully on both sides, it was a model of architectural simplicity and functionalism. The walls were trellised so as to assure proper air circulation, which is necessary to keep the yams from rotting.

The building, to all appearances, is merely a place for storing yams. In practice, it is also a religious edifice. The people here practice a cult of the yam, which is intricately connected with the cult of the dead. That, no doubt, is why the villages, although located on the coast, have not given up agriculture in favor of the sea. To give up the yam would be a renunciation of their culture and of its ceremonies and rites, for the yam is the foundation of the village's social and religious life.

I went with my guide, who had suddenly been transformed into my host, to one of the houses. We sat on the raised platform, or porch, in front of the building. Soon, we were joined by a number of village elders who wandered slowly onto the porch and, without so much as glancing at me, sat and chewed their betel leaves. From time to time, they spat, emitting jets of reddish saliva that traveled for a surprising distance before falling to earth. I sat there quietly, completely at ease, watching the sky blacken and the jungle disappear in the darkness. The fires of the village twinkled in the gloom, and the women bustled about their household chores. Dogs and pigs lay quietly on the hard, packed earth of the clearing, their fur glistening in the firelight.

No one seemed surprised to see a Westerner suddenly appear on my guide's front porch. No one expressed the slightest curiosity about where I came from, what I was doing there, or where I was going. I was treated with that vague and disinterested politeness normally reserved for a transient who will soon be gone and who will never be seen again.

The detachment of my hosts was not difficult to understand. These villagers had seen, in their lifetime, strangers wage a savage war around them. They had witnessed slaughter and bombings and suffering on a scale incomprehensible to them and for reasons unintelligible to them. They had experienced an American occupation, with its senseless waste, its openhanded generosity, and its total indifference to their own culture and traditions. Then, they had been told they were "independent." Yet, they knew that they were still very much dependent on Port Moresby, whence came a steady stream of officials, medical supplies, and ethnographers. None of this really mattered to the inhabitants of the Trobriand Islands. They had survived the war unchanged. They would survive, unchanged, the Port Moresby regime. Life on the Trobriand Islands goes on. A strange white man, making himself at home on their front porch in the cool evening air—what difference could it possibly make?

The Trobrianders are perfectly right to put their faith and their hope in the Chinese yam. If I were a Trobriander, I would do the same. Of all the peoples I encountered during the travels in the Pacific, the inhabitants of this island are undoubtedly the wisest, the most reflective, and the most aware of the peril to their way of life presented by the modern world. Their natural pride, evident in their demeanor, is perhaps their means of salvation, their bulwark against "progress." They have raised to an art the ability to keep a stranger at a proper distance— while, at the same time, treating him with exquisite courtesy. The Trobrianders, in a word, have succeeded in combining Polynesian nobility with the common sense and realism of the Melanesians.

The flower-crowned maidens

During my stay at the Trobriand Islands I managed to see the island of Kiriwina almost in its entirety, visiting villages in the jungle, gardens, and settlements along the shore. My earlier impression was confirmed by what I observed. The Trobrianders, having seen their way of life imperiled by the war, have no intention of allowing it to be threatened once more by the tourist industry. They know how to go about protecting it: they are completely impervious to the curiosity of strangers, and, while never discourteous, they are content simply to ignore the presence of visitors.

The villages in the interior of the island have well-constructed and ingeniously arranged houses.

I discovered that many of the islanders speak English, although they will not do so until the visitor has won their confidence. One Trobriander even knew of Malinowski and was delighted to know that the ethnographer had familiarized the outside world with the customs and traditions of the island. I came to suspect, however, that this man was something of a professional informer—the kind of man who, in order to satisfy an investigator, will supply an abundance of information embellished with subjective interpretations and with details of his own invention. I could not help wondering how many ethnographers had fallen into the hands of "cooperative natives" of this kind.

The layout of the villages appeared to conform to the most sophisticated requirements of urban design. Each one consisted of a large outer circle formed by the houses of the people. In front of the houses was a smaller circle: that of the storehouses for yams. It happened often that these handsome storehouses were more numerous, and more painstakingly constructed, than the houses. Moreover, they were always in a state of perfect repair. In the center of the circle there were always two structures, decoratively painted, ornamented with rows of white shells. One of them was the house of the chief; the other, his personal storehouse for yams.

Wherever I stopped on the island, the first thing I saw in each village was a group of young women sitting on the stoop of one of the houses. These women—girls, actually—ranged in age from 13 to 16; almost invariably they wore either wreaths of flowers on their heads or hibiscus flowers in their hair. They seemed to have a great deal of leisure time on their hands.

The girls smiled readily, and many of them were quite attractive—especially when compared to the athletic matrons of the Asaro valley, or to the toothless fisherwomen of Lake Wissel in New Guinea. Their slender bodies were clothed only in short skirts made of three layers of grass, the outermost layer dyed in various colors. Their firm, well-formed breasts were, of course, bare.

This was their everyday dress. No doubt they were even more attractive in holiday apparel.

I often encountered Trobriand Island women along the jungle trails of the island, and, as a group, they are characterized by an elegant nonchalance that should be the envy of their Occidental sisters. They walked the trail in single file, all so marvelously alike that they seemed figures from an antique frieze, each of them carrying a conical basket on her head. Their burden served only to accentuate their graceful, straight necks, which were bare of jewelry or other ornamentation, and their well-formed, golden-brown breasts. As they moved, their grass skirts tossed and swayed like the tutus of a troupe of ballerinas.

According to ancient custom, the women of the Trobriand Islands are initiated very young into the sexual life of the community. From puberty, they are expected to indulge in free love, and they continue this practice until they marry. Even then, my informer volunteered (not without a touch of bitterness in his voice), some of the women are not addicted to total fidelity.

My impression of the women was that they are remarkably sure of themselves. And, in fact, their self-confidence is reflected in local practices. Unlike the women of Papua New Guinea, Trobriander women play an important role in the social life of the tribe. They are listened to with respect, and they have a voice in

The bows of Trobriander pirogues are carved in an intricate design framing a tiny human head and the stylized silhouette of an ancestor. (Photograph J. Oster, Collection Musée de l'Homme)

all important decisions. They are even allowed to participate in the cultivation of the Chinese yams, which is regarded as a privilege rather than as a chore.

The coral gardens

I had the opportunity to inspect the fields along the trails where the yams are grown. Actually, they are more accurately described as gardens rather than fields, since the yams are grown in relatively small clearings in the midst of the brush. The clearings themselves require much effort on the part of the Trobrianders. The trees must be removed by burning, and the vines, roots, grass, and brush cleared away. Finally, a stout fence is built around the plot, consisting of heavy vertical posts connected by interwoven branches. It is the kind of enclosure that one would expect to find in India, as protection against voracious elephants; or in Africa, where gorillas are delighted to harvest an unwary farmer's crop for him. Here, the only danger to crops is from a few wild pigs.

The men working in one of these yam enclosures allowed us to enter. They were digging in the earth, their tools a kind of stake sharpened into a wooden blade and a steel-bladed hatchet, the latter obviously imported. They were plant-

A chief's house in a village in the bush, near Losuia.

ing yams, as I expected, but there were also large round holes in the ground which, I was told, were for taro. Here and there, I could see banana trees, only recently cut down, beginning to sprout from the roots.

These enclosures are the famous "coral gardens," which have been raised to the dignity of an ethnographic curiosity, and which are visited as though they were historical monuments.

Here, as elsewhere, however, nothing is as simple as it seems. The garden is not merely a garden. Indeed, there would have been no garden had it not been planned and planted to the accompaniment of an elaborate ritual presided over by a magician, who is often also the chief of the village or of the tribe. It is not so much a matter of raising food as it is of preparing for the festivities that will result from the cultivation of this small piece of land. There will be a fertility celebration, during which the crops will be gathered. The fruits of the gardens will be piled high in the center of the village, and the yams and taros will be artistically arranged in stacks decorated with flowers. Wreaths of bananas and coconuts will be attached to the piles, so as to attract, and to appease, the spirits of the dead.

The celebrations on the Trobriand Islands, like those on other islands, have a social as well as a religious function. They present an opportunity for the inhabitants to display with pride the produce of their gardens, to compare the size of yams, to gossip, and to visit—as people do in the county fairs of the midwestern states in this country. In addition, of course, there will be a ritual meal, during which everyone will gorge themselves on the yams and on pork and fish.

The sides of yam storehouses are often painted in delicate designs. These storehouses are a matter of great pride to the villagers.

The fertility of the land on the Trobriand Islands varies enormously from one place to another. Sometimes the land is good in one spot, and bad only a few yards away, depending, obviously, on the thickness of the topsoil covering the coral underneath. Generally speaking, however, the tropical climate of the island favors a stupendous rate of growth. The human population of these islands is too scattered to have been able to challenge nature successfully. The yam and taro gardens are miniscule in comparison with the overall area and the jungle is quick to reclaim any human infringement upon its domain. Only fire is able to challenge the vegetation effectively.

The overwhelming growth of vegetation on the islands, however, is somewhat illusory. The truth is that the fertility of the soil is quite limited and quickly exhausted. A plot of land, such as one of the "coral gardens" of the Trobrianders, can be cultivated only once every six or seven years. Even then, agriculture is a laborious task, for the yam requires constant care and attention. The yam is buried horizontally in the ground. When the vines begin to appear, they must be carefully twined around stakes and held in place by pieces of string. The most difficult part, however, is the task of holding the leaves themselves on the stake in such a way that each one will receive a proper amount of light; for the more abundant the leaves of the vine, the larger the new yam.

Gardening, obviously, plays the major role in the life of the Trobrianders, and the average islander probably spends half his life at work in his garden. The seriousness with which a Trobriander views his yam plants is indicated by the fact that his language provides a distinct name for every single twig of a plant.

The terms *savage* and *primitive mentality* are generally taken to mean that the people so designated work only when forced by absolute necessity; and then they work as little as possible. The *primitive* is supposed to be lazy, and to depend entirely on the generosity of nature in the tropics for his survival. If that be so, then the Trobrianders are neither savages nor primitive. They not only work very hard in their gardens, but they work far more than is really necessary. Self-respect and pride, if not inclination, push them to it.

Given the energy and care which the Trobrianders expend on their crops, it is not surprising that production often surpasses need. In a good year, twice as many yams may be harvested as can actually be eaten. The islanders take great pride in this superabundance, and it does not bother them in the least that the extra yams may simply be left to rot. The success of one's garden is an all-consuming passion. A man who has no garden is a very poor man indeed; a man who does not work his garden is an object of universal contempt. The average adult, indeed, has anywhere from three to six gardens of his own. A particularly energetic man may have eight. Even children have one or two gardens.

Considering the time and work involved in cultivating these gardens and the fact that the crops are so large that much of the produce cannot be used, it is evident that the Trobrianders do not realize a very high material return on their investment. Yet, they are unconcerned about this aspect of their lives. The importance of the gardens is not material, but social and spiritual. An islander's self-respect and his standing in the community are measured by the amount of work that he does. And those considerations are accepted as sufficient reward in themselves.

The worth of a man is directly proportionate to the size of the garden that he is able to work. The gardener himself actually sees very little of the produce that he raises. Three-quarters of it goes to the chief of the tribe, and much of what remains goes to his sister's husband or his mother's family.

Disputes over land are virtually unknown on the Trobriand Islands, since there is more than enough for everyone. The location of a man's garden and the general distribution of land for gardening purposes is decided on a yearly basis by the village chief or by the local magician.

As soon as this distribution takes place, a series of rites begins. The first of these occurs before the land is cleared. It consists of an offering to the ancestors of the tribe. This is followed by a common meal for the villagers, during which the spirits are invoked and the village's hatchets are anointed with a magical oil.

The burning of the trees in the garden plots is also a ritual act. It is undertaken by the village magician, who uses consecrated torches.

The magical act *par excellence*, however, is the construction of a *Kamkokola* in each corner of a new garden. The *Kamkokola* is a "magical corner," where the owner of the garden plants, first, a taro root, and, later, a yam. Then a house, for the use of the spirits, is built, resting on four stones. The house itself consists of several pickets leaning against one another. Sometimes the structure is twenty feet high—a considerable effort on the part of the gardener. Yet, the effort is worth the result, for it insures that the spirits will protect the garden from all harm.

Vanity of vanities

Although gardening on the Trobriand Islands has taken on a sacramental form, in that it is justified as an offering to the spirits, there is no doubt that its essential motive is human vanity. The abundance, size, and beauty of the yams produced by a garden is a means of maintaining or enhancing the owner's social prestige in the tribe. There is not a gardener on the island who does not regard his yams as trophies. The yam storehouses, which are built with open walls, serve to reinforce this attitude, since they allow passersby to examine, and hopefully to admire, the contents. In this context, the Trobrianders are not above using the tricks common to produce growers the world over. The largest and handsomest yams are often placed where they are most visible in the storehouses, and the less desirable specimens, of course, are made considerably less conspicuous. Once, out of curiosity, I stuck my hand into a storehouse and reached under the nearest (and largest) yams to pull out a much smaller yam. The people around me watched curiously, apparently not quite understanding what I was doing. Then they began to laugh uproariously, delighted at my cleverness.

This is not to deny that the Trobrianders do indeed produce enormous yams worthy of blue ribbons in any competition. Some of these prize winners are as much as six feet in length, and proportionately heavy. These, of course, are the object of much admiration and envy, and are displayed between the pieces of painted and decorated wood which serve as a kind of litter.

As might be expected, there is intense competition among the yam growers. And, as it happens, the yams lend themselves well to expositions and displays and to social functions, for, unlike the taro root, the yam retains its freshness for a considerable period of time. This natural longevity is then extended by storage in the well-ventilated storehouses.

The riddle of father and son

It is paradoxical that, given all the work that the gardener may do, his own wife and children do not receive any of the produce from the garden. What does not go to the chief, goes to the gardener's brother-in-law, or at least to his household. The reason for this peculiar arrangement is that the natural father-son relationship, as universally accepted in the West, is not recognized on the Trobriand Islands. In fact, when a man's wife bears a child, it would never occur to a Trobriander to think that there is a blood-relationship between the husband and the child. The husband is only the closest and most beloved friend of the child. The true father of the newborn infant, according to Trobriand custom, is the brother of the mother. The function of the mother's husband is to play with the child, and gradually to teach him what he should know to become a great grower of yams. He is required only to love and to be loved. The legal obligations of paternity, therefore, all devolve on the child's maternal uncle. Custom requires even that the uncle bequeath most of his possessions to the child, although he may leave a part of his goods to his own wife's children. Thus, all of the legal obligations of paternity on the Trobriand Islands lie with the maternal uncle. The function of the natural father is purely an emotional and sentimental one.

From what I observed, I could only conclude that the system works remarkably well. I saw children everywhere: playing in the villages, splashing around in the water in the midst of the pirogues, waiting on the beach for the fishermen to return with the day's catch. All, without exception, seemed unusually happy. They laugh constantly, and they are quite obviously alert and intelligent. Even at an early age, they begin to exhibit that dignified reserve in the presence of strangers, that seems characteristic of the Trobriander people. They are, as the psychologists would say, "well-adjusted" children. And why not? They enjoy the unique privilege of having two fathers playing two different roles.

The argonauts of the Pacific

The inhabitants of the Trobriand Islands, as we have already remarked, are an exceptional example of a people who are both seafaring and agricultural. The expert gardeners are also experts in the use of the pirogue. The latter skill is the basis for the marvelous adventure known as the *kula*—the expedition of the "Argonauts of the Pacific," as Malinowski calls it. The *kula* is, in fact, a maritime excursion in which hundreds of boats participate running in a double circuit from the eastern tip of New Guinea toward all the small neighboring archipelagoes. It occurs on a given date, and its purpose is to transport, in two opposing directions, two articles of no practical value: *soulava* (necklaces of pink shells) and *mwali* (armbands of white shells). These armbands or bracelets are made of a large shell (*Conus millepunctatus*), the tip of which is cut off. The bottom section of the shell is then polished into a ring. *Mwali* are prized in New Guinea as far south as the Gulf of Papua and in the Port Moresby district. The *soulava*, or necklaces, are made in New Guinea as well as in the Trobriand Islands, and I have seen them as far away as the Solomon Islands. The necklaces are made of flat, pierced disks, cut from spondylus shells, and are sometimes fifteen or sixteen feet long.

The excursion itself, the *kula*, covers a very large geographic expanse, beginning at the southeastern tip of New Guinea and including the neighboring groups of islands: D'Entrecasteaux, Louisiade, Trobriand. Thus, it serves to bind together, in a complicated intertribal circuit, the numerous islands situated on the periphery of the Coral Sea. The two articles being transported move in a double circular route. The *soulava* are carried from Dobu, the Amphletts, and the Trobriand Islands toward Woodlark (Murua) Island—that is, in a clockwise motion. The *mwali* move counterclockwise, from the D'Entrecasteaux Islands toward Misima and Laughlan Islands.

All this seafaring activity seems a bit absurd if one considers only that its ostensible object is the continuing exchange of items of personal adornment. And actually, the necklaces and bracelets do not even serve that purpose, since no one keeps them permanently. Actually, beneath the puzzling surface of this ceremonial and profitless exchange, there lies a complex and substantial commercial enterprise. Along with the bracelets and necklaces, there is much traffic in more useful

The cultivation and upkeep of gardens is a very serious matter to the Trobrianders. The garden must be protected by magical means at all times.

The Losuia lagoon is bordered by large trees that grow even on the coral in the water.

items—and, of course, the opportunity for human contact with its resulting recip- rocal influences. Among the items traded during the *kula* are the handsome green stones used as blades in ceremonial hatchets and the ebony sculptures of Kitava Island. The areca (betel) nut was brought by the *kula* from Massim Island.

Although the Trobrianders spend much of their time in their small, graceful pirogues, it is obvious that the *kula* requires larger boats, capable of navigating the open sea. The islanders are quite expert in the construction of such boats, and the building process (like that of the pirogues, for that matter) involves much magical ritual.

The *kula*, being an exchange of merchandise among various islands, implies the existence of a partnership of sorts among the participants. Actually, it is based on an association by virtue of which the individuals of different tribes and islands are bound together. This bond continues throughout the lifetime of the partici- pants, who comprise a fair number of the individuals of each village. Each of them receives one or more bracelets, or a necklace, but he does not keep these gifts. If he has received a necklace, he must pass it on to one of the other partici- pants; in exchange, he receives bracelets. Both necklaces and bracelets, although they have no intrinsic value, are regarded as precious gems, and they must be kept in continuous circulation among the members of the *kula* chain. The recipient of one of these ornaments may keep it for a year or two, at most.

Until Malinowski's study of the Trobrianders, it was generally accepted that the *kula* was nothing more than a primitive system of barter, that it was sporadic, and that it dealt in objects of recognized utility. And, as in any barter system, it was supposed that the traders were concerned primarily with getting the better of the bargain. One of Malinowski's great contributions was to point out the ceremo- nial, social, and commercial reality of the *kula* as it exists in fact.

A surprising aspect of the *kula* is that it involves individuals separated by the sea and disparate in language and culture. Even more surprising, it unites these in- dividuals by means of magical rites, well-defined regulations, and solemn public transactions.

This maritime activity among the islands by no means dispenses the inhabi- tants of the various archipelagoes from their agricultural duties. At Dobu, for ex- ample, the gravest of all insults is to accuse someone of being at sea while he should be tending to his garden. Not to care for one's yams is worse than a social *faux pas*; it is an act of great imprudence and an insult to the spirits. There is no human activity in these islands that does not have a supernatural aspect. But, even among the islanders of the *kula*, magical considerations require that man fo- cus his care and his anxiety on the land and on plants rather than on the sea.

Local artists

Every morning, a group of young sculptors was waiting for me when I emerged from my cabin. Their purpose, of course, was to try to get me to buy some of their works. It was hard to resist the temptation to accommodate them. I was often struck by the originality of the small, carved statues that they displayed. These young men seemed to have been influenced not at all by the art of nearby New Guinea. I wondered whether their inspiration might not have come from further away—from Indonesia, perhaps.

The local artists excelled particularly in the carved decorations on everyday items such as spatulas, platters, mortars (for grinding betel), ladles, and pirogue paddles. As far as I was able to determine, they make neither masks nor statues of ancestors, but there are many representations of pigs, birds, dogs, and crocodiles.

Jean Guiart, a well-known anthropologist, faults Malinowski for having neglected, in his otherwise rich study of the Trobrianders, the subject of the artistically sculptured bows of the islanders' pirogues. It is a lack that is truly to be regretted—particularly since, as I came to realize, there are so few of these works of art on the boats actually in use nowadays. Soon, there will be none, since the Trobrianders have taken up the practice of selling the carved bows when a pirogue is too old to be of use any longer.

These bows generally are composed of two separate pieces: the tip of the bow, and a panel of wood to which the tip is attached and which, in turn, is attached crosswise to the front of the boat. Both elements are carved in a delicate and complex motif, a series of interwoven spirals, arabesques, stylized figures of birds and evocations of the human form. "All these stylized festoons and plumes," explains Maurice Leenhardt, "all these dots which represent eyes, the days, the tides—this entire elegant construction rears up on both sides so as to frame, protect, and enhance a tiny human figure."

From the little that I was able to see of these works of art, from the little that is known of them, and from the very little that is left of them, we can only surmise how regrettable it is that they have disappeared before being studied thoroughly.

It is possible that such a study might have taught us a great deal more than we know about the relationship of the Trobrianders to the sea. There are so many questions that remain to be answered in that respect. Are the islanders really, as some have maintained, essentially land-dwellers rather than a maritime people? Is it true, therefore, that they are only "amateur fishermen" because the official magic is lacking in their fishing activities? There is no doubt that, compared to gardening, fishing is curiously lacking in magical rites. On the other hand, we might point out that the *kula* is undoubtedly a major maritime undertaking, and that the *kula* boats are certainly built in accordance with a strict ritual. By the same token, the carved bows of the pirogues are as much a part of Trobriander culture as the islanders' storehouses for yams. All things considered, the more probable opinion lies in the middle between two extremes, as it usually does. It seems reasonable to conclude, therefore, that the people of the Trobriand Islands are at home, and that they excel, simultaneously, on land and on the sea.

6

volcanoes and messiahs

*A myth is less the imaginative rhap-
sody of an idle mind giving free rein
to its fantasies than it is an extremely important cultural force the impact of which must be reckoned
with.*

BRONISLAW MALINOWSKI

After the Trobriand Islands, Port Vila (Fila), capital city of the New Hebrides, seemed a mass of streets, shops, hotels, and traffic jams. I resigned myself
to it wearily, having already made up my mind to leave as soon as possible for the
more accessible islands and islets of the archipelago.

There are two things that a visitor must never say to a citizen of the New Hebrides. One is that it is raining; the other, that there are mosquitoes.

I did not complain of mosquitoes, but I could not help observing that, when
my plane landed, it was raining heavily. To make matters worse, I had arrived in
the midst of an electoral campaign. It was the worst possible moment for a stranger, fond of tranquility, to be in Port Vila.

Municipal elections had already been held throughout the archipelago, and
the present contest was to alert delegates to a representative assembly. It was the
perfect occasion for a manifestation of Franco-British rivalry; for, until then, the
islands had been afflicted with the most baroque political regime imaginable! It
was governed jointly by the French and the British.

This bizarre arrangement came about in 1906, when the two colonial powers
grew weary of years of haggling over possession of a group of then virtually

A coral landscape off the island of Efate.

worthless islands. They therefore agreed to rule them together. Thus was born the so-called Condominium of the New Hebrides—more familiarly known to the British as the Pandemonium. Port Vila, on the island of Efate, was designated the capital of this political monster. The British governor chose to locate his residence on an island in the lagoon, remote from the people he was to rule. The French governor situated his residence high on a hill dominating the surrounding countryside and bay. The respective choices of the two governors were indicative of the respective approaches to government of the nations they represented. The Condominium was off to an inauspicious beginning.

The Hundred Years' War

The continuing rivalry between the British and the French—a condition described locally as The Hundred Years' War—often attained the proportions of a comic opera or, rather, of a burlesque. The situation was not greatly helped by the massive inefficiency of the governmental apparatus. Everything was in doubles so as to satisfy the vanity of both nations. There were both *gendarmes* and constables; customs inspectors and *douaniers; juges* and judges. Whiskey tried to coexist with cognac, and cricket with *pétanque*.[1] Everything had to be in both French and English—while most of the people spoke Beachlamar, a variant of pidgin English. It was indeed pandemonium.

Neither the French nor the British appeared to have learned much during the preceding three-quarters of a century. When local elections became imminent, both nations chose sides. Great Britain supported the National party, which demanded immediate independence. The French gave their support to more moderate candidates, those who wished to see independence come gradually through progressive stages of autonomy.

No one was able to explain to me why either the English or the French could possibly want to meddle in the affairs of the New Hebrides. The islands are, to all appearances, totally devoid of mineral resources of any kind. As far as anyone knows, there is no oil. And even copra, one of the traditional resources of Oceania, is a glut on the market.

The roots of the conflict go back more than a hundred years. What is now a petty administrative rivalry began as a petty religious rivalry.[2] In the nineteenth century, European Catholics and Protestants shifted their battleground from the Continent to the Pacific, to Polynesia and the New Hebrides. At one point, the contest for souls became so heated that the antics of an English missionary, the Reverend George Pritchard, brought France and England to the brink of war. En-

---

[1] A French game similar to bowling.
[2] See Appendix II.

glish interests were represented by Presbyterian missionaries; the French, by Catholic missions established by the Congregation of Mary, a religious order.

Today, Catholics and Protestants live cheek by jowl, in commendable harmony. Guerrilla warfare has shifted from the religious to the administrative arena.

Sixty isles

Viewed from the air, the most striking feature of the New Hebrides is the height of the mountains. On Espíritu Santo, there is a peak of almost 6,000 feet and at least one volcano nearly the same height.

Many of the islands are volcanic in origin, and there are still many active volcanoes. Three on them—on Ambrym, Tanna, and Lopevi—are in permanent eruption. The Lopevi volcano is the most dangerous, emitting flows of lava that necessitate the periodic evacuation of the inhabitants. Earthquakes are frequent occurrences, but rarely do serious damage.

The archipelago comprises about sixty islands and islets. A few of them are accessible only by air, on flights of a local airline, Air Melanesia. Other than these—Espíritu Santo, Malikolo (Malckula), and Tanna—the rest can be reached by boat or pirogue. Government boats, which deliver mail and supplies and transport the sick, do not run on a fixed schedule. Despite these unpredictable factors, I was able to visit several islands of the archipelago—enough to become aware of the physical differences among the islands and of the degree to which they have been cleared, cultivated, and Christianized. For each island of the group has its own history and its own people. In addition, each has its own, and sometimes several dialects, totaling more than a hundred in the entire archipelago.

Corals and volcanoes

The New Hebrides usually now are approached by air rather than by sea. The visitor no longer sees them rising up out of the water like great ships. Instead, he views them on the horizon, then drawing nearer. From that vantage point, it is immediately obvious that there are two kind of islands: volcanic and coral.

The masterpiece of the archipelago, an exquisite design of blue and green, is a ring of coral fringed with palms and surf. It is Hollywood's idea of what a tropical island should be. It is relatively flat, and its unique beauty lies in its lagoon. But the island that at once draws the eye and inspires awe is a land of mountains and jungles, a volcanic island where the earth trembles and the fertility is so great that the vegetation is like an elastic wall resisting man's every attempt to penetrate

The Efate lagoon. The landscape is as beautiful beneath the surface of the water as it is above.

it. Above the volcanic island rises a *morne* covered with vegetation, like an ominous green skull.

These islands exist only in the eye of the beholder. What we see is only a tip of earth rising from a base on the ocean's floor. Beneath the islands is a chain of mountains, a world submerged.

An island can be understood only from within the sea itself. For that reason, I had decided to do as much diving as possible during my stay in the New Hebrides, so as to see what each island owed to coral and what to volcanoes.

Cannibalism and religion

Of all the New Hebrides, Tanna is the island with the most intriguing history. It has a reputation for violence as unrestrained as its fertility, for cannibalism and intense religiosity. It was my first stop after Port Vila.

Air Melanesia's small aircraft flew above the shoreline of Erromango. I could see the island's carpet of vegetation, black and green, so dense as to seem a solid mass. From the air, Erromango appears hostile, even sinister. Perhaps my impressions were colored by a book I had read as a youth, and had re-read shortly before leaving: *Erromango,* by the French writer Pierre Benoit. *Erromango* is not the most depressing of Benoit's novels, but it is not an inspirational tract either. I did find, however, that most of Benoit's descriptions of the New Hebrides were accurate, particularly that of the omnipotence of the vegetation in the tropical dampness and of the sadness that overcomes a white man, isolated in the jungle, when he hears, night after night, the sound of drums. No doubt, what Benoit recorded was even more true thirty years ago than it is now.

The island of Tanna, viewed from the air, seemed hardly more prepossessing than Erromango: a compact mass of green rising from the water, its strange, flat-topped mountains shrouded in wisps of fog under lowering clouds. There was no town in sight, of course. Not even a village or a single hut. I had the feeling that I was about to set foot on a land consisting of nothing but mountains and jungles. I did not know what I would find. Perhaps nothing more than creatures from a magical dream world.

The island has been called Tanna for a comparatively short time. For the inhabitants, the islands of the archipelago had no names. The island where Port Vila is located is now called Efate. It has also been known as Vaté and Sandwich. The people who live on Erromango call their island Itara; the inhabitants of Futuna know it as Ekiamo. The present name, Tanna, is the result of a misunderstanding. When Captain Cook landed on the island in 1774, at Weasisi Bay, he gave the bay the name of his ship: Port Resolution. Then, in an effort to christen the island, he questioned the natives, pointing stubbornly at the ground until one of the men gave him a name: Tanna. Cook was satisfied. What he did not know was that the man who answered him gave him the native word for what Cook was pointing at: land.

The French delegate on Tanna was hospitality itself. He was delighted that I arrived with a knapsack. "Ah," he said, "I see you're well equipped. Good. To-morrow, we leave at dawn for the bush. I'll give you the grand tour. I can do my work while showing you around. But we'll have to do a great deal of walking, you understand."

Of all the islands of the New Hebrides, Tanna is, in my opinion, the most interesting because of its fertility and its vegetation. The French representative, with commendable effort, has encouraged model gardens and agricultural projects with such success that the island is in a position to supply Port Vila with vegetables and fruits—if only an economical means of transportation could be found.

When I arrived on Tanna, the islanders were preparing to vote for the first time for their representatives. The actual vote had to be preceded by a census and by the distribution of ballots—no easy task when the voters are scattered among mountains and throughout jungles. It also made it difficult for anyone interested in local politics to meet the electorate. My host's intention, during the three-day tour that he planned for me, was to ferret out the voters.

Our chief destination was a mountainous area where, only two years before, an adventurer had, in the style of the nineteenth century, carved out a kingdom for himself. Tanna had seen such men before. In 1860, one Rosso Lewin had established a similar fiefdom, where he maintained a force of a hundred men. The latest in this distinguished line of adventurers was a Frenchman from Lyon, a gun-smith by trade and a former paratrooper, who had created a redoubt for himself in the heart of the island. The least of this man's idiosyncracies, it appears, was his habit of cleaning his fingernails with a commando knife whenever he made a public appearance. Among his other foibles was that, after fortifying his redoubt, he drafted the natives into the army, created uniforms and decorations, and declared war on Great Britain and France. It became necessary to dispatch troops to subdue him, which was accomplished without bloodshed. The man was tried before a tribunal in Nouméa, where he was treated with indulgence. He is free today; but the French delegate was interested in discovering what had become of the former troops of the gunsmith.

A former rebel

We left the Landrover at the foot of a trail and began the climb up the mountain. I noted that my aerial view of the jungle had been somewhat misleading. Seen from above, the trees are an almost solid mass of greenery. The winding trail, however, offered unexpected relief from the trees: a ravine covered with ferns, a stream of sparkling water inhabited by freshwater shrimp, like those of

The people of a village on the island of Tanna are holding a meeting on the occasion of local elections.

A gardener on Tanna uses a long, sharp pole to dig holes for planting taro.

Polynesia. Scattered shrubs and young trees marked the sites of former orange, lemon, and coffee plantations. There was nothing left of the buildings on these plantations. Similarly, the orchards, fields, and clearing had been repossessed by the jungle. Only an occasional lemon or orange tree, struggling for survival among wild plants, recalled the former human presence.

I was delighted to discover that the French delegate was an expert botanist. Nothing escaped him. He knew by name the flowers growing everywhere in the treetops and the wild fruits, many of which are edible.

After a long walk, we reached the village where the gunsmith from Lyon had incited to rebellion against the British and French. We were greeted warmly by the man who had been the rebel's chief lieutenant. We shook hands. Everyone smiled. No one seemed to have hard feelings of any kind about the uprising. Order reigned once more, and all was right with the world.

The delegate consulted his list of voters and distributed ballots with the help of the local schoolmaster. Meanwhile, I photographed the women and children of the village—and especially a young coquette, her face painted yellow and red, who ran shrieking in mock terror from tree to tree as I pursued her, clicking away relentlessly.

An initiation

We had to hurry to reach the next village before sundown, fording rustling streams, leaping from rock to rock, climbing muddy cliffs. We followed a mountain trail offering specimens of almost every kind of plant life on the island; but what struck me was the absence of animals in this abundance of vegetation. In the African jungles, and in those of certain parts of Asia—the Malayan Peninsula and Vietnam, for example—at this time of day the air would have been alive with the screaming of monkeys, the sound of wild boars and gaurs crashing through the underbrush, the screeching of parrots and calaos. Here, there were only a few birds and not a single snake. The only sound was that of the leaves blowing in the wind.

The village was what one would expect to find in the bush and the mountains: tiny, squeezed between the jungle and the peaks, poor but not poverty-stricken. Late that night, we slept in the infirmary, which was otherwise empty. Upon arrival, however, we had been initiated into a rite, a ceremony, consisting of a sacramental libation of kava. I had heard so much about kava that I wondered how I had managed to drink it.

Tanna is the island of kava. It was here that this drug first came into widespread use and developed into an elaborate ritualistic observance, although it is actually of Polynesian origin. I saw kava on other islands as well, especially at Fiji.

My initiation took place in impressive surroundings. The village boasted a large public square with splendid trees: a giant banyan, loaded down with interlacing aerial roots, and an immense filao, with featherlike foliage and a huge trunk. Beyond the clearing, there was a backdrop of wooded mountains and valleys stretching into the distance until they were lost in the darkness of approaching night.

On the opposite side of the square was the *Nakamal*, the house of men, which is also the dwelling place of ancestors and the storehouse of skulls. The houses of the village were beyond the *Nakamal*, in a shallow depression. I could see fires, women moving about, children and dogs playing.

The drug

Late in the afternoon, shortly after our arrival, the men of the village had begun to gather in front of the *Nakamal*. Squatting on their heels, they took out their pipes and conversed softly. They were naked, but the night was mild and dark and there was no need for clothing.

A group of young men arrived, carrying bundles of roots. Two of the older men took the roots and carefully separated them, then cut them into pieces and distributed them to the other men. This is the precious kava, a wild pepper, *Piper methysticum*. It is a drug. Beyond that, I had no idea whether it was a euphoric, a depressant, an addictive, or a non-addictive substance.

By then, all the men of the village had gathered in the square. No women were allowed. For them, kava is taboo. If a woman had happened to enter the square while the kava drink was being prepared, there would have been a great uproar. At the very least, the kava already prepared would have been discarded.

The first step in the preparation is the chewing of the roots. The elders of the village divide the roots among the younger men, and the latter begin chewing and spitting into bourao leaves. It would be a serious breach of propriety for a man to chew his own kava roots.

The men around me conversed in low tones. There was considerable movement and much coming and going on mysterious errands. Finally, fires were lit.

Suddenly, small packages of food appeared from nowhere. It was *lap-lap*, a paste of yams and taro wrapped in banana leaves. I was familiar with its hot, bland taste, which can be improved somewhat if one adds a bit of grated coconut.

It was now almost dark, and the jungle was black around us. The *Nakamal* was only dimly visible under the trees, guarding its skulls and its secrets. Beyond it, the tiny village had become invisible, as though its fires had now been extinguished. The only light in the square was that of the fires at our feet. Around me, I heard the sounds of constant spitting.

A young man approached, his skin golden in the firelight, carrying two

This woman is preparing *lap-lap,* the traditional dish on Tanna. (Photograph Aubert de la Rue, Collection Musée de l'Homme)

lengths of cut bamboo which served as containers for water. A man took the bamboo, poured the water into the masticated kava, and then filled half a coconut shell with the yellowish liquid. Ceremoniously, he held it out to me.

I knew the proper ritual response. I was required to stand and walk to the end of the square, turn my back to the setting sun, and drink the entire mixture slowly and without pausing. The final drops are sprayed out between the drinker's lips, and he finishes by uttering a cry. I did what was expected of me as best I could. The kava was cold and had a sour taste, like tree sap.

Now, there was nothing I could do but wait to see what would happen.

Libation

The young men who did not drink kava[1] now filled the cups and distributed

---

[1]Young males are not allowed kava until they have been circumsized.

Tanna's volcano, Mount Yasur, shoots out a shower of red-hot stones every three minutes.

them among the others. Seated around the fire, the men drank, and then ate their *lap-lap*. I discovered that I could observe the amenities and still be spared the *lap-lap*. I simply took one and casually held it behind me until I felt first a moist

muzzle, and then a mouth. Almost immediately, the unwanted *lap-lap* disappeared silently into one of the village dogs.

Gradually, the sounds of conversation ceased. There were a few moments of utter silence. One of the men rose and moved toward the fire. He picked up a burning brand and began walking with measured steps, his eyes on the ground, his body in a stooping position. Quietly, the others got to their feet and followed. Kava, whatever else it may be, is not a soporific. It does not immobilize the user. I watched as the silent ghosts filed past me, toward the village.

An entire book could be devoted to the implications of the use of kava. Here, its use is primarily a communication among men, a participation through the mingling of saliva and through the solemnity of ritual. It is also a common excursion into a dream world created by the drug. And it is a communion with plant life and the jungle through the use of the kava roots. It celebrates the power of darkness, but also the power of nature. The true grandeur and social significance of its use can be measured only in such an environment, among naked, silent men.

It appears that the essential chemical effect of kava is to plunge the user into a state of interior communion with himself. This is called "listening to the kava." In that state, the user can perceive neither light nor sound. He does not fight against darkness as we Westerners do. He fuses with it, entering into complicity with the night and the jungle.

The man sitting next to me complained that I was talking too loudly. The reason was that, somehow, the drug had practically no effect on me.[1] I felt neither intoxicated nor euphoric. I was entirely myself—although I had been given, I was told, a strong dose.

Kava is usually described as harmless and non-addictive. It can be dangerous, however, if it is chewed; for this is a region where many communicable diseases flourish, among them tuberculosis and syphilis.

It is not for hygenic reasons, however, that the white man has sought to wipe out the use of kava. This struggle is one of the strangest chapters in the history of Tanna, and it is an integral part of the story of missionary activity in the New Hebrides. The most tragic phase of the drama was not played out in the interior, but along the coast, where the whites had settled and where Western and native cultures were in confrontation.

The perfume of sandalwood

After leaving the village, my companion and I made our way down toward the coast. Once again, I marveled at the contrast between the almost suffocating vegetation of the interior and the openness and light of the shore, with its fringe of cor-

---

[1] I tried again, on several occasions, but, alas, with the same lack of results.

al reefs, pounding surf, whitecapped waves, and, above all, delicious salt air. It is hard to believe that these two worlds, so different, are hardly more than a stone's throw from each other.

The coast of Tanna, at the spot where we emerged, is fairly typical of the entire island. Gray volcanic rocks, covered with shrubs, rise from the water, like tiny green dots in the sapphire sea. The shoreline itself is deeply indented by narrow, irregular bays. Gold-hued branches of trees, their bark removed, were piled against the dunes, waiting for the arrival of a boat to carry them away. It was sandalwood, which in the nineteenth century was regarded as a luxury and was in great vogue.

The sandalwood tree is of moderate height but is a slow grower. Its trunk contains an aromatic oil; but the oil does not appear until the tree is fully grown—a process that requires forty years. Sandalwood falls into three categories, according to its color: red, yellow, and white. The darker the wood, the richer it is in aromatic oil.

For centuries, the Chinese used sandalwood in the construction of perfumed boxes and chests and also as incense in their temples. At that time, the wood was imported from India, the coasts of Malabar and Coromandel. In the nineteenth century, when an insatiable thirst for tea seized the British, merchant ships regularly called at Chinese ports for that commodity. It occurred to the owners of these ships that, given the popularity of sandalwood in China, it would make an ideal cargo for the voyage to that country.

Tanna, despite its inhospitable coasts and lack of good anchorage, had sandalwood. Thus, the island attracted more than its share of beachcombers, adventurers, and sandalwood-hunters, none of whom were even remotely interested in becoming bona fide settlers. The quest for sandalwood—I have seen the stumps left in the island's jungles—led to friction with the inhabitants of the island, and the friction, to violence.

Since the English colonies were as avid for tea as the people of London, seamen and businessmen from Sydney also took to the Pacific in the search for sandalwood, which they could sell in China in exchange for tea. The trees on Fiji were cut down without any attempt at conservation and were quickly exhausted. Then, new sources were discovered in the south of Tanna, on Erromango, Anatom, Isle of Pines, and New Caledonia. It is true that the quality of the wood on these islands was inferior to that of India or Timor Island; but it was still sufficiently good to enable the traders to make enormous profits on a single voyage.

A secret history

By 1860, the flow of sandalwood slowed because all known sources were virtually exhausted. Then, a new supply was discovered on Espíritu Santo Island,

the largest of the New Hebrides, which gave new impetus to the sandalwood trade.

At that time, the New Hebrides were more or less unknown in the Western world. The sandalwood-cutters, along with the whalers, were the first white men to set foot on these islands. The natives already had a reputation for ferocity; that reputation was soon to grow by leaps and bounds.

Polynesia, since its discovery by Count de La Pérouse, was well known to Occidental ship captains, but Melanesia, the New Hebrides, where Captain Cook had almost died, inspired nothing but terror among mariners. Yet, the Polynesians had been practicing cannibals when the Europeans discovered them, like the inhabitants of the New Hebrides. Nonetheless, they somehow enjoyed a better reputation than the latter.

The relations between the sandalwood-cutters and the natives were such that the era of sandalwood is the story of a succession of ambushes, massacres, reprisals, and atrocities. Savagery and violence abounded on both sides. Landing parties were captured and eaten by the cannibals, and the wives and children of na-

Mount Yasur's explosions are accompanied by clouds of smoke which drift out to sea and are dissipated there.

tive warriors were imprisoned in a cave and then asphyxiated with smoke by the whites.

Evangelization

The arrival of missionaries from England coincided with that of the sandal-wood-cutters. In 1839, John William, a clergyman dispatched to the New Hebrides by the London Missionary Society, the first missionary to set foot on Erromango, was killed.

Fifty years later, the islands were still the scene of violence. Labor recruiters, as they were euphemistically known, periodically raided the New Hebrides for laborers to work the cotton fields of Queensland and the sugarcane fields of Fiji. The forced seizure of the New Hebrides inhabitants was known as "black-birding."

All these rather obscure historical events made of Melanesia a lawless archipelago, where violence was supreme. The islands existed on the margin of international life, a spot of romance and danger peopled by adventurers of every ilk and by idealistic missionaries. The adventurers and the missionaries were often irreconcilable enemies, although they shared the common dangers posed by the climate, malaria, and the red-hot stones of the cannibals' cooking fires. (Contrary to popular belief, humans were not boiled in a cauldron. Their flesh was cooked on a bed of hot stones.)

The volcano

Thanks to the hospitality and help of the French delegate on Tanna, I was able to remain there long enough to inspect the island in some detail. The principal geographic feature is the volcano, Yasur.

The trail to the summit of the volcano leads through a vast plain of gray ash. The trail begins, unexpectedly, at a shimmering lake of clear water, Lake Siwi. The water seemed impossibly pure at the very foot of the volcano with its slag-covered and, one suspected, crumbling slopes. Children, shouting happily, were splashing in the lake. I saw a woman approaching the lake, leading a child by the hand. She undressed the boy and bathed him in the water.

It was my unexpected good luck to have magnificent weather for this excursion to Mount Yasur. It had rained constantly for the preceding three days. By the time I reached the summit, at around ten o'clock in the morning, there was not a cloud in the sky. The column of smoke rising from the volcano's crater drifted upward in regular puffs, as though from the pipe of a giant smoker.

Below me, I saw a man on horseback at the edge of the field of ashes. He put on a show of horsemanship for my benefit, making his mount gallop and turn with an expertise that was truly professional. There are many wild horses on Tanna, no doubt brought there by white men at some time in the past—perhaps by the English missionaries of the nineteenth century. A troop of several hundred of the animals live in complete freedom on a plateau near Lenakel, feeding on white grass—which, rather than grass, is a kind of tender fern. Curiously enough, the plateau on Tanna is the only place where these animals are now found. In any event, the Man Tanna, as the inhabitants are known, have developed a taste for riding, and they are quite skilled at breaking and training the horses—as I had just had occasion to witness.

As I stood staring at the smoking crater, the ground around me shook. I heard the muffled roar of distant explosions, and the volcano belched out a cloud of soot and ashes that momentarily darkened the sun. I looked around. No one except me seemed concerned in the slightest. It was as though the volcano had put on this display for the amusement of tourists.

For an active volcano, Mount Yasur is comparatively inoffensive and accessible. It takes about forty-five minutes of easy climbing to reach the summit, where the crater yawns like a gateway to the infernal regions. I could not overcome the feeling that it should have been more difficult to gain access to such an exotic spectacle, and I felt vaguely guilty, as though I had sneaked into a circus.

Here is an excerpt from my notes on that occasion:

"The sound of the volcano seems to roll in the ground under my feet, grows louder, subsides for a moment, and then explodes like a bomb. There is an explosion every three minutes. Tongues of fire shoot from the crater; then, simultaneously with the deafening roar of the explosion, a column of black smoke and gray ash rises into the sky. The smoke is like velvet, with shades of dark and light and accents of thick soot contrasting with the gray of the ashes. The smoke mushrooms, still climbing, and covers the sun. For a moment, it is dark as night. Then the cloud thins and is carried out to sea, where it drifts between the clear blue of the sky and the emerald green of the sea.

"Standing at the very edge of this witch's cauldron, I look down. At my feet, a vertical wall descends to a narrow ledge, then drops again. At the bottom of the pit I can see lava flowing, twisting like red snakes. Blue and pink fumes spiral upward. I think I can distinguish three holes, three sources of fire. There is a large one, like a pool in which the lava lies flat. Another, smaller, sends up showers of molten lava, like tracer bullets from a machine gun. A third, the smallest of all, seems hardly more than a crack of red between two solid masses. I cannot be sure, since, with every explosion, the pattern is wiped out and begins again."

As night fell, the lava at the bottom of the crater turned from dark red to blood red. Darkness was moving across the plain, but the sky remained clear and bright between the explosions of Mount Yasur. Below me, the plain of ashes spread like a lunar scene, treeless, in the twilight. Beyond was the dark jungle and, somewhere in that unbelievable vegetation, the village of Ipekel, from which my guides and companions had come.

I decided to remain on the lip of the crater for a part of the night. Despite the rumbling and the explosions, I felt somehow comfortable there, sitting at the edge of an intermittent cataclysm, watching the increasingly visible showers of glowing rocks spewing from the yawning pit. As it grew darker, the display became more spectacular. The fire blotted out the ashes, soot, and smoke. The red seemed to climb higher and higher with each repeated explosion, and the lava shifted, bubbled, spurted, and then fell back with the grace of a fountain. It was impossible to tire of watching it. My companions, who were in charge of my equipment, cameras, tapes, and recorder, shouted and leaped with every explosion—clearly an expression of joyful admiration. They knew the volcano well and loved it.

Their affection for the volcano was once a source of trouble to a friend of mine, Haroun Tazieff,[1] a geologist who visited Tanna to "listen" to the volcano. Tazieff spent two days situating his geophones and hooking them up to his recording devices at his camp. His purpose was to measure the volcano's tremors so as to compare them with the tremors of Stromboli, off the Italian coast. (Stromboli's explosions are similar to those of Mount Yasur.) The villagers of Ipekel thought that Tazieff was a magician summoned by the government of the Condominium to capture Devil Iarpopangi, the tutelar spirit who lives in the volcano. The electric wires, running from the geophones to Tazieff's camp, were clearly intended to bind the giant who protected the people of Tanna. Amid general indignation, poor Tazieff was forced to dismantle his equipment and leave in haste.

I was not suspected of harboring any evil intentions with respect to Devil Iarpopangi. Or it may have been merely that the people of Ipekel were less tolerant twenty years ago than they are now. In any case, my companions did not see any cause for alarm in my photographic equipment and tape recorder, and I was left in peace to photograph and record to my heart's content.

A misguided missile

The aspect of Mount Yasur, in the darkness of the night, becomes somewhat more threatening than during the day. The flowing lava, the showers of sparks, and the flying rocks rose from the crater on trails of fire. It may have been only my

---

[1] Cf. Haroun Tazieff, *Vingt cinq ans sur les volcans du globe (25 Years on the World's Volcanoes)*, Fernand Nathan.

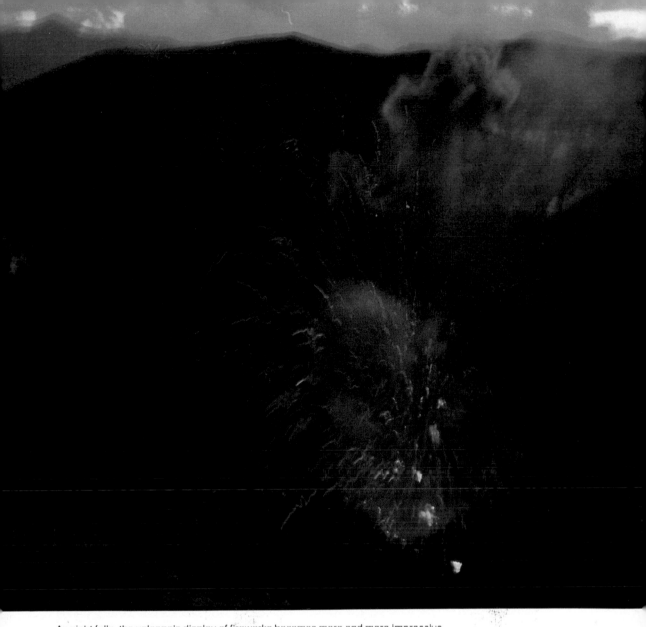

As night falls, the volcano's display of fireworks becomes more and more impressive.

imagination, but it seemed to me that the explosions were more powerful, the underground roars more deafening, and the tremors more violent. Fiery jets shot into the air and fell to earth with the sound of hail.

Suddenly, a large rock shot out of the crater, passed just over our heads, and landed with a dull thud somewhere behind us. I wondered if I had actually felt heat as it passed overhead.

My companions, who until then had been laughing and joking, were terrified. Shouting, they rushed about, gathering up my bags and equipment. Their intention was clear: to flee. I tried to calm them, but was met with a barrage of stories about what had happened to other foreigners who had tampered with Mount Yasur: an Australian tourist had received a jet of lava in his face, a young girl had been injured by a large rock, etc. Finally, I was informed that I could stay if I wished, but that I would stay alone.

A shower of stones

I refused, of course, to leave the crater. With as much dignity as I could muster, I snatched back my equipment from my companions, hoping to shame them into staying. To my dismay, they turned and started down the trail.

I reconsidered. The night was dark, and I could not be sure of finding my way back alone. I offered a compromise. We would move back fifty feet or so from the crater, where there was a protective ledge of rock. Agreed. We withdrew. A few moments later, there was a great explosion, the sky lighted up, and a veritable rain of sizeable pebbles fell around us. Once more my companions began gathering up the equipment. This time, there was no discussion and no arguing. They were already scurrying down the trail. To this day, I do not know whether they were really afraid of the volcano, or if they merely did not want very much to spend the night away from their families in order to satisfy the whim of a white stranger. It is likely they thought that I had seen enough, and that no reasonable man could ask for more. Moreover, it was true that Devil Iarpopangi seemed particularly restless that night.

I hurried down the trail behind them.

The Rome of Tanna

Mount Yasur belongs to the people who live at its base, and no one is allowed on the volcano's slopes without their permission. They spend their lives weighted down under the threat of an eruption, putting up with the explosions and the showers of ash and soot. Nonetheless, they live comfortably enough on the shore of a deep-water bay near the spot where Captain Cook's *Resolution* first dropped anchor.

The village is enclosed by a stout fence and is well fortified. The neat, well-constructed square houses line both sides of a broad square. In the middle of the square, there was a wooden cross painted red, with a low fence around it. The cross was surrounded by empty cans containing artificial flowers. It looked like a well-tended grave. In fact, it was not a grave, but a repository of the John Frum cult. The village of Ipekel is the Rome of the John Frum religion, and the village's chief is the pope. There are many such crosses on Tanna, and it is estimated that ninety-five percent of the population are adherents of the new cult.

The name "John Frum" is sometimes said to be derived from the word *broom*—representing the broom that will sweep the white man from the island and thus give freedom to all the people. If it were that simple, the story of the John Frum religion would be only of passing interest. The truth is much more complicated and more beautiful. The cult is actually a variant of the cargo cult which has grown so popular, since the beginning of the twentieth century, in New Guinea, the Solomons, and elsewhere in Melanesia.

On Tanna, there were Protestant missionaries at Port Resolution, Kwangera, Whitesands, and Weasisi. Originally, they were all Presbyterians, sponsored by the London Missionary Society. They preached the gospel with great assurance, and with great intolerance for the traditional beliefs of the people. They also tried, as they had done elsewhere, to gain control of the local sources of copra, and thus to establish what has been called an "economic theocracy." Their authoritarian faith, a sort of militant puritanism, led them to attempt to outlaw traditional ceremonies and festivals—while leading them also to despoil the natives of their land. They also made great efforts to facilitate a British seizure of the islands.

The fatal mistake of the missionaries was to attempt to ban the use of kava. In their ignorance of local practices, they were unaware of the effect this new regulation would have on the people. All they knew was that kava—like the dances and other ceremonies of the people—was a pagan manifestation, totally at odds with the true religion. They even went so far as to close their churches to anyone who used kava.

Until then, Christianity had made considerable progress in the New Hebrides. A number of villages had been built on the shore, around the missions and their chapels. Now, however, the converts began to wonder about the value of a religion in which the white man kept all secret knowledge for themselves. The natives, meanwhile, were robbed of their lands, and what little money they had went to the mission stores for the purchase of European goods. Moreover, they noted that what their children were being taught in the mission schools had no practical use. They learned only to sing hymns and to read the Bible.

The native in the mission schools was the first to become disenchanted with this system and to break away from it.

This red cross at the foot of Mount Yasur does not mark a tomb. It is a symbol of the John Frum cult, a messianic religion invented by the people of Tanna.

Opposite: The weather in the mountains of Tanna is chilly. The children are naked, but their mothers hold them in their arms to warm them. The women themselves wear nothing more than grass skirts and pieces of cloth, which serve as shawls. The reddish-brown hair is typical of the inhabitants of Tanna.

The appearance of John Frum

The missionaries did not know that the kava ceremony was a part of the cult of ancestors. The final drops of kava, sprayed from the lips of the user, are intended for the spirits of the dead and are an appeal for their protection. To forbid the use of kava was to close the hereafter to the people, to unbalance them emotionally, and to damage their social cohesion.

In the first years of resistance to the missionaries, the people of Tanna drank kava excessively, at all hours of the day. Even children drank it. It was an act of defiance toward the white man's beliefs. It was also a way of ridding the people of the belief, taught at the missions, that kava was evil and restoring their faith in it as a religious and ceremonial manifestation. At the same time, it was planned to restore the traditional dances and festivals of the island.

The name John Frum was first heard in January 1941. It was time to prepare

for his coming. He would come in an airplane; therefore a landing field must be built for him in the bush.

Everyone waited for John Frum, "the ally of Rusefel [Roosevelt], king of America." The preaching of the imminent coming of John Frum took on a military and nationalist tone. John Frum's militia paraded with wooden rifles on their shoulders.

The British and French were astonished when, in the middle of the war, the religious crisis exploded. They knew so little about the beliefs of the people that they were unaware of any religious, social, or political unrest—a situation that had been brewing for years and that might have proved fatal.

At the same time, it was hard to know what to believe, even when the John Frum religion began to spread rapidly. There are numerous legends and stories, many of them contradictory. According to some, John Frum was everywhere and had many forms. Others maintained that he had come and had left, but would return. Others argued that they had received orders directly from John Frum.

Today, it is generally accepted that the movement was conceived and launched by a handful of men familiar with the secrets of kava. These leaders, with remarkable intelligence and psychological skill, manipulated the people in such a way as to prevent domination by the Presbyterian missionaries.

By opposing the white man's mission with one of their own, they succeeded in emptying the mission villages along the coast. The schools were closed. The mission families returned to their ancestral homes in the bush and once more took up their traditional beliefs and practices. The kava ceremonies, the ancient dances and feasts, were all resumed on a large scale. At the same time, a widespread disaffection with the white man set in. All contact betwen the whites and the blacks became difficult. It was no longer the Protestant church that was responsible for duping the natives, but all white men.

The British Resident, John Nicoll, made every attempt to renew contact with the people, to reestablish confidence in the government. Everywhere, his efforts met with open hostility. Frightened, he organized an expedition against the followers of John Frum and succeeded in arresting a few of them at random. They were sent to Port Vila and jailed there.

The French representative remained neutral in the crisis. But at Port Vila, as on Tanna itself, the white man still did not understand the power of the John Frum myth or the sociological importance. It was easier simply to talk of a "revolt."

Nowadays, John Frum's followers are no longer persecuted. They are left in peace to honor the red cross which evokes, it is said, the red cross on John Frum's white shirt. For Frum is believed to have been a medic in the American army.

It is difficult to know if the inhabitants of Ipekel truly believe in their messiah, if they still are convinced that he will come one day in a plane or on a ship. Or is it possible that the cult is only a symbol of resistance to the Franco-British administration? If the latter is so, then the cult will lose its reason for existence when the New Hebrides become independent.

I asked these questions in Ipekel. The answers I received were unequivocal. Yes, it was all true. John Frum would come.

I had to believe these answers. On a Friday, John Frum's day of rest, as on every Friday, I saw the men of the village parading in the square, marching in step, wooden rifles on their shoulders. The army of John Frum was drilling.

the night for dancing

Art and the supernatural are integral parts one of the other.

MARGARET MEAD

As I was climbing the steep incline leading to the village of Enfitana, a group of young men hurried past me on the trail, talking and laughing excitedly. There was, I had noticed, a festive air prevailing in the brush. That afternoon was scheduled to begin the festival known as *Toka*, which is the greatest event of the year on the island of Tanna.

The people of Tanna seem to be superior meteorologists. For a month, the weather had been incredibly bad. Then, as soon as the *Toka* had been announced, ten days beforehand, the sky cleared, the sun shone, and the weather was magnificent.

It was a fortunate change. Rain or shine, the *Toka* goes on: a day, a night, and then the following day filled with singing and dancing. As many as two thousand people attend the festival.

The trail I was following passed through the jungle for a stretch, and then ended suddenly on a spacious opening, a wide esplanade such as one hardly expects to find in the jungle. There were two immense banyan trees in the opening, both of them with an abundance of aerial roots.

There were many people already in the clearing, seated on a rise in the ground, greeting one another and chatting—the same sort of pleasantries that one hears in a Broadway theater before the curtain rises. I looked around. I was the only Westerner present at the festival.

It took several minutes for me to sort out the details of makeup and dress in this colorful, restless, and shifting crowd. It was obvious that the young people especially, both boys and girls, had taken extraordinary care with their face paint. The upper parts of their faces, from the nose to the ears and up to the hairline, were painted red. Eyebrows and mouths were outlined in yellow and black. Large

For the *Toka* celebration, these young men have donned their best feathers and necklaces. The striking facial makeup is part of the traditional holiday attire.

feathers were attached to their hair. The girls wore necklaces of flowers, while the men sported streams of grassy fibers tied around their biceps.

All of the women, regardless of age, had had their hair "done" for the occasion, just as Western women would. Here, however, hairdressing is a very serious matter indeed. A newly coiffed woman is not allowed to have sexual relations even with her husband. And what coiffures they are! The strands of hair are enclosed in a ribbon of tree bark, from which dangles a knot of kinky hair. The hairdresser's finishing touch is to douse her customer's hair with perfumed coconut oil.

The really elegant women of the island had not yet put in their appearance. They were, no doubt, in the midst of last-minute crises over their dress and their hair. It was certain that they would be on time for the celebration to begin, for the women open the ceremony.

Several shelters had been erected at one end of the opening, in a small valley. These were merely shed-roofs held up by four posts, and they seemed to be used as combination nurseries and powder rooms for visiting women. I could see children playing, and young women making last-minute adjustments in their dress, their hair, and their makeup, uttering little shrieks of despair or delight—I could not tell which.

The young men, meanwhile, disported themselves as young men do everywhere. Naked, crowned with feathers, carrying clubs or bows, they strutted from group to group, assuming the poses they considered most becoming and doing their best to appear as ferocious as possible.

I watched a group of new arrivals enter the clearing, carrying pigs on poles. A few moments later, a stately matron emerged from one of the houses and moved into the clearing, her grass skirts swaying gracefully with each step. I sensed that the festival was about to begin.

The dance of the women

It was about 4 o'clock in the afternoon. Immediately, the hum of conversation fell. The crowd swayed, moved to free the central part of the clearing. The first group of women appeared and gathered under one of the banyan trees. Their skirts of colored grass, worn low on their hips, reached to their feet; but, whenever they moved, the grass parted to reveal smooth golden thighs.

The dance began quietly. The women turned, advanced toward the audience, withdrew, stamped on the ground with their bare feet. As they moved, they sang, softly at first. Then one voice became louder, and the others also increased their volume. The beat quickened. The rhythm of the swaying skirts adjusted to the new beat; yet, the effect was graceful rather than sensuous, and strangely moving.

After a while, the first group was relieved by a second; and the second, by a third. Finally, the three groups joined together in a finale, and the beat accelerated once more. I could feel the vibrations in the ground from the stamping of their feet. Dust, golden in the sunset, partially obscured the dancers from view. A wave of odors swept over the clearing, a mixture of jasmin oil, sweat, and dust.

It appeared that almost every woman present took part in the dance and moved in time to the simple, obsessive rhythm. The steps performed by the danc-

This man, his face vividly painted in red and yellow, is one of the moving spirits of the celebration.

ers seemed easy enough, but they were executed with obvious conviction and utter seriousness. The only exception was on those few occasions when a collective sign of appreciation swept over the spectators, or a sound of approval, and then the faces of the dancers would be wreathed in smiles, teeth flashing whitely in the dark, painted faces.

The question of whether the women are "beautiful" is one that sprang naturally to my mind—although I was aware that this was a reaction to a purely Occidental view of women. Actually, it was difficult to tell, given the masklike appearance of the faces under the multi-colored paint. In fact, I could do little more than distinguish between the matrons because of their more solid (though vigorously dancing) figures, and the slim, more delicate bodies of the younger women. I wondered for how many of the latter this was, so to speak, their "first dance."

The opening part of the festival, which I had just witnessed, is called the *Napënapën.* The dance movements and the chants are traditional and rigorously choreographed. Not even the slightest improvisation is allowed. The *Napënapën* celebrates the gardens of the island and the fertility of the earth. The dance itself, like the gardens, is strictly a women's affair.

A night made for dancing

Night fell, black, impenetrable. The three groups of women dancers, which had dispersed briefly, gathered together once more and once more began their dance. Now, they danced as a single, solid, tightly knit phalanx, using a small drum to set the beat of their movements. Their bodies bent forward rhythmically, their heads bowed low. I was now able to distinguish several movements and chants that were being repeated. The rhythm of both the dance and the songs was pervasive to the extent that I was aware of nothing else.

The men were gathered in a circle around the women, and the circle expanded and contracted as the women moved closer or farther from its rim. But the men were not simply spectators. Now, they were dancing too, without moving from where they stood, their naked feet beating a tattoo so powerful that the ground shook. Their shouts and cries mingled with the chanting of the women. In their growing excitement, the men pressed in toward the dancers, and were pushed back by other men who, apparently, were acting as ushers or sergeants-at-arms—or perhaps they were simply the husbands of the dancers.

There came a moment in the night when the men actively began to participate in the dance, forming a troop which encircled the women and began to move in the direction opposite to that of the latter. The excitement of the dancers reached a climax. Shouts and screams rose from both men and women, and it was impossible to know if they were declarations of love or meaningless expletives. Light from the carbide lamps, which were hanging here and there in the clearing, cast an eerie glow over the frantically moving bodies; more eerie yet were the areas not touched by the dim light, where painted bodies writhed in an abandonment which seemed the acme of passion and sensuality but which was without the least trace of vulgarity, and was wholly without violence. Desire, mutually felt between the two groups of dancers, was almost tangible in the night air, like the dust.

It was no longer possible to follow all of the action of the dancers. It was like a vast, deliberate scene, conceived and staged by a mad genius, comprehensible to the participants but baffling to a spectator. It was pandemonium, and it was to last throughout the night.

Under the hypnotic rhythm of the beat and the chanting, the men and women broke into long ranks, then intermingled, brushing against one another. They withdrew, re-formed their ranks facing one another and again touched. Groups formed or disintegrated haphazardly, in accordance with the desire or the exhaustion of the members. Electric lights occasionally spotted one group, which instantly vanished into the surrounding darkness. A flashlight cut through the night briefly, then was not seen again.

The children danced too, alongside the adults, naked, clumsily painted, until they were exhausted. Then, they slept wherever they wished, until they had rested sufficiently to dance again.

Throughout the festival, I had been fascinated by the behavior of the many children present. They had been integrated in the festival in all respects, and consistently danced and sang along with the adults. Not once did I see the children playing among themselves, apart from the adults. And never did any child appear to create the sort of disturbance that we are accustomed to expect of Western children at adult gatherings. Throughout, their little painted faces were serious, almost grave, as though they were fully conscious of playing an adult role and participating in an important social act by which their family affirmed its ties to the community.

Until dawn, the groups of men and women mingled, separated, mingled again, withdrew, their feet pounding an exotic rhythm on the hard ground, their chants rising and falling like the waves of the sea. Exhausted, hot, I could not help longing for the end of the night, which would dissipate the acute tension pervading the air and allow the celebrants, finally, to sleep. The evident excitement of the dancers, which never abated, was born of the dance, the songs, the cries; and, of course, from the unrelieved desire of the men and women for one another. It can perhaps best be described as an intoxication of sorts—a "high," as the current expression has it—although neither alcohol nor drugs of any kind were used by anyone. It would have been superfluous, in any event, since the general exhaustion and lack of sleep were sufficient to act as an intoxicant.

Finally, my ears throbbing, my senses overwhelmed by the din, I stretched out on a bed of banana leaves under one of the shelters. Lying in the darkness, the pounding feet and hypnotic chants still breaking in the distance like the surf on a beach, I tried to sort out my impressions of the incredible spectacle I had just witnessed. But it had been too much for me. I fell asleep almost immediately.

A year's work

A visitor assisting at the *Toka* celebration, and particularly a foreigner like myself, has great difficulty in grasping either the meaning or the significance of the ceremony.

It is true that the *Toka* serves many purposes. It is an annual occasion for "letting go" on the part of the celebrants. It is an opportunity for meeting all one's friends, renewing old acquaintances. More important, it is also an occasion of

The *Toka* festivities are approaching their climax. As the women continue swaying in their colorful grass skirts, some of the men carry in the pigs suspended from long poles.

central importance in the life of the community, the climax of a whole series of preparatory ceremonies, of work and of creativity which, all taken together, constitute the *Nekowiar.* This night of dancing and the following day—even more rich in celebration—is the result of a whole year of work.

The basis of the celebration is a friendly competition and a challenge to a display of wealth between the tribal groups. The challenge itself, once given, is regarded as a sign of empathy and affection. An entire year must be spent in creating new gardens, planting kava, accumulating taro roots and Chinese yams, raising new pigs—all so that one will not lose face on the day of the ceremony. Thus, before the joy of the ceremony itself, there is the joy of preparing for it and looking forward to it; then, on the great day, there is the pride of showing oneself to be richer than one's rivals, more handsome, a better dancer, and a more accomplished singer.

The chanting and the dancing is rehearsed for three or four months before the ceremonial encounter between the two tribal groups. Those who organize these rehearsals are by no means slaves to tradition. They introduce variations on what has been done in the past, and occasionally they create new chants and steps. The careful planning of dress, and subsequently the beauty and elegance of the participants, also contributes greatly to the impact of the groups competing in the festival.

The tribe issuing the challenge plays host to its rivals, and it is traditional that the hospitality offered will be openhanded and without stint. The visiting tribe, in its turn, is determined to make as great a display of its wealth as possible. Yet, "wealth," in the sense that it is understood by these islanders, covers aesthetic as well as material goods; hence the great importance attached to the choice of songs and dances, for which official directors of music and choreographers are appointed well beforehand.

The function of the director of music is to develop the tribe's repertoire and to compose a new song. This song's worth is judged on the basis of the degree to which it communicates the composer's magical inspiration. The greater that degree, the greater the power that the song will exercise over the spectators.

The composer's effort is judged by a committee of the tribe. If the song is of sufficient quality and originality to be accepted by the committee, then the entire host tribe learns it by heart. At that point, the dance rehearsals may begin.

These rehearsals take place in a secret spot in the jungle, access to which is guarded by rigorous taboos. In order to swell their numbers, the tribe calls in its allies from the surrounding area, and everyone rehearses together. This period of preparation is itself regarded as a preliminary celebration, offering as it does numerous occasions for meetings and talking. Everyone, it appears, takes great delight in the planning and rehearsing.

The date of the festival itself is usually sometime in October, but it is always kept secret. Elaborate stratagems are employed to guard the secret. Once the two tribes have agreed to a specific date, it is not revealed until ten or twelve days before the appointed date.

The single-mindedness and dedication with which all these preparations are made are an indication of the underlying seriousness of the festival. It is more than a keeping of faith with tribal traditions, more than an occasion for social encounters, more than an affirmation of solidarity between two tribes. It is also a spiritual function: an evocation of ancestors, an excursion into the past and into the future. It is, in the words of Jean Guiart, "a climax of collective life."

The Toka

The first grayish-green rays of dawn had already touched the sky as the feet of the women executed the final steps of their dance. Simultaneously, the chanting was stilled. At that moment, a new group was gathering at one end of the clearing. This was the competing team, the visitors, who were scheduled to perform the dance from which the entire festival took its name: the *Toka*. Still fresh, they advanced vigorously toward the center of the clearing, each one brandishing a long staff painted white.

One man bore on his shoulders a structure made of palm leaves and feathers, topped by a bouquet, which swayed precariously as he walked. Around him, his companions used their staffs to steady the structure. As soon as the group had reached the clearing's center, the palms and feathers were discarded and the dancers formed two ranks. The dance began, the ranks of performers stamping and turning so as sometimes to face one another and sometimes both to face the same direction. The white staffs moved ritualistically in time to the chants and the rhythm of the dancers. Some of the dancers let their belts slide over their hips and fall to the ground, whereupon there was a rush of young men, the quickest of whom succeeded in pouncing upon these precious souvenirs as the spectators shouted their happy approval.

An air of joyful celebration permeated the clearing as the dancers performed, bodies bending forward, staffs moving, plumes and grass accoutrements swaying, penile sheaths jiggling to the beat of the dance, and, everywhere, white teeth flashing in faces painted scarlet and ochre. The message of the dance, however, is not joy, but power: the power of the tribe.

When the visitors had completed their performance, they moved away to make room for the local dancers, who were to perform the *Nao*, the response to the *Toka*. During this dance, the men hold bundles of dried twigs and small branches which they use to set the beat of their chants and dance steps. In my opinion, the *Nao* is the most unusual—and certainly the most moving—of the ceremonial dances. The syncopated rustling of the branches, interspersed with pauses and moments of silence in which only the sound of moving feet was audible, is so complex, so subtle in its artistic use, as to astound and disconcert the uninitiated observer.

The end of the *Nao* is the signal to begin the central ceremony of the festival: the presentation and slaughter of the pigs, which had been specially fattened during the year preceding the ceremony. The pigs are carried into the center of the clearing, their legs tied over a pole, borne on the shoulders of the men. A child, crowned with flowers, rides on the head of each animal. As the procession advances, the spectators sing in praise of the beauty and value of these living offer-

Around two thousand people take part in the *Toka*. Each one of them arrives in feathers, flowers, and grass streamers.

ings. First, the hosts, and then the visitors, place their pigs on the ground. As the animals grunt and struggle, they are closely inspected by the whole populace. Then, the executioner approaches, carrying a ritual bludgeon—a heavy mass of carved wood, which he brings down with all his might on the snout of every animal.

The animals do not die instantaneously. Sometimes, a second, or even a third blow is necessary. Meanwhile, one hears the dying animals groaning amid the general indifference of the onlookers, as the dogs of the village run forward to lap at the blood running from the victims' snouts.[1]

The ceremony lasts as long as there are pigs to slaughter. On this occasion, I counted over forty of the animals, waiting their turn to be sacrificed while the hosts and visitors inspected them with admiring, and sometimes critical, eyes.

---

[1]The role of the pig, in this ceremony particularly and in Melanesian culture generally, does not admit to easy analysis. The pig is undoubtedly a privileged animal and very likely a sacred one. At the same time, it is not, to all appearances, a totem.

The women wear long grass skirts that sway gracefully to the rhythm of the dance.

The stalks of kava, piled in two competing stacks in the clearing, are constantly surveyed, and their respective sizes are the subject of much speculation and comment. The kava, like the pigs, once the slaughter of the latter has ended will become the subject of a ceremonial exchange between the hosts and their visitors.

Finally, the men of the *Toka*, still carrying their white staffs, come in procession, with measured steps, to make their official inspection of the pigs and the kava. Once this is done, both visitors and hosts are allowed to take possession of their respective gifts and to begin butchering the pigs.

Victory through generosity

At the moment of this division, the dancers were suddenly transformed into bearers and they were loaded down with quarters of pork. The meat had to be cooked no later than that evening; otherwise, it would spoil. Therefore, the paths from the clearing were swarming with men and women, still painted and crowned with feathers and flowers, hurrying toward their villages as best they could with their loads of pork and kava. But that was not the end of the festival. From all sides, I could hear shouts and songs. As dusk fell, campfires, like blazing stars, illuminated the countryside. It seemed that every corner of the jungle was in celebration, with everyone gorging themselves on pork during the next few days before returning to their customary diet of yams and taro roots.

The purpose of the *Nekowiar* challenge, as I mentioned, is to allow the challenging tribe to make a display of its power and wealth. The number and quality of the animals led to slaughter, and the riches displayed in the center of the clearing, are a measure of the status of both the hosts and the visitors.

The exchange of this wealth, as reciprocal gifts, is at the foundation of social life in Oceania. The offer of pigs and of kava requires a counter-offer of pigs and kava, with each side trying to outdo the other in generosity. Those who offer the most are regarded as the winners, as being the superior tribe, as the moral victors.

Although the practice of gifts and counter-gifts is the fundamental social law of Melanesian culture, the *Toka*, which is the ceremonial application of that law, is the particular privilege of the island of Tanna. Nowhere else does this highly codified and living institution exist. On Tanna, however, it is the central event of tribal life, the cement that assures the unity of the community.

It would be virtually impossible for one man, no matter how highly organized, to observe and especially to film the *Toka* in its entirety. It is not a Western-style ceremony, designed to be viewed by an audience. In fact, at the *Toka* there is no distinction between participants and spectators. Everyone, at a given moment, becomes a performer. No one sits and contemplates the spectacle; rather, all the people take part in the dancing and singing and the general enthusiasm. Participation is in the air, in the very nature of the *Toka*. Even I, a Westerner and a visitor, never felt alien or "left out" of the activities. No one paid the slightest attention to me; everyone was too involved in the festival to be concerned about the presence of a stranger.

Frankly, I felt a secret envy of the enthusiasm and courage of these hundreds of men and women who had spent months, day after day, preparing this celebration, and who, when the time came, were able to throw themselves into it without reservation and without pretense, but with a simple, all-encompassing joy.

Melanesian art has a gift for expressing, with appropriate sobriety, man's interior life. This large wooden statue was sculpted in the New Hebrides, on the island of Vao. (Collection Musée de l'Homme)

8

the Big Nambas

*In reality, there is no such thing as
a "child-like people." All peoples
are adults, even those who have no
record of their childhood and
adolescence.*

LEVI-STRAUSS

Norsup, on the island of Malikolo (Malekula), is little more than a tiny cluster
of buildings. There is an airport (a mud hut with a thatched roof) and a grass landing strip; a few government buildings surrounded by gravel; a road along the
shore, with a few large trees, dominated by two flags flying high on their poles:
one British, one French. There are no houses in sight, and no village in the usual
sense of the word.

That is not unusual in Oceania. White settlements are often scattered and
very small, with the houses tucked away here and there. Somehow, it is strange to
see a colonial "possession" without any colonial city.

From the air, Malikolo seemed an island of coconut trees, rows of them
stretching into the distance, swaying gracefully. There is an enormous coconut
plantation, dating back to the time when the copra trade was flourishing. Copra
has had many ups and downs since that time.

The importance of Norsup to me was that it was my jumping-off point for the
country of the Big Nambas. The name "Big Nambas" itself is enough to stir the
imagination; in fact, it had stirred mine for as long as I could remember. I had read
everything available on these "cannibals" who live in a remote and inaccessible

Viriambat, High Chief of the Big Nambas. The Big Nambas, who live in the bush on Malikolo Island,
have managed to preserve their tribal traditions.

area; and I had often studied the few, and mostly unsatisfactory, maps available of their country.

The Big Nambas are bushmen. On Malikolo, as on many other islands, the origins of the bushmen are veiled in obscurity. All that is known is that they appeared, carrying with them, in their pirogues, a few domestic animals—dogs, chickens, pigs. Having landed, they disappeared into the bush and remained there, totally isolated, for a thousand years. They were indeed cannibals at one time, and today they still live in nostalgic remembrance of that time. They are not seamen, but live off the land. In the Pacific, this means that they have chosen the more difficult and uncertain way of life.

Big Nambas do not come to the white man. They remain in their villages, surrounded by the jungle, watching from a distance the advent of progress. If one wishes to see a Big Nambas, he must go in search of him. And that was precisely what I had in mind.

Preparations

Visitng the Big Nambas is an easy plan to formulate, but a difficult one to carry out. The tribe's isolation is protected by dense jungle, by hills and cliffs of mud, and by a certain reputed intolerance of strangers. One's welcome, I was given to understand, depended entirely on the *Meleoun*, or High Chief, of the Big Nambas, a man of high rank and a well-developed sense of his own importance. I had read of this chief—his name was Viriambat—in books written twenty years before. It seemed to me that the time to worry about my welcome was when I had succeeded in reaching the Big Nambas. For the moment, the problem was whether or not I could get there. At Port Vila, the difficulties in the journey through the brush had been described to me in vivid detail; it was pointed out to me candidly that such an expedition might well be beyond my endurance.[1]

At Norsup, I called on the French representative, who had just taken up his post. Both he and the local gendarme—the latter had also just arrived—were eager to give me any help they could, but they knew hardly more about the Big Nambas than I did. My first dead end.

I did learn one thing of importance that no one, either in Paris or in Port Vila, had bothered to tell me. The one indispensable item, if one is to reach the country of the Big Nambas, is a pair of boots with rubber soles and deep treads. Otherwise, there is no way to get through the mud. Naturally, the local store had none in my size. I have small feet, and footwear is always a problem. In this instance, the gendarme's kind wife came to my assistance. She let me have her boots,

---

[1]Much of what I knew of the country was based on a remarkable work titled *Malekula: A Vanishing People in the New Hebrides*, compiled by Camille Wedgwood from the notes of English anthropologist, Arthur Barnard Deacon. It is significant that Deacon died on Malikolo, at the age of twenty-four, after living for two years in the bush.

which were a tight fit but a fit nonetheless. There is nothing lacking in the hospitality of Norsup.

Now properly shod, I turned my attention to the next step. I needed six porters and a guide, which I was able to find easily enough. I also bought enough provisions for myself and my seven companions—and a stack of gifts for the High Chief of the Big Nambas. I did not stint. There was enough of the vile local tobacco, matches and whiskey to insure his good will twice over, if it turned out to be available at all.

Despite all that I had been told about the difficulties of a trip into the bush, I was not discouraged. Nor was I unduly disturbed by rumors about High Chief Viriambat. I had been through Africa and Asia on foot, by jeep, in pirogues, and by camel. I knew that there were very few "exploits," and even fewer expeditions, that were truly beyond human endurance. After all, the Big Nambas had somehow gotten to where they lived; and so had a few other people, including white men. Why not I? And as for Viriambat, I would deal with that riddle when I came to it.

The night before I left, I lay in bed, listening to the rain on the roof and wondering if, after all, I was not being too optimistic. I was no longer twenty years old, I reminded myself. Perhaps the jungles of Malikolo were somehow different from those of other islands. And what if High Chief Viriambat and I did not hit it off?

My sleep was uneasy that night.

The gate to the bush

I had planned to leave at dawn, but my plan went amiss. It took a while for my companions to arrive from their village nearby and then to divide up the load to everyone's satisfaction. I had been through this before many times, and the division followed the usual pattern. There is always one porter who is cleverer than the others. For some reason, he always seems to wear a pair of bright red shorts. He quickly looks over the bundles and instinctively knows which is the lightest. He seizes that one. In this instance, his choice was the tripod for my camera, and a small bag of film. The heaviest load—the canned goods and the whiskey bottles intended for Viriambat—went to the most reticent and puniest of the porters. Actually, this initial division was purely ceremonial, since we were driven to the end of the road in a pickup truck.

The road does not go into the bush. It leads through the coconut plantation, where the trees are planted in lines so straight and long that they make one dizzy, to the edge of the bush. At the foot of the road is the gate to the bush: a sliding gate, like that found on any farm. We opened the gate. There was an air of solemnity to the act, as though we were crossing the boundary between the known and the unknown. Beyond the gate, there was what can only be described as a wall of vegetation: the bush. On the ground, we could barely distinguish a bare spot that passed as a trail. It would lead us to the Big Nambas.

The only way to reach Big Nambas country is to pick one's way along jungle trails.

This wood sculpture, with deep, rectilinear features, stands in the middle of the bush. It was probably part of a *Nakamal* at one time. My guess is that the *Nakamal*, or House of Men, was abandoned and then somehow was destroyed.

There were a few arguments about the division of the load, which I settled arbitrarily, before we set out. I told the man carrying my photographic equipment to stay directly behind me. Then we entered the bush.

I had never felt in better shape. The clear sky, the jungle around us, the fresh morning air—everything contributed to a sense of well-being.

The men at the head of the line disappeared into a stretch of tall grass and the rest of us followed. When we emerged on the other side, there were three leeches attached to my thigh. I removed them quickly. Leeches can be dangerous, as I knew from my experience in the Malayan jungles.

Once again, I was struck by the absence of fauna (other than leeches) in the bush. Elsewhere, the trees would have been alive with monkeys screaming and doing acrobatics, and with screeching hornbills. Here, there were only a few birds and nothing more.

Occasionally we found a fallen tree across the trail. The path grew even more difficult to see, let alone to follow, and the vegetation thickened. We had been walking for three hours, and our boxes and bags seemed to grow heavier by the minute.

I sniffed the odors of the jungle. A surprisingly sweet smell, not unlike that of tuberoses, emanated from some hidden flower; a warm, heavy perfume. It was shortly replaced by the smell of chlorophyll, as though from cut grass.

There was a surprising diversity of scenery in the bush. The jungle is far from being monotonous. Sometimes we had to fight our way through a thicket of shrubs. In some places, the branches were so low that we could get by only by walking in a crouch. There were hills and clearings, and a small stream with muddy banks where I found a growth of treelike ferns, the branches spread like parasols, which seemed to radiate light. Beyond, the dense vegetation began once more, so thick that the ground was totally hidden. It reminded me not so much of a hothouse as it did of the sea bottom overgrown with algae.

The porters were now rather far ahead of me on the path. I could not even hear them. The young man with me, carrying my cameras, was staying very close. It suddenly occurred to me that he was afraid. I turned and glanced at him. Fear was evident in his face, in the way he looked at me. Afraid of what? Of getting lost in the bush? Of me? Probably he was experiencing nothing more than the vague unease of a "man salt water," as the coastal inhabitants are known in Beachlamar (a local variant of pidgin English), when he is surrounded by jungle. I looked again and smiled encouragingly. He smiled back, weakly. I looked forward again just in time to avoid an enormous spider whose web was strung across the path.

Two lost statues

We passed through an area of dense shade crowded with low-growing plants of every kind. Thick masses of epiphytes grew on the trunks of trees. I would have liked to be able to stop a while and examine the plants, but I was afraid that we might lose our porters entirely in the jungle if I delayed.

We hurried on. Suddenly, like a scene from a South Seas adventure film,

This photograph, taken from atop a banyan tree, gives an idea of the density of the jungle in the interior of Malikolo Island.

there rose before us, from between the twin trunks of a large tree, a greenish statue, its empty eyes staring at us from a square face. Another, similar statue lay on the ground next to it. The two statues had apparently been abandoned here, in the middle of the bush, far from any village. These were the first ones that I had seen on the island that were not meant for the eyes of tourists. I examined the two faces with their deep, rectilinear features. It was obvious that the artists who had carved them believed, not in the possibility of a sale, but in the statues themselves.[1]

Our wayward companions had decided to wait for us at the statues. It was obvious that they, being inhabitants of the coast and therefore pupils of the missionaries, were singularly unimpressed. Their only concern was to avoid all contact with the *nangalat*—the bush nettle, which causes a painful burning sensation and raises an enormous blister.

And, still from an adventure film, as we stood there two men appeared before

[1] They were probably statues that had, at one time, been part of a Namel (House of Men) which was now abandoned.

Among the Big Nambas, the relations between father and son are characterized by a marked tenderness.

us on the path, their bows and arrows in their hands, their golden skin glistening. They were naked, except for red loincloths. It was too perfect. Too much like an old Dorothy Lamour picture. I was tempted to applaud. Then the two men disappeared as quickly and as silently as they had come. If I had been alone, I would have wondered if I were dreaming.

Our path led to a break in the plateau, an opening in the vegetation. I could see the sky again, and I caught a glimpse of water. There was a dull, rhythmic sound: the surf. We had reached the sea. The guide led us down a muddy embankment, with a great deal of sliding and slipping. Then we were on the beach, standing on sand of incredible whiteness. The freshness of the salt air was like a bath as we stood watching the waves move majestically toward shore and break against the gray rocks.

While in the New Hebrides, I was often struck by the contrast between the humid darkness of the bush and the blue and green of the sea flooded with light. Our eyes had not yet adjusted to the glare of the sun reflected on the sand.

The beach was narrow, littered with smooth stones and pieces of dead coral. There was no lack of vegetation. Shrubs, thick plants with pink flowers, and mangrove trees with rock-bound roots, grew to the edge of the water. There was a small stream, emptying into the sea.

It seemed an ideal spot for a rest. We sprawled in the sand for a short time, long enough to allow the sun to dry the jungle dampness on our clothes. Then we set out again.

The path followed the general line of the shore, sometimes turning away from the sea and then returning to it, until we reached Unmet. Unmet is not even a village. It is a mission, with a surprisingly large school building.

I knocked at the door of the mission. It was answered by a lay brother. The priest was not at home, I was told. Was there anything that he could do for me?

I had some difficulty in understanding the brother. He was a French Canadian, but he had been in the islands and had spoken Beachlamar so long that he had almost lost his native language. There were two things that he wanted to convey to me, once he understood why I was there. The first was that I was welcome to share whatever food he had. The second, that he knew Viriambat, who often came to the shore at Unmet, and that he would send a message to him or send someone to take me to him. Touched by this good man's openhanded generosity, I accepted his offer gladly.

The high chief

It was soon time to rejoin my companions who were having their lunch in the mission yard, in the shade of a large tree. The brother accompanied me to the door. As I emerged into the sunlight, I felt his hand on my arm.

"Viriambat!" he said, pointing.

I saw a man standing in the yard, naked except for a tuft of red fibers covering his genitals. His expression was tranquil, neither smiling nor frowning. My impression was that he was a man who was sure of himself. He was tall, solidly built, well muscled. A powerful body, I thought, but not the body of an athlete. It was obvious that he was in the prime of life; around forty, perhaps, but a very young forty.

Our eyes met.

I smiled. He smiled.

I had a bottle of whiskey in my bag. Not one of the bottles that I had bought as a gift for Viriambat, but one intended for my personal use. I took out the bottle and walked toward the High Chief.

Two minutes later, we were all sitting in the mission, having a drink. I say "all" because Viriambat was not alone. His entourage was with him. There was a small man, older than the chief, dressed in a shirt and shorts, who smiled constantly and thought he was speaking English when he spoke Beachlamar. He was Viriambat's most intimate councillor, his "prime minister." Then there were courtiers, guards, hunters, officials—too many people for me to have remembered them all at our first meeting.

I was fascinated by the Big Nambas uniform, simple as it is. It consists only of a large belt made of a dried leaf, held in place by a western-style leather belt.

Under the belt, below the stomach, is the *namba*, from which the Big Nambas take their name: a turf of fibers, wine-colored rather than red.

The brown-amber color of the Big Nambas seemed to emanate from beneath the skin. Their expression is impassive, distant, detached, and they have an air of simple dignity about them. Their overall appearance is more natural and impressive than that of the penile-sheathed Papuans of New Guinea.

A cash basis

The name of Viriambat's prime minister, I learned, was Willy. Willy served as interpreter for the chief; mine was the mission brother. I directed my questions to the brother in French, who addressed them to Willy in Beachlamar, who passed them on to Viriambat. I discovered later that Viriambat himself understands Beachlamar perfectly and speaks it. An interpreter was not a matter of necessity, but of protocol. The High Chief did not address strangers except through an intermediary.

Yes, I was informed, Viriambat will allow me to visit his village. Yes, there will be a place for me to stay, a house for me and my companions. However, I will have to pay. For the house. For taking pictures. For filming the village. For the food. For everything. And in cash.

The word *cash* occurred frequently in the conversation. It is undeniably a part of the Big Nambas vocabulary.

The Big Nambas' appetite for cash, which I had frequently heard about, irritates the white people of the islands. Actually, it is not greed, but prudence, that motivates this insistence upon "cash." People who live in the bush have learned by experience to be wary of outsiders. They are an intelligent people who have no wish to be "taken" by strangers. They have had their fill of adventurers of all kinds, all of them more or less penniless, who arrive out of nowhere and expect to be fed and lodged indefinitely at the expense of the village.

It should also be remembered that the social system of the New Hebrides is based on a profit motive. Everything is bought and sold quite openly; even social status. Pigs and pigs' teeth are used as a medium of exchange; but Western style money is also acceptable.

I would be expected to pay the Big Nambas in New Hebrides francs, and I gathered that we were talking about a large number of them.

Big Nambas country

We were well into the afternoon, and it was time for us to leave if we were to reach the Big Nambas village before dark. My porters and I set out, slightly the worse for wear. My pack was lighter than before, by the weight of a bottle of whiskey.

Viriambat was still in Unmet, shopping. He would catch up to us in the bush.

This part of our journey through the jungle seemed to me to be the most arduous. The rumors concerning the difficulty of access to the Big Nambas, as it turned out, were more than just rumors. There was a deep ravine to be crossed, and, at the bottom of the ravine, a river to be forded. It was, nonetheless, beautiful country. The enormous trees were garlanded with orchids—a sight which lessened the discomfort of sliding down one muddy slope on my backside and climbing another on all fours.

The shade of the trees was like night, and the thickness of the vegetation reduced visibility to almost nothing. I could well understand how dangerous this region must have been twenty years before, when the Big Nambas roamed, spreading terror throughout the bush. For then they protected their solitude with every means at their disposal. In order to throw curious white men off their trail, they turned their trails through the bush into impenetrable labyrinths in which only a Big Nambas could find his way. At the time, they were in continual warfare with their neighbors, the Dirak, whom they finally defeated, with much bloodshed, and forced to take refuge on the coast, near the missions. During this struggle, a handful of grass placed on a path meant that the path was taboo. To violate the taboo brought instant death.

I became suddenly aware that we had been joined on the trail by two naked men carrying bows and arrows. I had no idea if they were hunters or warriors. They walked with us for a while, without speaking. When I looked again, they were gone.

By late afternoon, Viriambat himself had joined us, and it was a pleasure to watch him move quickly and gracefully through the bush, his feet seeming barely to sink into the soft mud. Every muscle in his body moved with the supplety and effectiveness that we normally see only in large animals living in the wild. Needless to say, he quickly outdistanced me.

Soon, I began to see signs of former gardens in the bush. Then there was a clearing. Someone in our group shouted, a long, modulated cry. There was an answering shout from somewhere ahead. We had arrived at the Big Nambas village. There was a fence. Dogs barked, children shrieked. We were led to the *Nakamal*, the House of Men, and told to wait there. Viriambat was having our house prepared for us.

It was growing dark, and the men of the village were assembling for their kava, when Willy appeared and motioned for us to follow him. He led us to our house, which was set slightly apart from the others. The women of the village had hidden themselves as we followed in Willy's path, but we had picked up a sizeable escort of children along the way.

Finally, we were alone. I was too tired to try to cook anything, and we ate out of our supply of canned goods.

I inflated my air mattress and looked for a corner to lie down. The house had been cleaned, the dirt floor covered with banana leaves, but it was small, and there were nine of us.

I selected a spot and made myself comfortable.

I could hear the porters talking, laughing, teasing one another like high school girls. My God, I wondered, don't they ever get tired? Then I slept like a dead man until morning.

The house that I rented from Viriambat, in the village of the Big Nambas, was set apart from the other houses.

A village asleep

The following pages are taken from my diary:

"September 13. I awake at 5:30. The interior of the house is damp. I see that it rained during the night. My companions are still asleep, piled one on top of the other. Dawn is breaking, and the light is faintly green. Outside, it is cold and damp, with water dripping from the houses and trees. The enormous leaves are wet, shining. An alien substance. Looking out through the door into the green light and the jungle, I can imagine how it must feel to live inside an aquarium.

"I hope that the rain will stop soon. With the trail as muddy as it was yesterday, it will be absolutely impassable if there is any more. To say nothing of the river at the bottom of the ravine.

"Behind me, I hear someone moving about, lighting a fire to make coffee. I had better heat some water to wash and shave.

"I see that it is raining harder than ever. There is no point in going outside, and I don't know what to do with myself. My friends seem to be at a loss, too. They are not nearly as lively as they were last night.

"It is now eight o'clock. After a great deal of yawning and scratching, most of my friends have gone back to sleep. How discouraging. The whole village seems to be sleeping. Who would believe that the Big Nambas are late-risers?"

An understanding

Later in the morning, the rain slackened somewhat. Viriambat appeared in the doorway, trailed by the village council. He seemed in a good mood, unaffected by the bad weather. He gave an order, and two men carried firewood into the house. Soon, there was a blazing fire. I stood shivering under a heavy sweater.

Viriambat and I looked at each other. I wondered what I should say. Should I mention the weather, as though we were chatting at a cocktail party? I decided against it. The Nambas were no doubt accustomed to rain; moreover, the polite conversation of one society may be the taboo of another.

Willy was seated at the fire on a kind of stool, his short, thick legs as close as they could get to the flames. I decided to use him in order to engage Viriambat in conversation. I tried, but it was not much use. Willy, with all the good will in the world, really spoke nothing but Beachlamar. He did not understand most of what I said in English. One of my porters came to the rescue. Apparently, he knew enough English at least to guess, with some accuracy, at what I was trying to say.

Most of my questions had to do with Viriambat himself, his personality, his psychology. First, I tried to find out what his function was among the Big Nambas:

"Does a chief have much power?"

"Yes."

"Absolute power?"

After much consultation with the other men, Willy decided not to answer the question.

"How is a chief chosen? Does age have anything to do with the choice?"

"Not necessarily. The most important men are chosen as chiefs."

"Who are the important men? What makes them important?"

Willy shrugged helplessly. How could he make a white man understand what was important to men who lived in the bush, surrounded by mud and jungle.

"Is it important to be able to walk in the bush without falling in the mud? To be able to walk in the rain without catching cold?"

Willy laughed. "No, no. It's much more complicated."

Eventually, after many questions and answers, I began to understand that the characteristic of the Big Nambas is cohesion: the cohesion of a group of men, of a village, of everyone and everything that has to do with custom and tradition. Custom, no doubt, covers much territory, from cannibalism to the cultivation of yams to the way a Big Nambas carries himself. The social and psychological structure of the community appeared to be perhaps monolithic, but not secret or intentionally surrounded by mystery.

I also gathered that Viriambat had adopted a strange mission for himself: to bring his people, whether or not they are willing, to a state of political awareness. If the vote comes, they will vote. Viriambat has decided.

I looked at the High Chief standing before me. He glanced at me. I felt a solidarity between us, an almost ironic complicity, such as I had not experienced elsewhere in the Pacific or in Africa. I understood him. And he knew that I understood. The Big Nambas were poised on the edge of the unknown, but Viriambat was there to guard them against harm. How hard it was to believe that, only ten years ago, the world of the Big Nambas ended at the foot of their trails through the brush. They did not even have a name for the island in their language because, for them, the universe did not extend beyond their trees.

Lovers and friends

Toward noon, the sky began to clear. Viriambat and his entourage left, and I began a leisurely tour of the village. Despite the rain, everything seemed neat and well tended.

Before every house there was a clearing where the children, dogs, and pigs of the house roamed. The most valuable of the pigs, however, those with spiraled tusks, were kept in roofed pens. These were the "money-pigs," too precious to run loose with the others.

The houses have only one opening, which is so low that one must enter on all fours. The interior of the houses is quite large, but dark, and equipped only with primitive utensils. Sometimes, pigs are kept in the house; I was warned more than once to be careful, or else the pig would bite.

I photographed a naked man sitting on the ground with his son. Or possibly it was his grandson. The boy was no more than nine or ten years old, as naked as the man and with the same air of gravity and concentration. The two seemed bound by an obvious tie of affection.

I had already noticed how serious children are in Africa and Asia. This child was particularly impressive; so delicate and yet sure of himself, as though sustained by courage and will. He did not run away as the other children did, but sat looking at me.

By then, I was certain that I had photographed one of those couples which, strange though they may seem to Western eyes, are within the traditions of the Big Nambas. Young boys become the wards, or rather the lovers, of their paternal grandfathers, who are responsible for initiating them into sexual life. Males are not allowed to have relations with women until they are old enough to wear the *namba*. Thus, homosexuality is an institution among the Big Nambas. And, like heterosexuality, it has its dramas and its jealousies. I was told that Viriambat himself, as a young man and a candidate for the position of High Chief, was the victim of a jealous feud. Homosexuality is also common among women, and there are many instances of passionate attachment between such lovers. The Big Nambas obviously are far advanced along the path of social sexology. Unfortunately, the anthropologists, as far as I know, have done little work in this area.

To all appearances, the ties that bind the Big Nambas to their way of life in the bush are very strong. That is evident on days when the weather is bad. The people, though they look neither unhappy nor undernourished, are naked and exposed to the rain and the cold, to say nothing of the mud. Yet, only a half a day's walk from here, in the village not far from the mission at Unmet, the inhabitants keep dry under canvas roofs, they have clothing to protect them from the cold, shoes for their feet (if they want them), and a nearby store for food. Most of all, they are spared the terrible isolation of these mountains smothered in mud and vegetation.

Yet, we must remember that, on the coast, there is a mission—and Viriambat is wary of missionaries. He is on excellent terms with the priests and brothers. He visits them and accepts their hospitality and their gifts. But he makes no concessions on the spiritual plane, and he is willing to make none.

There are Big Nambas who live on the coast, having been drawn there by the attractions of an easier life. Their children go to the mission school, and as Viriambat knows, they have given up the traditional practices and beliefs of their own people.

Viriambat, in fact, knows pretty much everything that goes on at Unmet, both in the mission and in the village. Willy, the prime minister, lives there; and he serves as the chief's eyes and ears. The chief, however, chooses to remain loyal to his two small, poor villages.

Why? The answer to that question intrigued me. There was no doubt at all in my mind that Viriambat has carefully analyzed the situation and made a deliberate choice.

Nudity: a symbol

Viriambat and his faithful followers, if they chose to come down from their mountains, would live a much more comfortable and an easier life. I do not believe that the fact that they remain in the mountains has anything to do with timidity or a fear of civilization. The Big Nambas know what they will find. Viriambat is not a simple "native" who is terrified by the white man's technology. He is familiar with airplanes and automobiles, and he has a radio of his own. In that respect, none of the Big Nambas are naïve.

Though they stand on the edge of the modern world, the Big Nambas seem to regard it without admiration or astonishment. They lack entirely the enthusiasm of the Africans for "progress." Rather, they seem extremely cautious. And, because of that caution, the tribe is a unique example of victorious resistance to the white man's influence. The fact that there are so few Big Nambas no doubt has something to do with that successful resistance. Not many people from the outside world believe that they are worth bothering about, and this has protected Viriambat's people from the effects of foreign ideological propaganda. It has also

The author with Viriambat (center), High Chief of the Big Nambas.

isolated them from the political mainstream of the region, for the Nambas' potential as a voting block is negligible.

The fact that the villagers remain naked today is an important factor in this respect. It represents a steadfast refusal on the part of the Nambas to bow to the white man's sense of modesty, and especially to the authority of the missions. Nudity is a decisive psychological and moral commitment. It justifies everything else. It symbolizes the traditional way of life of the Big Nambas.

Fidelity to nudity is the Big Nambas' strongest defense against the outside world. When a Namba consents to wear clothing, the white world has begun to assimilate him. Nudity is an open refusal to conform to the white man's customs or to accept his standards. This courageous stubbornness leads to a turn-about in value judgments. Ridicule is heaped, not upon those who are naked, but upon those who do not understand why the Big Nambas are naked.

What of the Big Nambas who have gone to live along the coast and who, by way of concession, now wear shirts and shorts? Do they represent a trend? And will Viriambat lose all his people in an irreversible movement down from the mountains?

There is no way of knowing. Material comfort (which, as it exists on this island, would be unbearable to most Westerners) does not necessarily exercise an irresistible attraction. Man, in the final analysis, serves his ideals rather than his needs. One has only to observe the Big Nambas to realize how simplistic it is to believe that man is instinctively materialistic. Their attachment to their way of life is part of their history and of their physical and psychological well-being. They truly like to walk along their slippery, muddy trails. They are truly fulfilled in raising their pigs and planting their yams.

The women

As hard as life may be for the men who live in the bush, I think it is even harder for the women. I went out one morning, after another night of rain. Everything was soaked. It was early, and the sun was just rising behind the trees.

If the menfolk of the Big Nambas sleep late, the women do not. I saw them filing through the village, their eyes on the ground, on their way to work in the yam gardens. They carried sharp sticks with which to dig and baskets. Some of them were also carrying infants. The women, Willy had already explained, are allowed to use only certain paths in and around the village. The others are taboo to them.

I hesitated to approach the women. The last thing I wanted was to offend them, or to give the men of the village any reason, however far-fetched, for jealousy. I therefore followed the women, at a respectful distance, to the gardens.

The gardens are truly junglelike, overgrown with an inextricable tangle of vines from the yam plants. Even the paths through the gardens are barely visible. There were two plots, however, which were quite bare. Nothing yet grew in the rich black dirt. And it was in these that the women worked, while a male supervised the women and gave orders.

The fact that the women work while the men watch them is not a sign of male laziness or male chauvinism. Agriculture is the province of women because women, it is believed, assure the fertility of the land. Moreover, not very long ago, when warfare raged in the mountains, it was necessary that the Big Nambas stand guard, with their weapons at the ready, while the women worked the land and cultivated the yams. Today, of course, the role of the males is much easier than that of the women, and has lost all of its dangerous aspects. The men, obviously, are content. They are unemployed warriors. They occupy their time in interminable conversation and libations of kava within the *Nakamal*. Their lives are simple and rather pleasant, and they see no reason for a change.

The fondness of the Big Nambas for the yams cultivated by the women is another factor in their reluctance to abandon their traditional way of life. In the mountains, there is no lack of space, or of rich earth, to grow as many yams—to say nothing of bananas and taro—as one wishes. Along the coast, which is already inhabited, it is by no means certain that they would have the same advantages. The gardens in the bush provide enough food for the families of the village. Along the coast, there might not be enough food. And, perhaps as important, it is possible that the men of the tribe, once they gave up their mountains, would no longer be able to enjoy the same life of leisure that they do in the bush.

Those are all considerations that certainly have occurred to the ordinary villager in Viriambat's domain. But, so far as the High Chief himself is concerned, I had no doubt that his reasons for remaining in the bush are much more subtle and calculated. There is, first of all, the question of preserving his authority. His regime, half autocratic and half democratic, is contested by no one in the mountains. He is free from interference by both the government or the missionaries. Rather, they seek his good will and support. Thus, he is favored by isolation. I noticed that when the French representative on the island was attempting to persuade Viriambat to attend a meeting of the chiefs, he treated the High Chief as a power to be reckoned with. This status, this recognized dignity, Viriambat owes largely to the isolation of his people in the jungle. In the bush, he is able to preserve his prestige, and he makes independent use of the kind of tribal diplomacy in which he was trained and in which he has had enormous experience.

The prestige of virility

The High Chief's situation is not the same in both of his villages. At Amok, where he lives, it is easy enough for Viriambat to collect his customary tribute of

Double page following: Although the Big Nambas could choose to live along the coast, where medical care and a certain amount of physical comfort are available, they prefer to remain in the cold, dampness, and mud of their mountain jungle.

whiskey and tobacco; but at Unmet, on the shore, it may not be quite so simple.

In my own mind, I have no doubt that Viriambat's motives in preserving the traditional life-style of the Big Nambas rise above sordid concern with his own petty profit. There are so many factors to be considered and so many repercussions if a single one of the customs of the tribe is abandoned, that he hardly knows where to start. There is, for example, the question of polygamy. Wives, like pigs, are a sign of wealth, and polygamy is indispensable to Viriambat for economic reasons. But it is also necessary from the standpoint of sexuality and psychological well-being.

Viriambat has had as many as thirteen wives at one time—all of them beautiful. Today, he has seven. His father, Nisaie, had twenty-seven. It is not that Viriambat needs seven or thirteen women to satisfy his sexual appetite. It is, above all, a question of the image of virility that he must project. His reputation for strength and courage, and his prestige among his subjects, all hang in the balance, for virility is an obsession among all primitive peoples. There is, of course, an aspect of sexual enjoyment involved in Viriambat's devotion to polygamy. I could understand why. From the little that I saw of some of his wives, I can say that they are not without charm. It is also likely that they have a certain behind-the-scenes influence on their husband's attitudes and decisions.

It would be easy to go too far in referring to the influence of women in the tribal life. That influence is undeniable; I have witnessed it with my own eyes. At the same time, the salient fact of life among the Big Nambas is that one is dealing with a male society. Officially, women have no voice in tribal life. Even unofficially, they must find it difficult to exercise any influence that they may have over the males, for husbands and wives live apart. The husband must visit his wife, in the House of Women or in her family's house, in order to perform his conjugal duty. His own residence is the *Nakamal*, or the House of Men, where he lives with the other males of the tribe.

It is not surprising, in these circumstances, that life among the Big Nambas is decidedly tinged with homosexuality. The *Nakamal*, where the men live, is not only the place where kava is drunk and where interminable discussions on local affairs take place. It is also where the grandfathers of the tribe initiate their grandsons into the mysteries of sexuality.

This aspect of Big Namba society plays a part in Viriambat's attachment to his village in the bush. In the exclusively male society of the *Nakamal*, he is able to exercise the kind of domination, partly ideological but also partly sexual, that one occasionally finds among the leaders of juvenile gangs. And, just as the gang-leader's authority seldom survives the onset of maturity, it is likely that Viriambat's authority would not survive his tribe's initiation into modern life.

To one who has had no experience with the Big Nambas or with Viriambat, much of the above may seem a kind of projection on my part: a gratuitous attribution, to the leader of a small group of naked primitives, of comparatively sophisticated motives for keeping his people safe from the influence of Western civilization. Actually, by Big Nambas standards, they are not "sophisticated" at all. The people who live in the remote interior areas of the New Hebrides have been forced by circumstances to consider in depth their relations with the world of the white man. Their experiences in that area have taught them to exercise caution.

Sometimes, they seem to carry caution to extremes and to attach too much importance to past experiences. In any event, one thing is clear: they are determined never again to be the dupes of the white man.

The same kind of determination is evident also on some of the other islands in this region, where the chief rules by the force of his personality. Chief Tofor, on Ambrym, is one such leader. Another is the chief of Pentecost Island, who, while protecting his people from unwanted aspects of Western civilization, has made a tourist attraction of the Gaul Leap.[1] Each one of these tribal groups is a microcosm, the evolution of which is a fascinating spectacle. The situation of these groups is different from that of other "developing nations." Social structures and social cohesion are much stronger here than in Africa. And, unlike the Africans, the islanders have not been divided by colonialism into artificial and sometimes incompatible groups.

A beauty

During my stay among the Big Nambas, I was determined somehow to learn what I could about the women of the tribe. Once or twice, during my walks in the village, I encountered women who had smiled at me. But almost always, the women—and especially the young women—fled as soon as they caught sight of me. And, when I tried to observe them while they worked in the gardens, they made such a hue and cry that I fled.

With many circumlocutions, I discussed this problem with Willy. I explained that the women of the Big Nambas were indeed beautiful, as everyone knew, but that they appeared very shy. I had only the most honorable intentions toward them, I pointed out. I wanted only to be able to photograph one or two of the women.

Willy's features took on a mysterious and mischievous look. He grinned broadly. And then he turned and walked away without saying a word.

The next morning, Willy appeared at my door. Motioning me to take my camera and follow him, he led me to the House of Women. I could hear voices, and occasional shrieks, through the low doorway. We waited a long while. Then a girl emerged into the sunlight. She smiled and looked directly at me. There was no trace of shyness.

She was truly striking. Her skin was the soft, shining copper color of all the Big Nambas tribe, and her breasts were firm and well shaped. She wore her tribal dress with elegance: a skirt of grass, dyed the same dark red as the *nambas* of the men, through which I caught tantalizing glimpses of shapely thighs. Her hair was covered by a wiglike arrangement of grass, of the same color as the skirt, which hung down her back to the base of her spine. Her black eyes were large. When she smiled, I saw glistening, perfect teeth.

A crowd had gathered around us, and everyone was laughing. It occurred to

---

[1] The hero of this spectacular attraction is a performer who leaps from a tower about a hundred feet high. His fall is slowed—but not broken—by vines tied to his body. The vines break as the falling body gains speed, and the performer lands on his feet, intact.

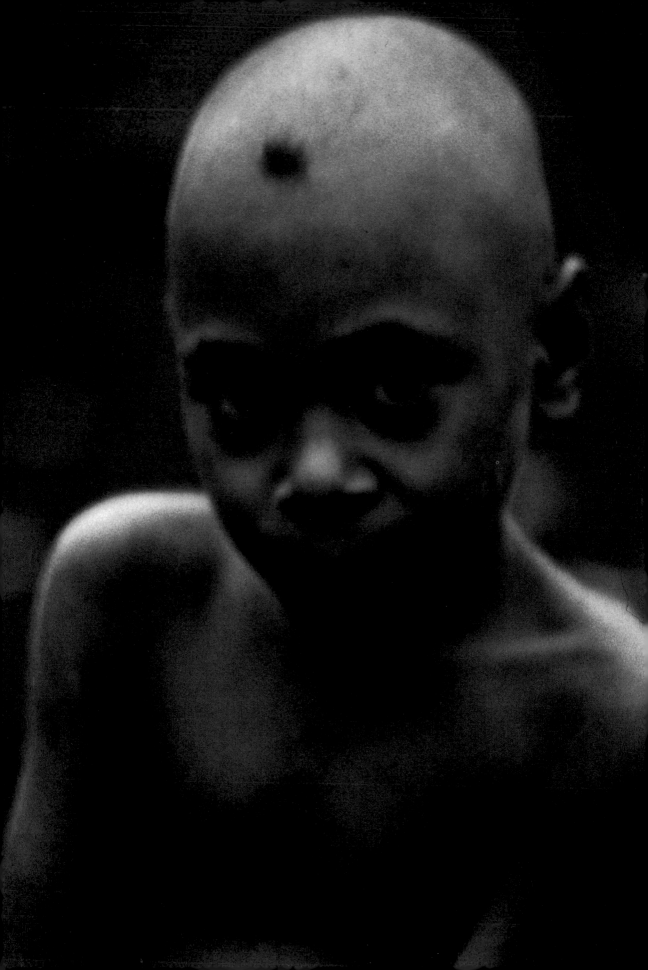

In front of the *Nakamal* (House of Men), these befeathered warriors, covered with sweat, are performing a dance for my benefit.

Opposite: This Big Nambas child, his head shaved except for one tiny tuft of hair, was raised in the bush. One wonders what life among the Big Nambas will be like when he is a grown man.

me that I might be the victim of a practical joke. I was indeed, in a way. The girl, I discovered, was Viriambat's own daughter—a choice dictated by the knowledge that she, of all the women of the village, would certainly come to no harm at my hands. This also explained the girl's air of self-assurance. She could afford to take chances that other girls could not. She was, after all, the daughter of the chief.

The Nambas

The film that I planned to shoot of the Big Nambas and their village was the subject of constant discussion among the menfolk. Everyone had something to say, or suggestions to offer. And, above all, no one seemed in a hurry to arrive at any decision. This was something entirely new to them. It was an opportunity for everyone to have his way and to express his ideas, and, above all, for each one to feel that he was making an important contribution. There was a surprising similarity between these protracted discussions and those held at staff meetings the world over. Nothing really useful was accomplished, but everyone had the satisfaction of speaking his mind.

It occurred to me that, if I had to wait for a decision, I might be with the Big Nambas for another month. I would not have complained if it had been so. I was learning a great deal about the village life—beginning with the *namba* worn by all the men. I had a demonstration of how it was worn. A young warrior, under Willy's supervision, showed me how to put it on and take it off. Then, amid general hilarity, I was required to prove that I had learned my lesson—by donning one myself.

The *namba* is essentially a twist of wine-colored fibers that is wrapped around the genitals. The ends of the twist are passed under the belt of treebark worn by the men, and then held firmly in place by a leather belt worn over the treebark belt. Part of the *namba*'s popularity no doubt rests on the fact that it makes the genitals appear much larger than they really are. But the essential question about the *namba*, as it is about the penile sheaths of the Papuans of New Guinea, is its significance. In other words, is its use dictated by considerations of modesty, or does it have something to do with a fertility cult which also manifests itself in the Big Nambas' gardens?

The only thing that I know for certain is that the *namba* is regarded neither as an ornament nor as an accessory. I am inclined to believe that it is somehow related to a concern for fertility, rather than to any innate sense of modesty. The menfolk of the island are not nearly so reticent in removing their *nambas* as my friends at Wamena were in doffing their penile sheaths. Indeed, they seem more inclined to exhibitionism than to modesty. It is probably safe to conclude that the *namba* is at least an affirmation of sexuality and, perhaps further, of homosexuality.

Visitors from the coast

By now, Viriambat and I had established a working relationship. He had developed a taste for conversation with me, and often came to visit. On those occasions, we sat outside, under the overhanging roof of my house. At first, as soon as he appeared, I placed my air mattress on the ground for him to sit on, and I sat in the mud. Later, when I knew him better, I insisted on sitting on the mattress with him.

By then, most of our discussions had to do with what I would film and when I would film it. Once we had agreed upon a subject—it was to be a dance—the question of price was raised. I would, of course, have to pay for the privilege of filming the ceremony. Viriambat named a sum. It was exorbitant, and I flatly refused to pay it.

I really was not greatly concerned about the film, or about the dance. What interested me was Viriambat himself and his people.

One day, the High Chief came to my house with a large entourage of people whom I did not know. They were, Willy explained, from the coastal villages—Big Nambas who had turned to visit the home of their people.

Unfortunately, since everyone spoke only the Big Nambas dialect, I could not understand a word of what was being said. I did understand, however, that Viriambat, who had only about a hundred men in his village in the bush, was very eager to continue exercising his authority over Big Nambas in the coastal villages of Tenmaru, Leviamp, and Brennwe, as well as Unmet. That, of course, is why he made so many visits to the coast. And, in that scheme of things, Willy, who lived much of the time at Unmet, was engaged in a diplomatic and public relations campaign designed to keep those exiles from breaking their ties with the village in the mountains. The fact that they were here today represented a success for Willy and a victory for Viriambat.

There is still some question in my mind as how to describe Viriambat's position with respect to the Big Nambas who live on the coast. Superficially at least, Viriambat represents tradition, and the coastal dwellers represent progress. But it is not that simple. The visitors that day were champions of the transistor radio and the refrigerator. But it is possible that they were also champions of the Bible and the white man's hierarchy of values. If so, Viriambat, in his determination to resist the white man's way, is more a revolutionary than a traditionalist, and the coastal Big Nambas are reactionaries. Which does not exclude the possibility of some revolutionary spirit among the villagers, directed against their High Chief. Given the complexity of the actual situation, and the ease with which labels become interchangeable, it is difficult to know who stands where among the Big Nambas. If we use accomplishment as a criterion, we must conclude that Viriambat's historical role is that of a modern man. He was the first chief of the New Hebrides to be able to pacify his island without compromising with the white man. His attitude is certainly more original, and more praiseworthy, than that of the more "developed" Big Nambas along the coast who have more or less assimilated the teachings of the missionaries.

I sat and listened as everyone else spoke. Occasionally, Willy translated something for me, but very little. What was important was that my presence was tolerated by the Big Nambas. Some of the warriors made a point of smiling benevolently at me now and then. I was proud of having won their confidence, of being treated like "one of the family."

The dances

Late the next afternoon, Viriambat sent Willy to extend an invitation to the *Nakamal.* All the men of the village were there when I arrived. I was struck by the

There is neither road nor trail leading from Big Nambas country to civilization. After leaving the mountains and crossing walls of mud, the traveler must follow the coast.

appearance of one of them: a fat albino, with women's breasts and a hairless face. He was evidently a person of some influence in the tribe, but there was no mistaking the expression of contempt on his face when he looked at me. Somehow, I no longer felt like one of the family. I was a visitor once more.

With a royal gesture, Viriambat ordered the fire to be lit. In the dimness,

Opposite: Two Big Nambas in official garb. The man on the right is Willy, Viriambat's "prime minister."

the old men of the tribe sat smoking their pipes, giving off fumes which overpowered the smell of the green wood burning in the fire. They all had wooly beards. In their ear lobes, they wore pieces of shell and wood.

The young men of the tribe, according to custom, distributed *lap-lap*. My stay among the Big Nambas had not given me a taste for this insipid food. I would gladly have traded my watch for a decent stew. But, like a good guest, I ate with every sign of appetite.

A small group of men, with much chewing and spitting, was preparing the evening's kava. I was not invited to partake. Indeed, after the *lap-lap*, it was made known to me, very gently, that the evening was over so far as I was concerned. Viriambat, to soften the blow, walked me back to my house.

Willy arrived the next morning to tell me that the matter of making a movie had been decided, I would be allowed to film the dance after all. The price had been reduced. All I had to do was present a small gift to the High Chief. An appropriate selection, I was told, would be my air mattress.

I knew that Viriambat was fond of the mattress. He never missed an opportunity to sit on it. Nonetheless, I was very reluctant to part with it, since it would be difficult to replace and I still had need of it. In its place, I offered a blanket. Willy was openly unenthusiastic about the situation. Viriambat would have to decide, he told me, and left.

Willy returned the following day to re-open negotiations over the gift. After much haggling, I added all that remained of my cigarettes and tobacco, and Willy left with the package for Viriambat. He returned an hour later to lead me to the *Nakamal*, where I found the High Chief surrounded by his council. I concluded that the "deal" had been accepted. Actually, it was a matter of indifference to me. I had little enthusiasm for a dance ceremony that would be organized solely for the purpose of filming it and for which the preparations might go on forever. But Viriambat had a surprise in store for me. Almost immediately, the drums began beating. The men and male children of the village gathered in the *Nakamal*, followed shortly by the dancers themselves, their heads covered with feathers and their faces blackened with soot.

To my astonishment, Willy, the most "developed" of the Big Nambas, was among the dancers. He caught my eye and winked, waving his arms and shaking his feathers for all he was worth, his grinning face dripping with sweat. I filmed as the dancers moved three steps forward, then two steps back, and crowned this intricate maneuver with a shout. They began again: three steps forward, two steps back. . . .

For my blanket and tobacco, I got three dances.

The end of the dance was the signal for a general pillage of my bag of provisions. Everyone knew that I was leaving the following day, and they assumed that I wanted them to have my canned goods. They were not mistaken.

I was returning to a place where there were real houses with chairs to sit on and tables to eat at. I would no longer have to wash out of a pot. Strangely enough, I was eager to leave. I felt—disloyal. My friends here would remain on their muddy mountain, with the skulls of their ancestors, to defend their land and their traditions against the encroachment of the white men.

The next morning, I made my farewell to Viriambat. Willy guided me back to Unmet, where the brothers offered me hospitality for the night.

The overall impression, as I came away, was one of uncertainty. It was true, as I had suspected, that the country of the Big Nambas was not nearly so difficult to reach as I had been led to believe. And the High Chief was certainly more hospitable and friendly than I could have hoped. Those are the only absolute statements that I feel able to make about my visit.

For the rest, I am left wondering at the incredible complexity of man, regardless of the color of his skin or the location of his homeland. I left the Big Nambas with the conviction that Viriambat was even more of an enigma than I had thought when I first met him. And Willy, of course, not exactly a choirboy, must qualify as a true statesman. He may well be the Talleyrand or the Metternich of the tropics, with a very broad and certain overview of the destiny of his people. It is a pity that his conversations with Viriambat will never be recorded for the sake of posterity. I console myself with the thought that we can never know everything that there is to know. It is perhaps enough to admit that there are many things we do not understand.

9

the drums

*There are a fair number of Oceanic
artifacts offered for sale here and
there which are not authentic.
These are made for commercial
purposes by artisans who do not
play the game. Being without roots
and without inspiration, they have
the same value as the elephants of
Ceylon or the shrunken heads sold
to tourists in Caracas.*

PATRICK O'REILLY

Ambrym Island is more difficult to reach than Malikolo. There are no landing strips, and one must depend entirely on surface travel. Even then, there are no scheduled boats, and a traveler must pretty much depend on the kindness of strangers. That is, he must "hitch a ride" on a government boat or a commercial boat of some kind. This struck me as rather a strange situation, since Ambrym is quite close to Malikolo—right across the strait from Lamap (Autoua). The ostensible problem is that the weather is frequently bad, and the tides and currents treacherous. Since the inhabitants of Ambrym are no more inclined to a seafaring life than are those of Malikolo, they are not tempted to brave these dangers in their frail pirogues.

Despite these problems, I was eager to get to the island. By all accounts, it was the center of remarkable artistic activity. It occurred to me that its very inaccessibility might have contributed to the preservation of some originality in that activity.

After investigating all possibilities of travel from Norsup to Ambrym, I decided that I might have to wait for weeks in that town before anything turned up. I was advised to go to Retelimba, on the northeastern coast of Malikolo, where my chances of finding transportation would be better. As luck would have it, I was

This dance mask, from Ambrym Island, is made of a paste of leaves and then painted.

preparing to leave for Retelimba when a government supply boat, the *Artois*, arrived at Norsup. I learned that the *Artois* was bound for Port Sandwich, and that—as a result of the kind intervention of the French representative on Malikolo—the captain would be happy to have me as a passenger.

Port Sandwich

The *Artois* was probably the most picturesque of the government boats plying the wholly unpredictable waters among the islands, carrying supplies, delivering mail, and transporting the sick. Not the least of the boat's attractions was its captain, a man right out of a novel by Robert Louis Stevenson. We became friends immediately. His hospitality and his knowledge of the inhabitants of the islands, both natives and European, made the trip a delight.

In the morning, after a night of tossing and turning in my berth, in rhythm to the tossing and turning of the *Artois* in a rough sea, we entered the quiet waters of Port Sandwich Bay—a calm expanse, walled in by jungle, where Captain Cook had dropped anchor two hundred years earlier. The place has changed since Cook's time. There was a short wooden bulkhead along part of the shore, a hangarlike building and three small boats on the beach. The bay itself, I observed, cuts deeply into the shore, and its circumference is marked with a band of fine beach.

Port Sandwich was simply a point of debarcation for me. Retelimba, a modest town comprising mostly governmental buildings, was on the other side of the island, and I reached it easily by automobile. My first task was to arrange transportation to Ambrym, which I could see looming on the horizon. I found a Tahitian fisherman who owned a seaworthy boat with an outboard motor. Well, the man explained, he would be happy to accommodate me, except that his motor was not in running order. Moreover, he pointed out, the sea was too rough to go out. The latter observation seemed superfluous, since, if the outboard motor was broken down, it didn't matter what the sea was like. I think the problem was neither the motor nor the sea, but the fisherman was afflicted with a disease common among Tahitians. It is known locally as *fiu*, and its chief symptom is a total repugnance for all activity.

Finally, luck was with me, in the shape of another government boat, the *Armagnac*, which docked at Port Sandwich. The captain generously consented to drop me at Ambrym, although, he explained, the island had no dock and no port facilities of any kind. If I had not been able to see Ambrym in the distance, I might have begun to suspect that it did not exist at all. Certainly, the inhabitants of Malikolo were totally oblivious of their neighbors across the strait.

The black sands of Ambrym

When the captain of the *Armagnac* told me that he would "drop" me, it turned out that he had meant exactly that. Off the island, a small boat was lowered. I was dropped into it and rowed to shore. Barefoot, carrying my camera, my shoes, and my bag over my head, I waded the last few yards onto a beach of black sand. I stood waving at the *Armagnac* as it moved away. There was total silence. Not a footprint on the black sand except for my own. Watching the *Armagnac* disappear, I knew how Alexander Selkirk, the prototype of the marooned traveler in Defoe's *Robinson Crusoe*, must have felt, stranded on his island.

Clutching my bag and my equipment, I struggled over the dune and into the brush. Still not a sound. Not a sign of life. I walked a short distance, looking for—I have no idea of what, perhaps for my man Friday. At any rate, I was not disappointed. Not one, but two Fridays appeared, both children: a boy and his sister, equally naked. They stared at me in silence. I stared at them. I spoke, and they ignored me. I tried again. Nothing. It occurred to me that they might be deaf-mutes.

In silence, the children turned and picked their way back to a trail. I followed, knowing that the trail must lead somewhere. We walked for a half an hour without speaking, until, by chance, we encountered a small group of men along the trail. I was greeted with smiles. Through signs, gestures, and assorted sounds we were able to communicate—to a point. I was given to understand that we must walk some more. To my great relief, one of these gracious gentlemen picked up my bag and hoisted it up onto his shoulder. We formed a line and began walking.

Everyone seemed to know exactly where we were going—everyone, except me. This is a situation to which one becomes accustomed in the brush, no matter in what part of the world. There are always ways of doing things that are perfectly natural to the people living there, but totally incomprehensible to visitors. I had learned long before that one must simply bow, submit, and trust the good intentions of one's hosts.

In this instance, I was not disappointed. The trail led to a hangar, and within the hangar was a jeep. One of my guides jumped into the driver's seat and motioned me to climb aboard. I did so, and everyone else piled into the back. The driver started the engine and we roared down a trail barely fit for walking, let alone for driving.

As the jeep leaped from one pothole to another, I wondered where on earth we were going in such haste.

Then, coming toward us on the trail, I saw another jeep. My driver grinned in obvious relief. "Father!" he said, pointing excitedly.

It was, in fact, Father Clementi, director of the local mission at Olal. The mission was only a few miles from the spot where I had come ashore on Ambrym; and, I discovered later, my jeepload of guides were taking me to the priest's house.

The Christianization of Ambrym

As it turned out, it could not have been a better choice. Father Clementi—an Italian who spoke excellent French—was the soul of hospitality. Moreover, he took charge of seeing that I got around the island during my stay on Ambrym, and

Opposite, upper: Next to the human face of this drum is a virtuoso who is able to make the drum speak a secret language.

Opposite, lower: In the villages of Ambrym, isolated in the bush, pigs are capital wealth and are cared for with great tenderness.

A missionary at Olal has Christianized this vertical drum by adding a cross above the head.

he was a fount of information on every conceivable aspect of life on Ambrym. He had, after all, lived there for fourteen years.

His mission, which is run by the Marist order, is a large place. Situated between two villages, it compromises a school with several classes, a hospital, and a concrete church. The center of the mission is a football field, where there seemed always to be a game in progress. The rules of these football matches, however, seemed to be made up as the encounter progressed and, to the uninitiated spectator, confusion reigns supreme.

The most remarkable sight in the area is a large human-faced wooden drum standing in front of the church. It is carved in the best style of the island and is typical in all respects save one: the head is surmounted by a cross. Thus, the pagan drum was converted into a Christian symbol.

Father Clementi was not the innovator in this case. The Christianized drum is also found in other missions. If truth be told, the human-faced drum, of all the symbols in these islands, is the one most in need of sanctification, at least if one believes all the stories told about it. According to tradition, these drums were once used for nonmusical purposes. A human victim was tied to a drum and then beaten to death.

I was understandably eager to see as much as I could of Ambrym, and Father Clementi made it as easy as possible for me to do so. As a guide, he gave me the mission's agricultural expert, a native of the island who knew every village, but whose brilliant green shirt, vividly patterned, made me nostalgic for the nudity of the Big Nambas.

I must admit that what I saw was not what I had hoped to see. I had thought that, since Ambrym was so isolated, its art would be relatively intact. I had hoped that I would discover many authentic works of art—modern, to be sure, but original in inspiration and execution. It was not to be.

Certainly, there are two or three artists in every village who continue to work in the forms traditional on Ambrym. These artists are not reticent. They are proud of their work and eager to show it to visitors. Perhaps the problem is that the artists have become so specialized. Some work only in hardwood, others in gray, pourous volcanic rock, and others only in fernwood. As a result, there is no variety in the artists' work. From one village to the next, I saw the same few objects, reproduced over and over again, in different sizes. Very little that I saw seemed to be the result of wholly mechanical labor, completely uninspired, and intended for the tourist market. It was sad to witness the deterioration of an artistic spirit that has lost its reason for existence.

Not for the sake of art

Even so, I continued to look, hoping to find something different, of genuine aesthetic value. I went from village to village. At each place, a group of two or

This remarkable drum has a human figure above the usual head.

three men—alerted by the sound of an approaching jeep and standing in the midst of a crowd of children, pigs, and chickens—were waiting for me. They all insisted that I visit their houses and inspect their sculptures. Occasionally, one or the other of them tried to do business on the spot, proudly holding out a statue and thrusting it into my hands at the first opportunity, eager for either a sale or for a look of admiration. Since there are so few visitors to Ambrym, tourists or otherwise, there are few opportunities to make a direct sale. And, since buyers are so scarce, they feel that their wares must be exorbitantly priced to compensate for the lack of turnover.

In going from one village to the next, I was merely going from disappointment to disappointment. Today, there is nothing in Ambrym art that rises above banality. The reason, undoubtedly, is that the island's production of carvings has only one purpose: to be sold in boutiques of Port Vila. This produces a certain small income for the inhabitants of Ambrym. The sculptor's work is a product, not a work of art.

I found on Ambrym a repetition of a phenomenon that I had observed elsewhere in "primitive art," notably in Africa. Our Western ideal of "art for the sake of art" simply does not exist among so-called primitive artists. We value a statue solely for the sake of its beauty. The artists of the Pacific, however, or the African artist who carves a statue has only one purpose in mind: the utility of his work. Moreover, the artist's "patron," the one who has commissioned the work, is also concerned only with the work's utility. The statue is something that will be useful on a day-to-day basis and perhaps even indispensable to the purchaser.

There is probably a connection between the loss of the ideal of "art for the sake of utility" and the loss of true creativity among primitive artists. Statues are carved now to be sold to tourists as souvenirs, not to be used by a fellow islander. This was very obvious on Ambrym. The exaggerated prices I was quoted for worthless carvings were always stated in New Hebrides francs. In the old days, the artist was paid in pigs or in pigs' teeth. Somehow, even in so remote an island, we have succeeded in degrading art by creating in the artist both a lust for profit and an unbecoming vanity. Both are entirely alien to their artistic tradition.

Statues of rank

Every human society, even the most democratic, has its own symbols of rank. And the citizens of Ambrym have their statues. All the carvings that I saw in the villages were copies of "statues of rank"—sculptures the social significance of which are far more important than their aesthetic value, and which are the symbols of a social system combining taboos and magic with ritual objects and minutely codified ceremonies.

These copies bear only a superficial resemblance to the originals. They are made of the soft wood of the island's treelike ferns, which is virtually incorruptible. (This is a major consideration in a place where dampness and insects make short work even of the hardest wood.) The modern artist barely manages to imitate the general outline of the original statue. Obviously, to him sculpting is a livelihood rather than an artistic undertaking.

There was a time when statues of rank symbolized all that was worthy of attainment in Ambrym life. Then, the very thought of such a statue having a function outside of the island's rigidly hierarchical social system would have inspired disbelief.

The ideals of the system may have been lost, but the system itself, the *nimangi*, still exists despite the inroads made by the souvenir industry. The *nimangi* is characterized by twelve or thirteen ranks (the number varies from area to area). Each rank has a name, which also differs from one place to the next. When a citizen rises a degree in rank, he is required to erect a statue, which he commissions from a sculptor. This is a "statue of rank." Promotion to a higher rank is not based on merit or achievement. It is bought from the local elders, and is paid for in the dearest medium of exchange in the region: pigs.

Each of the twelve or thirteen ranks confers the right to wear a particular kind of dress at ceremonial dances and a particular kind of flower in one's hair. The distinctive badge of the rank is a belt of leaves. Another rank allows the initiated to give his house the name of the rank he holds.

Aside from considerations of personal vanity, a rise in rank imposes more restraints than it confers privileges. Men initiated into the higher degrees may no longer eat food prepared by women, or even vegetables raised by them. They must therefore cook their own meals individually, or take turns cooking them for everyone else in the same rank. So stringent are these dietary restrictions that the old men at the very pinnacle of the hierarchical pyramid are literally in danger of starving to death.

The *nimangi* is, in essence, a political formula according to which advancement is conferred on the basis of wealth, and which concentrates power in the hands of a group of old men. This power, however, is far from absolute. In fact, it is more the power to advise than anything else. The elders are councillors rather than chiefs. They are in a position to moderate certain ambitions, to restrain certain of the more hot-headed citizens and to temper excesses. Their influence, to a large extent, is based on their ability to "blackball" any candidate for admission to their own rank. From all this, it is evident that the various ranks do not confer any real authority over one's fellow citizens. What is important within each group is not the "power" of any individual, but his personality and his conduct in the community. The villages are quite small and the social groups very narrow. Everybody, in effect, knows everybody else. One can only imagine the in-fighting and the secret intrigues that dominate the struggle for upward mobility in the *nimangi*.

Social life on Ambrym, as elsewhere in the Pacific, is constantly in touch with the supernatural. Therefore, every member of society must constantly take into account the magical influences that are believed to be everywhere. Magic is regarded as a power to be feared. The most powerful magic, it is believed, is in the hands of some of the elders. Yet, no one is wholly without protection against an abuse of power; for there are secret rites of great efficacy of which one can make use. And there are always those poisons, made from plants, with which inhabitants of the brush are always familiar.

The drums of Ambrym

The jeep hurled itself along the trail leading from Olal, in the northern part of Ambrym. My driver would admit the existence of no obstacles. It seemed that two of our wheels were permanently in the air, while the remaining two served to propel us from bump to bump and from pothole to pothole at breakneck speed. By the end of the morning I felt as though I had spent several hours in a cement mixer. Yet, I had to admit that the driver's determination produced results. We reached villages that I had thought completely inaccessible except at the price of a whole day's march through the brush.

The village of Neha alone was more than worth the discomfort, to say nothing of the terror, of the trip. The *Nekamal* was hardly more than a hut with a thatched roof sloping to the ground. But the drum in the village square was the most striking that I had seen. The bottom section, or trunk, of the drum had a long vertical cut in it and appeared quite old and worn through constant pounding. The carving above the trunk was not of the stereotyped model that I had seen everywhere. The eyes were oblique, round, cloven, and appeared to contemplate an interior vision. The large-nostriled nose protruded above a sculpted curve in which mouth, tongue, and chin were all combined. It was an enigmatic monument, and one which inspired contemplation.

The face, or faces, sculpted on the upper part of the drums generally follow a traditional formula: a half-moon face, round eyes, hooked nose, chin and neck joined. Occasionally, however, one of these sonorous statues, like that at Neha, is highly individual and, indeed, awesome.

All the drums seemed to be sculpted of the same wood, that of the bread fruit tree. They varied in size, and some of them are over thirty feet high. They serve a number of practical purposes in the village: for example, to send messages between villages and to set the beat for dances.

In one village, I was greeted by the chief. I was surprised to see that he was nude, except for a socklike covering encasing his genitals. The sock was probably made of leaves. (I did not want to risk embarrassing my host by staring or by asking offensive questions.) The chief and I were quickly joined by several village elders, all wearing the same kind of covering as their chief. My guides led me to a clearing where there were two drums. The greenish light of the jungle, the enormous trees, the stillness, the isolation—everything contributed to confer an air of mystery on the scene.

An elderly blind man was seated in the clearing. His torn shirt, scraggly goatee and drooping head gave him an unprepossessing appearance. Yet, I was informed, this man was the supreme drum virtuoso of the island. As though cued by this explanation, the old man took a wooden mallet and began to pound the drums, softly so as not to alarm the village. The sound rolled like thunder from the stat-

These two young girls are examining the head of a woman for fleas. The examination has nothing to do with hygiene. The girls are visitors in a village on Ambrym, and their attentions to the older woman are a sign of respect.

ues, receding into the trees and evoking strange echoes. What, I wondered, was in the mind of the drummer? He did not know me and had not seen me. Yet, in exchange for a wad of tobacco, he was willing to set free all the spirits and ghosts held prisoner in his drums.

It is possible, as some have suggested, that the drums commemorate, in stylized form, an individual who once played a part in village or tribal affairs. According to that interpretation, the voice of the drum is the voice of the man it symbolizes. That is no doubt partially true, but, in my opinion, that explanation is too simple. The drums are not an integral part of the *nimangi*, or hierarchy of ranks, which dominates the island—even though the members of each rank are assembled by a drumroll peculiar to that rank. The actual making of the drum, and its

This is a House of Men on the island of Ambrym.

erection, is accompanied by ritual ceremonies which are still more or less secret. This is one area, fortunately, in which the inhabitants of Ambrym are still wary of the white man's curiosity.

At Port Vila, I have seen five or six drums—all of them handsome specimens—displayed for sale along the sidewalk, propped up against a building. It is fashionable, apparently, to have a drum in one's front yard. To anyone who has seen a drum in its proper habitat, the sight of it in a town, for sale, is a kind of desecration. The drums, made for use in the jungle, rise up in the midst of a sea of automobiles.

The Big Nambas also have drums with human faces. I saw two of them, both in the dancing square at Amok, but I did not hear them. In my opinion, the drums of Ambrym are not only more numerous but more impressive. Some of them seemed quite ancient, and the wood from which they were made shone with the patina of age and use. And, as I have already noted, some of the drums depart from the traditional forms and models. Certain of these individual pieces show hands on very short arms, under the faces. And the faces themselves, with their empty eyes, appear each to have an expression of their own—often one of restraint and almost sorrowful, intensity.

It would be difficult to define the essence of Oceanic art, and particularly that of the New Hebrides. Like New Guinean art, it is based upon a distortion of the human form, a disassembling of the parts of the face and body so as to elicit a feeling, not of violence but of compassion.

One of the drums I photographed had two heads, one above the other. Some of those I saw had four or five heads of varying sizes. Certain of these multi-headed drums seem to slant slightly, as though unbalanced by age. This was the case with one of the two drums I saw at Amok. I think, however, that the slanting position is intentional: the drum was erected on the bias, perhaps in conformity with a ritual requirement, or merely to alter the tone of the drum.

Most of the drums are painted. Or rather, I should say that the faces themselves are painted in colors so as to enhance their awesome appearance.

Not all villages have their drum in the public square. I saw several which, to all appearances, had been deliberately concealed behind a screen of trees. Why the location of the drums should vary is one of the mysteries of the New Hebrides, and one which has not yet been resolved. The fact that some of the drums are hidden, however, casts some doubt on the theory that drums are phallic symbols. The inhabitants of the New Hebrides are quite open about sex, and it does not seem logical that they should be secretive about phallic symbols. On the same basis, it seems more appropriate to regard the vertical slit in the base of the drum as the mouth of the person represented by the drum, rather than as a symbol of feminine sexuality.

The artist and the patron

The traditional sculptor of Ambrym—as opposed to the sculptor who turns out souvenirs for tourists—works only on the basis of a commission. That is, he is commissioned by a patron to execute a particular work. The nature of the work varies according to the needs of the patron, but all works of the traditional sculptor have in common that they involve a series of taboos and ceremonial rites.

The art of Ambrym is a very grave and complex undertaking, and one would be hard put to distinguish between "profane" and "sacred" art in the Occidental sense of those terms, since carvings generally have magical applications. One example is the small amulet stone, or "pig stone," made by the artists of Ambrym. These amulets are made of soft volcanic rock and are round. Usually, they have a sculpted face. They are used in all matters having to do with pigs—buying, selling, renting, or exchanging. Their purpose is to assure the success of one's negotiations, for upon the success or failure of a piece of business depends the trader's advancement to the next rank as well as his social standing. It is easy to understand, therefore, why the inhabitants of the New Hebrides take a very serious attitude toward business matters and why they use magic to ensure success. The magical power of a pig stone becomes operative when the stone is placed before the door of one's house, with the face turned toward the spot where negotiations are to take place.

On Ambrym, sculptors also make sledgehammers for the ritual slaughter of pigs, bamboo flutes, and dancemasks. The masks, it seems, are no more profane than the pigstones, for their manufacture is circumscribed by complex taboos and is carried out in secrecy. The masks themselves are made of wood, in the shape of a triangle. They are painted in bright colors and crowned with feathers. White, silken strips of banana leaf complete the decoration of the mask. Each color has

its own special meaning. A saw-tooth arrangement across the middle of the mask confers a sacred character on the work.

The dances for which the masks are intended are neither very complex nor very artistic. The important thing, apparently, is not the dance as art but the dance as ceremony, with its masks and long dresses of leaves. The dance is a present given to the village by itself, and village festivals are a primordial art in themselves.

Since the social system of the New Hebrides is based on profit, there is nothing that cannot be bought. Rank, of course, is for sale. But so are dances, which one village can buy from another village. One can also purchase designs, songs—even an entire ceremony, complete with costumes and accessories. All one has to have is a sufficient number of pigs or pigs' teeth. Then, of course, one's purchase can be re-sold, at a profit.

This commercial traffic in works of art is based upon the spirit of emulation that exists between individuals, from tribe to tribe, in the elaboration of festivals and ceremonies; that is, upon the desire to surpass one another in public spectacles. Thus, one purchases that which one's own imagination has not been able to supply. Since everyone uses the same means to attain this and purchasing dances and ceremonies is not, strictly speaking, cheating. No one takes unfair advantage of another in the pitting of influence, prestige, and wealth against one's neighbor to be officially recognized as the winner in this intense competition.

Opposite: The artist drawing on the ground is one of the last practitioners of this art left on Ambrym Island.

Vertical drums are used as a means of communication between villages, but they also memorialize the voices of the village's ancestors.

Lower: These statues of fernwood rise along the coast of the Olal lagoon.

A self-effacing art

Among all the practical arts of Ambrym, perhaps the most surprising is that of drawing in the dirt. It is also the most ephemeral of the arts and that which is in greatest danger of being lost. There are now on Ambrym only two artists skilled in this traditional form. Thanks to Father Clementi, I was able to watch (and to film) both of them at work.

One of these artists, a man perfectly aware of his talent and his importance, lives in the village of Olal where, in front of his house, he exhibited his skill for my benefit. Using the palm of his hand, he laboriously smoothed the earth, removing any small stones or pebbles from his "canvas." Once the smoothing was completed to his satisfaction, he stared at the ground for a long moment, as though planning his work. Then he began, by making several small holes at various points in the area. These, no doubt, were his reference points. Finally, with an air of great concentration, he began his drawing. The forefinger of one hand touched one of the holes, and moved away, drawing a line. Not once, until the drawing was complete, did the artist look up, raise his finger from the ground or retrace a single line. These things would have been violations of tradition. At first glance, the design of the drawing evoked a shark, or perhaps a basket. In fact, it represented, symbolically, the labyrinth which the soul of a dead man must follow in order to attain the hereafter.

There is nothing particularly secret about the interlacing designs produced by the artists—unless they are somehow associated with a taboo. In the latter case, it is forbidden to divulge the meaning of the design to women or children. A fairly common theme, representing the guardian of the country of the dead, is one such taboo subject.

The artist I was watching did not appear to attach any particular importance to his work. As soon as it had been completed and was properly admired, he erased it with the back of his hand. He was proud, not of having produced a skillfully wrought design, but of having the ability to produce it, so to speak, at his fingertips.

Father Clementi, using a schoolboy's notebook, has laboriously reproduced every one of the designs that he has seen. There are at least fifty designs recorded in the book—which may very well save at least those designs from disappearing forever.

The charm of Ambrym

Maurice Leenhardt noted that Pedro Fernández de Queirós, when he discovered (by error) the New Hebrides in the sixteenth century, "found the shores so pleasant and the country so beautiful that he thought he had found the Garden of Paradise." But then Leenhardt goes on to express his astonishment at the contradiction between "the charm of the country and the severity of local art."

I cannot bring myself to use the word *charm* to describe the central plateau of Malikolo, but that term may quite safely be applied to the island of Ambrym. No matter how torturous the trails may be, the countryside is far more pleasant, as well as more accessible, than that of Malikolo. There has been as little clearing away of brush and jungle as possible on Ambrym—just what was absolutely necessary to make room for the few cacao plantations on the island. The trails that narrow into nothingness and the cliffs of mud, which make travel so difficult on Malikolo, do not exist on Ambrym. On the latter island, nature seems less oppressive. For one thing, the topsoil is of volcanic origin, and thus it dries quickly.

I did not climb Benbow, Ambrym's active volcano, but I did feel several earth tremors during my stay on the island. The natives paid them no heed.

The art of raising pigs is an ancient and honored one in the Pacific, and, in my opinion, the inhabitants of Ambrym excel in that art. The islanders are vegetarians, and their staples are yams, taro, and, occasionally, sago flour. Pork is eaten only on feast days. The pig is a sacrificial animal and is slaughtered ritualistically, but it is, above all, an embodiment of wealth.

The raising of pigs on Ambrym is a difficult and painstaking process. Great care is taken to allow the teeth in the lower jaw to develop, since a pig's worth (and it's owner's) is measured by the lower canines. These grow in spirals, and sometimes there are two or three spirals. It is said that seven years are necessary to complete one spiral—which would mean that a pig with three spirals in its canines is at least twenty-one years old. The danger in letting the pig's teeth grow excessively is that, the longer the canines, the greater the chance that they will break. If that happens, then the animal is virtually worthless. It sometimes occurs that these tusks grow to such length that they pierce the upper lip and penetrate into the gum. The animal suffers terribly, and it depends entirely on its caretaker for its survival. In such cases, the animal is fed premasticated foods. According to tradition, the first pig with curved tusks was bred on Ambrym. Given the skill and care manifested on the island in the raising of pigs, the story appears likely.

The women of Ambrym do not breast-feed their piglets, but they are exceedingly proud of the animals that they raise. According to the guide assigned to me by Father Clementi, a man cannot sell or exchange one of his pigs without the consent of his wife.

My stay on Ambrym was now at an end, and I departed reluctantly. The drums, the statues of rank, even the tusked pigs, would stand out in my memory as the characteristics of an island like no other that I saw.

My Tahatian fisherman from Lamap had somehow overcome his fear of "rough water" and repaired his engine. He was on hand to ferry me back to Malikolo. I watched as the dark mass of Ambrym receded to our stern, reflecting on all that modern man could still learn from an encounter with "savages."

10

the shark cult

One's first love, one's first sunrise, one's first contact with an island of the South Seas—these are all memories which stir in us a kind of sensual virginity.
ROBERT LOUIS STEVENSON

There was great activity in the water off Malaita in the Solomon Islands. A dozen pirogues, some of them manned by children of nine or ten years, were circling, bobbing like corks, sometimes striking one another, but never capsizing and above all never heading toward shore.

It was not a game. There were also adults in some of the pirogues, and they were going about the work of fishing. Their job was to seize the fishes caught in their great circular net. From time to time, I saw one of them suddenly plunge his hand into the water and come up with a sparkling strip of silver, which he quickly dumped into the bottom of his boat.

One fisherman was in the water, naked, swimming around the outside of the net, sometimes on the surface of the water and sometimes beneath the surface. His job—he was equipped with a spear—was to catch the fish that escaped from the net. Sometimes he caught more than he could safely impale on his spear, and then he swam back to his boat, carrying the extra fish in his teeth. He made no use of modern diving or fishing equipment. He was a fisherman, not of the twentieth century, but a Polynesian fisherman, plying his trade in accordance with the ancient traditions of his people.

This young belle in her straw dress is adept at flirting. She lives on Laulasi, a man-made island in the Solomons.

These fishermen and their children were all inhabitants of Auki. It was my first encounter, in a long while, with a people so exclusively dependent upon the sea and so determined to gain their livelihood from it. The Big Nambas and the people of Tanna, I had learned, were afraid of the sea. Other tribes, while unafraid, preferred to tend to their yam and taro gardens rather than to venture into the sea where they could have found food with less effort than on land.

The population of the Solomon Islands is not like that of the New Hebrides. Most of them are indeed of Melanesian stock, with small, wiry bodies, tight curly hair and dark, almost black skin. But there are also many large, athletic natives, with straight hair and light skin—Polynesians, all; and they were the ones fishing so happily and effectively in the waters of Malaita. Neither they nor their forebears have withdrawn into the interior of the islands. They have remained in their villages, in direct contact with the life-giving sea. And they have retained their ancient skills as makers of pirogues and fishing spears.

Even more, they have built artificial islands for themselves along the shore by stacking blocks of coral in the lagoon so as to construct platforms rising above sea level. There, they build their houses, beach their boats, and pray to the gods of the sea. These artificial islands are now overgrown with palms and are garden spots in the sea. The lagoon serves as a moat, which once protected the inhabitants of the man-made islands from the warlike tribes that long ago dominated the highlands of Malaita and from the cannibals who could not swim, knew nothing of navigation, and moreover were afraid of the sea.

When the Polynesians first came to the Solomons, they carefully selected the sites for these islands just within the barrier reef, where the surf breaks, so that they had, and still have, easy access to the sea and its inexhaustible wealth: the marvelous edible fishes of the tropics, the splendid shells which are the source of mother-of-pearl, and the marine turtles from the shells of which the Polynesians make fishhooks. And, of course, there is also an abundance of sharks.

A complicated voyage

I was impatient to visit one of these artificial islands and to see what kind of life the Polynesians led there. There was one nearby—a bouquet of coconut trees near the edge of the Langa Langa lagoon. Between the island and a nearby village on the shore, there seemed to be a constant coming and going of pirogues. But I concluded that I would see nothing on the island that I did not see on shore: nets, well-fed children, pretty girls with flowers in their dark hair. I wanted to go further out, to an island at the far end of the lagoon, to the village of Laulasi. There, I was told, I would find that the people still lived exactly as their ancestors had lived. My source of information was a friend at Port Vila, and what he had told me of the divers and sailors of the Solomons whetted my curiosity enormously. I had come to Auki by way of Guadalcanal and Gwaunanui. The final leg of my journey, to Auki, had been by jeep.

And there I stood, more or less stranded on the beach, watching from a distance the people I wanted to observe so closely. In order to get to Laulasi, I needed a motorboat. An intensive search turned up a lead: there was one such boat in the whole area—and it belonged to the village of Laulasi. My problem at that point was to let someone in Laulasi know that I would like to visit the island.

The sole means of communication with the village, it appeared, was a Melanesian virago, a lady swindler, who happened to be also the proprietor of the small hotel where I had taken what I hoped was temporary refuge. She promised to convey my message to Laulasi. I waited. And waited. I suspected strongly that her intention was to delay my departure as long as possible so as to be able to fleece me at her leisure. The fact is, I would much have preferred to sleep on the beach rather than in the hotel's suspect beds. But I was trapped. My only hope of reaching Laulasi was through this tropical harridan. I therefore endured the hotel's food—frankfurters and canned asparagus, a hundred yards from the best fishing in the world. For the sake of Laulasi, I also endured the establishment's lack of a liquor license. There was no beer or whiskey on the premises, and none allowed. When I ventured one night to produce a bottle in the hotel lounge, the proprietress protested so loudly that I withdrew to my room in a rage. And I sat there, on a splendid tropical night, the sound of the sea in my ears, sneaking a drink in my room like a college boy, shattered by the indignity of it all.

The next afternoon, I stood on the beach. The lagoon was as smooth as silk. There was not a cloud in the sky. The climate of Auki is equatorial, which means that the weather is totally unpredictable. One never knows whether it will rain or not. There is no "good" season. At the moment, the weather was perfect. I swore to myself that, no matter what, I would get to Laulasi the next day.

I returned to the hotel and loftily informed my landlady that, first thing in the morning, I would address myself to the representative of Her Britannic Majesty in Auki, who would no doubt find transportation to Laulasi for me.

The artificial isles

The threat worked. The next morning, when I emerged from my room, a giant, half-naked Polynesian was waiting for me. He was, he informed me, the operator of Laulasi's motorboat.

Naturally, the weather had deteriorated since the previous day. Still, it was not raining. We walked to the "harbor," where a large pirogue was waiting for us. The boat had the sleek lines and perfect form of the best pirogues of the ancients, except that it was equipped with an outboard motor.

We set out directly and, as I watched the shore of Auki recede, I forgave my malicious landlady all her sins. The lagoon was beautiful, and the water transparent enough so that I could see the coral growths at the bottom. The channels through the coral were indistinctly marked by poles, but my guide seemed to know his way perfectly through the maze. Here and there, I saw reefs covered with mangroves. As the motor sputtered away happily, my guide, in pidgin English, told me what he could of his amphibious homeland.

Off Auki, on Malaita Island, the men fish all day in the lagoon.

Opposite: The Langa Langa lagoon is particularly good fishing for this man armed only with a spear.

Children learn to handle a pirogue at a very early age.

He pointed out ancient artificial islands that were no longer inhabited. Some of them had been abandoned, he explained, because of disease; some, because of fire. And others had been attacked and destroyed by enemies. From the lagoon, I could see no sign that these islands had ever had a human population. They were now completely overgrown with trees and brush. I could only imagine what life must have been like for this man's ancestors, caught between the cannibals of Auki and the sharks beyond the reef. It is the kind of situation that easily gives rise to superstitions and cults. And, in fact, in the Solomons, boats are surrounded by a complicated ritual and have their own "house," analogous to the House of Men of the Papuans.

This is a typical ornament of the Solomon Islands. It is also a ritual object: a disk of mother-of-pearl cut from a shell and decorated with a design made of scale. The design represents, in all probability, frigate birds and sharks. (Collection Musée de l'Homme)

My guide suggested that, before landing at Laulasi, we visit a village along the way. As we approached, he slowed our motor, and we were soon surrounded by waving children and a small fleet of pirogues paddled, quite expertly, by young women.

When we landed, I was surprised at how small the island appeared. Yet, it was large enough for about twenty houses, shelters for boats, and other roofed structures of various kinds. There was a village square, where groups of women in grass skirts stood talking and laughing. Smoke drifted lazily toward the sky, from household fires. Life seemed much easier and happier here than in the brush, and the jungle in the interior of the Solomons is said to be particularly impenetrable.

Even today, however, life on the artificial islands is not without danger. My guide showed me the bulkhead, a sea wall of coral, which protected the raised island from tides and waves. But they were no protection against storms which sent waves crashing across the barrier reef and sweeping across the lagoon, carrying away houses and boats on the artificial islands. Even more deadly are the tropical hurricanes against which nothing can stand.

We visited the village only briefly before regaining our boat. Laulasi, to my delight, was only a few minutes away. It was considerably larger than the village we had just left, and the coconut trees stood very tall against the sky. As soon as the sound of our motor became audible, every pirogue in the water gathered around to escort us to land. Flattered, I concluded that the arrival of a visitor was a great occasion for the village.

As soon as we docked, my guide leaped to the ground and began striking a piece of iron suspended from a tree. This, apparently, was the village bell, a signal that we had arrived.

People began to gather. My guide presented me ceremoniously to an elder among the crowd.

"Is this gentleman the chief?" I inquired.

"No."

"Who is the chief?"

Everyone smiled, but no one answered. Perhaps there is no chief, I thought. Or perhaps his identity is kept secret from strangers.

A barrier against the world

The inhabitants of these islands did not survive the hostility of cannibals, the colonization of white men, the occupation of the Japanese and the treachery of the sea by being careless. They are a prudent, cautious people. Having overcome so many dangers, they are in a position to overcome one more: tourism. Rather, they have succeeded in taming and housebreaking tourists. Since they seldom leave their islands, they encounter tourists only on their own ground. Then, they treat visitors with courtesy—and take them for a goodly sum.

The procedure is simple enough. Since time immemorial, Laulasi has been the center for the manufacture of *tafuliari*,[1] necklaces of pierced shells that were once the currency of the region. Today, of course, the necklaces have no monetary value, and the problem presented to the Laulasians was how to give it a value of another kind. The answer was not long in coming: sell them to tourists. And today, there is a brisk market for *tafuliari* on the islands at Auki and Honiara, where they are gobbled up by eager tourists—to the delight and profit of the Laulasians.

When I arrived in the village, everyone was at work making the necklaces. First, pink and white shells are broken into small round pieces. Then each piece

---

[1]These necklaces are very similar to the spondylus necklaces traded during the *kula*, described in Chapter Five.

This tree-covered island is man-made of blocks of trimmed coral. It is known as Laulasi, and the village has a population of about a hundred people.

Opposite: This elderly man is the priest of Laulasi. It is said that he is able to speak to sharks.

The drill used by this woman to pierce a hole in a shell is like those used by prehistoric man.

has a hole drilled in it. A vine is used to string the pieces into a necklace from three to six feet in length.

The women were seated under a shelter, dressed in grass skirts, their breasts bare, polishing and rounding the shells with tools of stone. The only metal tool was the drill, which has a metal shaft. Upon examination, however, I discovered that the bit itself was made of a piece of flint, chipped to a point. The bits are found in the interior of Malaita, at a site known to the people of Laulasi. In effect, the flint bit is a prehistoric tool, left by former and long-dead inhabitants of Malaita.

I was shown a small warehouse where finished necklaces were stored for distribution to the markets. A visit to this display is mandatory for all visitors to the island. It is like an old-fashioned church bazaar; that is, the merchandise is of no particular interest, the prices are exorbitant, and a dim view is taken of haggling. And yet, one gets no peace until one buys something.

Actually, the system is ideal. Once I had a necklace, I was left alone. No one asked me for money. No one tried to sell me anything else. I had made my contribution to the well-being of the village, and I was not expected to do anything more.

Despite the inconveniences and dangers of life on a fragile island at the edge of a tropical lagoon, no one seemed particularly interested in moving to more solid ground. The little village, the sea, and the sky seemed more than enough to satisfy the people of Laulasi. Their sole concession to progress was the outboard motor. I wondered how long they would be able to maintain their isolation.

Having been initiated into Laulasian society through the purchase of my necklace, I was free to go wherever I wished, and everyone I spoke to answered my questions freely. My most rewarding conversation was with a very old man who identified himself as the local priest. He was responsible for religious activity on the island, which is quite complex. The priest had his church, a spacious building within which I was shown a familiar sight: rows of ancestral skulls.

After a long and sometimes confusing conversation in pidgin English with the priest, and with almost all the men of the village as well, I finally grasped an essential fact about life on these islands: the sharks, which reign supreme in the open sea just on the other side of the barrier reef, are not objects of terror to the villagers. Rather, they are regarded as protectors and benefactors who have the power to grant a miraculously large catch to the fishermen and to allow their pirogues to return safely to port in a storm. The sharks are believed to be incarnations of ancestors; they tend to enter into agreements with the men of a village—as they have done with the people of Laulasi. And that is the reason why fish, and particularly bonito, are so plentiful in the waters near the village.

The old priest is said to have the power of summoning the sharks and conversing with them. I should have loved to witness this phenomenon, but I was told that that was impossible. I looked closely at the priest. He was a man trembling with age, nothing but skin and bones, his gray hair knotted and unkempt, wearing only a rag around his loins. Did he really have the power to summon sharks? No one can tell. With sharks as with witch doctors, nothing is impossible.

The pact between the sharks and the villagers was not the only mystery on Laulasi. Given the tiny area of the island, where each block of coral had to be carried by human hands and where every coconut tree is a miracle of growth, the inhabitants seemed to have devoted an inordinate amount of space to taboo places. There was an enclosure of stone, where periodically the stings of stingrays had to be deposited. There was an area forbidden to women. And there were various other spots the purpose and significance of which boggles the mind of an Occidental.

My interest in the history and life of Laulasi somehow won the sympathy of the villagers. Or perhaps it was that we spent so much time together talking about fishing. In any case, I was treated with remarkable hospitality. While I was talking about the mother-of-pearl and scaled fishhooks that I had already seen in the Solomons, a man held out a handful of the very same hooks to me. It was more than I had dared dream of finding. On each one, a hook of scale was attached by a link to a mother-of-pearl shaft. Some of the hooks were carved in the shape of a fish. There was, of course, no question of paying for the hooks.

My most surprising conquest on the island, and certainly the most transitory, was the belle of Laulasi—a girl of fifteen with amber skin and the most beautiful smile in the world. Timidly, she offered me what was no doubt a prized possession: a carving of a shark made from a piece of shell. When I climbed into the boat to leave the island, we exchanged a final look, the look of two separate worlds whose orbits had crossed only briefly.

I had looked forward to the trip back to Auki, if only to have a few quiet moments to work out my thoughts on what I had seen in Laulasi. But meditation was impossible. An enormous black cloud burst over the lagoon and my mind was suddenly occupied with but one thought: my misery. By the time we reached Auki, I was as drenched as though I had tried to swim across the lagoon. All of the papers and notes in my briefcase were equally soaked. To add insult to injury, the operator of the motorboat demanded double pay for having come out in such a storm.

A battlefield

As soon as one disembarks from a plane at Honiara airport, he sees cannons. In fact, they are everywhere, in the gardens, in the brush, covered by vines, smothered by trees, sometimes garlanded by flowers. The reason for their presence becomes clear when one recalls that Honiara is the capital of Guadalcanal Island, where the Japanese and the American forces in the Pacific waged one of the

Double page following: This woman is using a stone pestle to fragment shells. The pieces will be used to make necklaces. Note the ground which, on this artificial island, is made of pieces of dead coral.

A fish was carved out of a piece of dark wood to act as a resting place for a human skull, which can be seen in the middle of the fish. (Collection Musée de l'Homme)

most memorable battles of World War II. Combatants from both sides return today to visit the site, just as French veterans of World War I return to Verdun-sur-Meuse. The analogy between Verdun and Guadalcanal is appropriate, for in both places were fought the decisive battles of great wars. The Japanese had seized the island, as well as the neighboring islands, in April 1942. Guadalcanal was of strategic importance for two reasons: there was a broad plateau suitable as a landing field for bombers, and there was a deep-water channel between Guadalcanal and nearby Tulagi. For those same reasons, the American High Command needed Guadalcanal as the jumping-off place for its planned offensive against the Japanese Empire.

Neither the American army nor the marines had as yet undertaken large-scale landings. This was the first attempt. A formidable armada of aircraft carriers, cruisers, and destroyers escorted troop transports to the area. Meanwhile, a huge number of aircraft had been assembled on neighboring New Caledonia, New Hebrides, Tonga, Samoa Islands and Fiji Islands. The Americans were determined

Mother-of-pearl from a giant clam was the material used to make this elaborately carved gate. The gate was used at the entrance to a shelter or hut where the remains of the dead were preserved. (Photograph J. Oster, Collection Musée de l'Homme)

that Guadalcanal was to be the turning point in the war: a great victory after an unbroken series of defeats.

On August 7, 1942, the marines landed successfully on Guadalcanal. But, the following day, the American ships were taken by surprise and defeated in the Battle of Savo. On August 9, the navy withdrew its ships from the area, and the troops already ashore were left virtually without support. Nonetheless, the marines dug into the beaches. For a month the battle raged, with neither side gaining a permanent advantage. The Japanese were entrenched in caves and holes, from which they could be dislodged, not with mortars or hand grenades, but with sticks of dynamite equipped with fuses so short that they could not be thrown back at the Americans. Every night, the Americans sustained furious attacks by screaming Japanese troops armed with grenades and knives. Meanwhile, the fate of the combatants was being decided on the sea. At the end of August following an indecisive naval battle, the Japanese were able to land a reinforcement division on Guadalcanal. It seemed that the marines were doomed. Thereafter, Japanese

In the distant Solomon Islands, children play a game remarkably similar to our hopscotch.

heavy cruisers—the Tokyo Express, as they were known to the marines—regularly bombarded American positions on the island. Finally, there was only one American aircraft left on Guadalcanal, and the Japanese recaptured the landing field in a battle which cost over 2,000 American lives. Finally, on November 11, 6,000 American reinforcements landed while, at sea, the naval battle of Guadalcanal was under way once more. It was not until three months later, in February 1943, that the island was at peace once more. There had been heavy losses on both sides, but, at the end, there was not one Japanese soldier left alive on Guadalcanal.

As far as the native inhabitants of the island were concerned, no one gave

The womenfolk travel alone in their pirogues, from one artificial island to another, to buy and sell fruits and vegetables.

them much thought. Those who had taken refuge in the jungle, in the interior of the island, survived. The others died.

Honiara

Against such a background of devastation, it is not surprising to learn that Honiara, the most populous place on Guadalcanal, is an entirely new city. Its site is quite beautiful, with the usual lagoon, coconut trees, and white sandy beaches. The jungle is not far away. Honiara, in fact, consists of a single wide avenue bordered by one-story buildings and planted with bright flowers. In this, it differs little from other towns on Pacific islands.

The body of water lapping the shaded beaches is known as Iron Bottom Bay—a name derived from the number of sunken ships littering the bottom. French divers still support themselves by salvaging nonferrous metals from the submerged hulks.

Thirty-five years after the Battle of Guadalcanal, there is little sign of any permanent damage to the dense jungles outside Honiara. The coconut trees cut in two by machine-gun fire, the trees and great ferns destroyed by bombs—everything has grown once more and healed the wounds inflicted by the fury of war. The river now flows serenely through impossibly dense greenery, unmindful of the time when thousands were slaughtered on its banks.

The golden mirage

To my mind, the name of the Solomon Islands was one to conjure with. Their isolation, their distant past, their reputation for savagery, their role during World War II—everything about them attracted me. Yet, once there, I found only one satisfaction for my exotic dreams: a hotel called Mendaña. It is the name of a historical personage, Alvaro de Mendaña de Neira who, at the head of a Spanish expedition, discovered the Solomons in 1568. Mendaña's discovery was virtually forgotten for two centuries. It was not until Dumont d'Urville's expedition, in 1838, that the archipelago appeared on maps of the Pacific under its present name. The name "Solomon Islands," in fact, was something of a fraud. It was used by the Spaniards in the hope of attracting colonists from Spain, to whom it was suggested that the islands were richer than the fabled mines of King Solomon. Legend had it that the battle clubs brought back by Mendaña's men had heads of gold. The truth was that the little ceremonial clubs of the natives were encrusted with mother-of-pearl and ended in a gilt ornament made of copper.

Umbrellas and loincloths

In the many contented hours I spent in the marketplace at Honiara, I had ample occasion to observe the two distinct elements of the population of Guadalcanal. There are the inhabitants of Honiara itself, and there are the inhabitants of the brush who visit Honiara to shop.

Those who live in the town—both young people and adults—are relatively sophisticated individuals, as often happens among the natives of territories controlled by the British. They seem to have adopted the conveniences and even the luxuries of Occidental life, while adapting those imported objects and attitudes to their own taste and whim. They go to movies (there is one theater in Honiara), and they have automobiles and motorboats. But, at the same time, they have insisted on retaining their traditional hairstyles and preferences in dress. Boys and girls stroll along the shaded avenue wearing feathers and flowers in their hair. Young belles are fond of dresses of pistachio green and shocking pink, bright makeup, and high-heeled shoes. They smile easily, laugh frequently, and are wholly without pretensions. The matrons are easily distinguishable from the unmarried girls, for as soon as her first child is born, a woman does not appear in public unless shaded by a multicolored umbrella.

On weekend marketing days, the elegant ladies of the town rub elbows, cautiously, with a crowd of natives from the brush. The latter are barefoot and dressed in loincloths or rags. They come in family groups to sell their produce and perhaps to buy pots and pans. They always seemed to be loaded with children and packages, buckets and bananas. For them, a visit to Honiara is an entertainment as well as a shopping trip. Their smiles and laughter lead one too easily to forget the misery always present in the tropics. I was reminded of it when I saw their children digging in garbage cans for half-rotten fruit.

Artisans rather than sculptors

Despite the proximity of such active artistic centers as New Britain and New Ireland, the sculpture of the Solomon Islands exhibits an undeniable originality. The artists make profuse and skilled use of inlaid mother-of-pearl in all of their work—large wooden balls, shields, carvings of sharks, and human heads carved into bows of boats.

The customary form for such bows is that of a human head and shoulders with the arms propped up on the elbows and the thumbs supporting the head. This ritual posture memorializes a dead man, but it is reproduced today *ad nauseam* for the sake of tourists. There are so many of these mother-of-pearl-encrusted effigies in the shops of Honiara, that it is impossible to attach any value to them.

The success of the art of the Solomon Islands today lies more in decoration than in sculpture itself. The skilled workmen of the islands make combs of exquisite beauty characterized by a delicate mosaic of different plants.

Both men and women are adept at working the various materials provided in abundance by the sea, such as mother-of-pearl and scales. Round plaques, cut from shells, are used in pendants enhanced by motifs wrought in delicately cut scales.

Formerly, the artists of the Solomons used the shells of giant clams as containers for miniature huts in which were kept the skulls of the dead. These reliquaries, known as *bavara*, were deeply etched with human figures. The art of the *bavara* apparently has been lost.

In the streets of Honiara, capital of Guadalcanal, people from the bush quickly learn to make use of modern conveniences. This woman has found an ingenious use for the pan she has just bought.

The Solomons and the future

The Solomon Islands encompass a comparatively large mass of land. The seven principal islands, which are virtually unknown in the West, comprise forty percent of the area of all the Pacific archipelagoes—twice the size of New Caledonia and ten times that of French Polynesia.

Opposite, upper: The young women of the Solomon Islands are unusually charming and attractive.

Opposite, lower: This peaceful river on Guadalcanal was once the scene of bloody confrontations between Japanese and American soldiers.

The relics of war are everywhere on Guadalcanal, like this cannon rusting away under the trees.

Great Britain, having maintained a presence there for the past eighty-five years, seems to have no plans for the archipelago's future other than to be rid of the islands as quickly as possible. Local elections have been held, and two or three political leaders have emerged from obscurity. No doubt, independence is in the offing.

Independence, however, will create problems in the Solomons. It will not be an easy transformation for a people who, for thousands of years, waged savage war among themselves and who have never known a moment of national unity. The transition from an almost unbroken tradition of headhunting and ritual cannibalism to democracy will be an arduous one, and the traditional opposition between bush people and salt-water people, as they are known, will probably be a cause of constant conflict.

Throughout the nineteenth century, only whalers, adventurers, and labor recruiters visited the Solomons. They complained constantly of the "ferocity" of the natives, but they neglected to explain that the hostility of the inhabitants was due at least in part to the treatment that they received at the hands of these visitors—to say nothing of the kidnapping of laborers for the plantations of Queensland and the Fiji Islands.

In 1893, Great Britain established a protectorate over Guadalcanal, Malaita, New Georgia, and San Cristóbal. After World War I, the protectorate was extended to include the former German islands of Choiseul and Ysabel.

Bougainville Island, and its neighboring island of Buka, which also had been German colonies, were mandated to Australia by the League of Nations. The reason for this special treatment was that Bougainville was and is rich in copper, and, along with its copper, it has sold its soul. The development of copper mines has literally ripped the island to shreds. Millions upon millions of dollars have been spent on roads and refineries, and even upon schools and hospitals. Bougainville, therefore, is rich—so rich that she wishes to keep all of her wealth for herself. Thus, she has become a paradox. Although she is geographically a part of the Solomons, which will become independent in the foreseeable future, politically she is part of Papua New Guinea—which has already attained independence. The inhabitants of Bougainville, however, are loath to share their wealth with the Papuans. Instead, they demand independence for Bougainville.

Meanwhile, the mines are continuing to ruin the island's hills and mountains and to wreak havoc with her traditional moral values. Once, Bougainville and Buka were both artistic centers and they produced admirable wooden sculpture. It is quite obvious that artistic endeavor has now come to a complete halt.

The problem presented by Bougainville is one that threatens the political equilibrium of the entire area.

the death of the islands

*The coral grows. The palm trees
grow. Only man disappears.*

AN OLD SAYING OF THE
SOUTH SEAS

A philosophical tale

The inhabitants of an island have a hundred ways from which to choose if they want to disfigure their homeland. The people of Nauru, for example, have selected one of the more radical methods: they eat their land, the land of their ancestors. Figuratively, of course. Nauru (Naoero) is a tiny island republic of 3,600 millionaires that each year, exports two million tons of phosphate. The mining of the phosphate requires that, every year, a large part of the island is destroyed. To date, three-quarters of the land has disappeared in this manner. By 1990, at the latest, there will be nothing left except a lunar landscape: bare rock. Not enough earth will be left, literally, for a single one of the millionaires of Nauru to stand on. Meanwhile, the fifteen miles of highway on the island are covered with thousands of expensive automobiles, and the consumption of alcohol is the highest in the Pacific.

A philosophical tale, and perhaps a lesson.

Self-destruction and the tourist industry

If one is determined to spoil an island, tourism is as good a way as any—as is obvious, on a very large scale, in the Fiji Islands. Travel agents refer to this archipelago as "islands of Paradise." They are Paradise indeed, or at least a god-

It is fashionable among the young women of Tonga to make earrings out of flowers.

send, for the agents who inundate the islands with honeymooners and tourists. There are numerous hotels, and the attractions of the islands are as numerous as they are expensive. One such notable attraction is the spectacle of the "fire-walkers" of Suva, who dance across a bed of hot embers for the edification of tourists.

The natives of the Fiji Islands, if they have ever had an art of their own, have lost it irrevocably. They have also lost their ethnic identity. The immigration of foreign workers, who are drawn from all the Pacific islands in order to work the sugarcane fields, and the influx of Indians (who are now in the majority), have made of Fiji the melting pot of the Pacific.

The kingdom of Tonga: a study in degradation

A group of black gentlemen were playing cricket on a very British lawn. Their immaculate white trousers sparkled in the sunlight. Behind them rose the glistening walls of a red-roofed castle: the Royal Palace of the Kingdom of Tonga.

I was struck by the irony of it all. I had come halfway across the world, explored the fabled isles of the South Pacific—only to end up, one fine Sunday morning, watching British subjects playing the national game before a pale imitation of Buckingham Palace.

The degradation of the island kingdom of Tonga, which was the last of the Pacific islands I visited, is even more striking. Fiji, after all, is a relatively large archipelago, comprising some three hundred islands of which only ninety are inhabited. There is hope that, in some remote part of the jungle or on an obscure reef, a wise elder (or a maladjusted youth) is following the traditions of his people, worshipping the spirits of his ancestors, and coming to terms with his environment by means of magical incantations. Tonga, however, is a tiny island kingdom as well as an ancient and once-glorious nation.

The former sovereign of Tonga was the massive and smiling Queen Sálote, Tupou III, who cut such an exotic and sympathetic figure at the coronation of Elizabeth II of England. Today, her son, King Taufa'ahau, reigns over an island remarkable for its "progressive spirit." The tourist and hotel business is booming, and on the international exchange, the Tongan dollar is exceptionally vigorous, enjoying a rate of exchange higher than that of the Australian dollar.

The history of Tonga demonstrates that the islanders are an enterprising and courageous people. It appears that, beginning probably in the thirteenth century A.D., the Tongans set out in their boats, traveling to the Fiji and Samoa islands, subjecting to their authority and exacting tribute from peoples less well equipped or less courageous than themselves. The Tongans are not Melanesians, given to gardening rather than to maritime adventures. They are Polynesians—that is, they are marvelous sailors and expert shipbuilders.

The qualities that enabled them once to make themselves feared and respected throughout the South Seas still exist today. Now, however, the Tongans do not spread terror. They spread tourist brochures.

Glory in recollection

The memory of past glories, and a certain conviction of superiority, enable today's Tongans to confront with equanimity the invasion of whites. Four to five hundred arrive daily from Australia, New Zealand, the United States, and Canada. The tour ships have barely docked before the visitors are whisked away in hibiscus-taxis—red or gold tricycles which, one suspects, are quaint by design. The first stop for the tourists is usually a public marketplace stocked exclusively with objects which appeal to souvenir-hunters: make-believe spears, gaudy tapas, ridiculous hats—all very exotic, to be sure.

In the evening, shortly before the dinner hour, it is interesting to observe the tourists returning to their ships. Exhausted, irritable, they are now traveling on foot along the shore, carrying the bows and arrows and other junk merchandise that are the means by which the South Seas exacts its revenge.

There remain today only the vestiges of what was once a flourishing art form on Tonga. The tapas (painted thin sheets of bark) which hold such fascination for tourists, are made in the same way as always; but their stereotyped designs are without real interest or value.

The Tongans still have a love for dancing, a sense of ceremonial, and a taste for festive banquets. Their natural hospitality and gaiety are evident occasionally in presentations and spectacles that are not, as yet, altogether commercialized. They have also retained an aesthetic preoccupation, as well as a very sophisticated taste, for elegant clothing and striking feminine fashions. The real marketplace is a fashion show of graceful ladies in long dresses, wearing unusual fringed belts of a dozen colors and designs. Sometimes, less happily, the ladies envelop half their bodies in a length of sparterie.

Captain Cook called Tonga the "Friendly Islands." That reputation, however well deserved, may have proved the undoing of the Tongans. Today, they will go to any lengths to be "friendly." They do not offer hospitality as much as impose it. And they have no doubt that they are indeed the friendliest people on earth, that their island is the most interesting one in the world, or that the trinkets that they sell are artistic masterpieces.

There is one attraction on Tonga that is not mentioned in the publicity releases: the cemeteries. These, indeed, are like no other cemeteries. They are generally located in the middle of the brush, and they consist of an enormous pile of sand in which empty cans and beer bottles serve as vases for artificial flowers. Sometimes there is a canopy over a tomb, usually decorated with paper and ribbons of various colors. Occasionally, the tomb of a prosperous Tongan will be marked by a large painting of Christ, or of the Virgin—a most unexpected spectacle in the open air of the tropics.

No doubt, a Tongan would be astonished to learn that his cemeteries are actually the most unusual thing on the island.

Genocide, of a kind

It is not by chance that this book ends with a discussion of tourism in Tonga and a description of the island's supremely symbolic attractions, its cemeteries.

We have all been made aware, by the events of the twentieth century, that human societies as well as animal species can become extinct. The chief in full dress, the tribal magicians and witch doctors, the sculptors, the ceremonies and dances, the dialects and languages—all these things can vanish as easily as whales and tigers and eagles. If we are concerned about the endangered species of animals, we should be doubly concerned about the endangered communities of humans. Otherwise, they will go the way of the dodo and the dinosaur.

"Tanna, New Ireland, Tonga," wrote Maurice Leenhardt, "there is no end to the names that we could choose from the map of the Pacific. They all evoke the image of a dot of land, surrounded by the sea, without economic interest for us. Yet, each of these dots is the guardian of something of cultural value, of an art which confers on that dot the dignity of an important island."

The art, the cultural value of which Leenhardt speaks, may, one day soon, exist only in books and museums. The tidal wave of traveler's checks, Coca Cola, and Kleenex now breaking over the islands may bring some material advantage to the fishermen, gardeners, and artists of the South Seas. But it is difficult to rejoice in such prosperity if it entails, as it apparently does, the loss of their native moral and aesthetic values.

In Tonga, gentlemen in whites play cricket in front of the royal palace.

Opposite: Along Tonga's coast, blowholes shoot up spouts of water whenever a wave breaks.

The cemeteries of Tonga are among the island's curiosities. Countless artificial flowers are displayed on piles of sand, and large paintings rise among the tombs.

There was a time, recent enough to be remembered by most people living to-day, when the very size of the Pacific served as a barrier protecting the islands, the peoples, and the cultures of the South Pacific. With the advent of air travel on a mass scale, there are no more barriers. There is hardly a beach so remote, or a coral reef so inaccessible, that it does not contain its quota of discarded beer bottles and rusting cans. The white man is everywhere, in pursuit, no doubt, of his manifest destiny to remake the world in his image.

The truth is that it is hard to tell who is remaking what, and who is civilizing whom. It is both amusing and sad to watch herds of Canadians, Americans, and Australians being led around and lectured by Tongan guides as they move from mandatory excursion to paid spectacle to piles of junk souvenirs. One thing is certain in this parade: the tribal chief has been transformed into a latter-day P. T. Barnum, the warrior into an actor, and the child into a street-beggar.

There was a time when explorers bought the good will, or at least the tolerance, of islanders by giving them handfuls of worthless beads in exchange for pearls. Now, even the shoe has changed foot, so to speak. It is the whites who require the trinkets and fight for them among themselves in the marketplaces of the islands, and it is the natives who take hard dollars in exchange for trash.

It is not entirely fair, I confess, to blame the visible deterioration of the Pacific wholly on the tourist industry. There have been other invaders, some of them well intentioned, who have had and are having an equally disquieting input on the social and cultural integrity of the islands. The first of these, in chronological order, were the missionaries and the missionaries' wives, with their plague of "mission dresses." There were Chinese merchants with their shiploads of pots, pans, and other amenities; oil interests with their jeeps and their engineers and their dollars; and the nuclear powers, of course, with their fallouts and their threats. It is hard, in fact, to think of one economic, social, spiritual, or national force in the "civilized" world that has not contributed somehow to the degradation of the islands of the Pacific. We all, it seems, live in glass houses of extraordinary fragility.

The human truth

My purpose in voyaging to the South Pacific was to study the islands as they are today, whether improved or deformed by their isolation or lack of it, and to surmise what the chances are that these islands will survive the twentieth century.

I should say, first, that despite the enormous damage that has already been done, there is still much in Melanesia to astound us. The green mass of islands—Ambrym, Malikolo, Erromango—rising out of the sea are still places of secrets, taboos, and exotic flora and fauna. There are still beaches of tinted sand untouched by an oil slick. And, beyond the white line of breakers, there are still coral

These two young women, natives of Espíritu Santo Island in the New Hebrides, are representative of the long-limbed beauties who live there.

New Guinea and Melanesia both offer a wide variety of human types. What they all have in common is a fondness for self-embellishment. Among the ornaments most favored are shells, feathers, pigs' teeth, and necklaces of flowers.

Opposite, upper: A Papuan woman. She wears bird-of-paradise feathers on her head and a cuscus fur around her neck.

Opposite, lower: This warrior's necklace is made of a large piece of trimmed mother-of-pearl.

Upper: This gentleman is an official, as indicated by his cap. He is also wearing a mother-of-pearl crescent which goes from one ear to the other.

Lower: This warrior of New Guinea was one of the most splendidly decorated inhabitants that I saw.

reefs harboring the brilliant-hued fish of tropical waters. At the marketplace in Port Moresby, the women wear red feathers above their noses, as their grandmothers did, and sell parrot fish, triggerfish, and pink jewfish.

There are still undiluted pleasures available to those who envy Captain Cook and Louis-Antoine de Bougainville. I have seen women in grass skirts, their breasts bare, their heads crowned with flowers, dancing the traditional dances of their people—not in Tahiti, heaven forbid, but on Tanna and the Trobriand Islands. I have heard native drums, with human faces, resounding through the jungle. I have seen human skulls encrusted with *cauri*, and corpses laid out on platforms among the trees. None of these things, I am happy to say, had anything to do with tours or organized commercial displays. They were *true*—that is, the human truth, the reality that is actually lived by the people of the islands.

We must realize that not every island has developed in the same way or been exposed to the same dangers. If I had to choose one man, one figure to embody and symbolize the future of the Pacific, it would be Viriambat, High Chief of the Big Nambas, whose personality and position were described in Chapter Eight. Viriambat, I believe, is now invulnerable to ruin. He has been subjected to "future shock," and he stands firm. No doubt, he is somewhat protected by jungle and mud, but he could have fled, and yet he remained. He stands out in my memory as a man among men.

There comes a time when a traveler wearily resigns himself to a single hope: that he will find a man, perhaps the last man, who is not like every other man, and yet who deserves the title of man. To my astonishment, I found that there were such men in existence. They inhabit the mountains of Malikolo; and they live in Irian, wearing the penile sheath of Wamena. Their tranquil self-confidence, their innate dignity, protect them from corruption. I am less confident about the feather-bedecked people of Papua New Guinea. They have already experienced the delights of Coca Cola and of the Australian dollar, and they may be too narcissistic to be capable of resisting the wave of temptations emanating from the mysterious Occident.

Humanism and savagery

The future of Melanesia does not depend solely on fluctuations in the tourist trade. It has much to do also with the psychological makeup of the people, with their beliefs and social structures. Every island has its own customs, myths, and taboos. Every island tribe will undoubtedly make its own kind of debut in the modern world and succeed or fail in its own way.

What is happening in the South Pacific is that the islanders are preparing to make a transition from the Stone Age directly into the Atomic Age. The results of this cultural shock are unpredictable. The situation is quite different from that prevailing in Africa or in Asia. In Africa, we are dealing with a continent of young republics afflicted with the growing pains of violence, misery, and totalitarianism. Asia is a place of ancient civilizations that have become the pawns of the great nuclear powers. In Oceania, however, the game is not yet over; indeed, it is just beginning.

There have been great changes in economic and human relations. There will be even greater changes, and these will be accompanied by political upheavals in a region that has not known real change in a thousand years.

The Pacific phase of World War II demonstrated that the area bounded by New Guinea, Australia, and the Solomon Islands is the most strategically sensitive spot on earth. It was control of this region that guaranteed American victory in the Far East. And it is there that, today, the United States, the Soviet Union, and China—and perhaps Japan, once again—confront one another in their quest for strategic and commercial superiority.

The odds are that the islands caught in this web of international rivalry, transformed into the toys of giants, will lose both their cultural independence and their originality. A thousand years of magic and the worship of ancestors cannot prevail against the forces of radio, television, and political propaganda.

The fact is that the world cannot remain stationary. It is wrong to force people to change. It is equally wrong to force them to remain the same so that we may preserve their originality and their innocence. Cultural immobility exists only in the imaginations of anthropologists and curators of museums.

Who are we, in any event, to teach the way to happiness? Surely we cannot hold ourselves up as examples. Have we been able, with all our dizzying philosophies and our glittering technologies, to evolve a way of living that conforms to our interior needs and offers us contentment? It is not impossible that the forgotten peoples of the Pacific may become our teachers rather than our disciples. For the moment—only for a brief moment, I fear—their homes are sanctuaries of humanity. What would it be like, I wonder, if, in contemplating these last vestiges of the humanism of savagery, we were finally to learn the secret? The secret that we have always sought and always ignored? The secret of being at peace with ourselves and our environment.

Following: This precociously serious young man is the son of a New Guinea chief. He symbolizes the difficult future that awaits the forgotten people of the Pacific in the modern world. (Photograph Bernard Sonneville)

appendices
and glossary

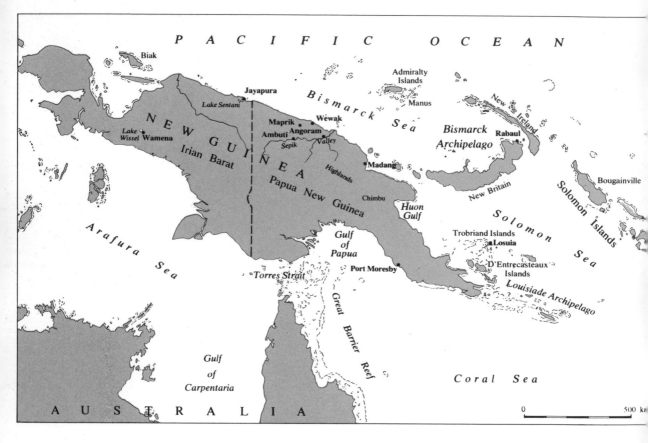

appendix I

The exploration of the Pacific was first undertaken by the Portuguese and the Spaniards.

In 1511, following Vasco da Gama's voyage around the Cape of Good Hope, another Portuguese, Alfonso de Albuquerque, claimed Malacca for his country, thereby gaining for Portugal a foothold of enormous strategic importance. In the following year, Captain António de Abreu, sailing from Malacca, reached the Moluccas by following a map found in Java. Shortly thereafter, Francisco Serrão, a friend of Magellan's, established Portuguese commerce at Ternate. Portugal was now mistress of the eastern spice route; and her superiority was assured in 1526, when New Guinea was discovered by Jorge de Meneses.

Still another Portuguese navigator, Vasco Núñez de Balboa, from a mountain-top in the Isthmus of Panama, discovered the American waterway of the Pacific Ocean in 1513. The best known of the Portuguese explorers, however, was Ferdinand Magellan, and his approach was also from the west. He sailed around the southern tip of South America, discovering the strait that bears his name today, and entered that vast expanse of water that he christened *la Pacifica*—"the peaceful sea."

Magellan was the first European to cross the Pacific. He reached the Philippines, but was killed at Cebú. Only one of his five ships, the *Victoria*, under the

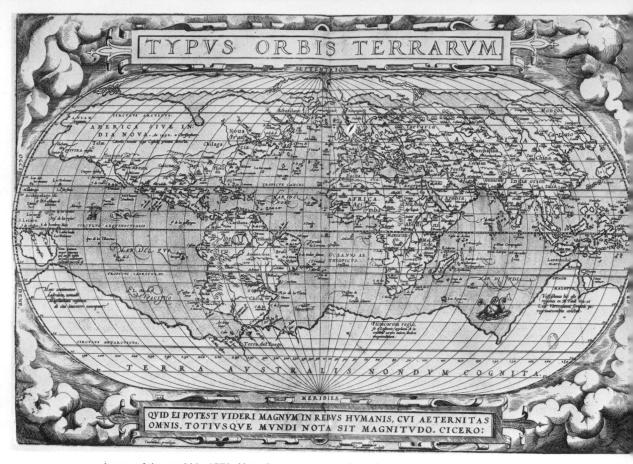

A map of the world in 1570. Note the enormous "unknown austral continent" across the lower part of the map. (*Theatrum orbis terrarum,* by Abraham Ortelius, Photograph Bibliothèque Nationale)

command of Captain Elcano and with a crew of eighteen men, survived to return home. The *Victoria* was the first ship to sail around the world, returning to Portugal by way of the Indies and bearing a fantastically rich cargo of spices.

As of 1565, the Spanish were solidly ensconced in the Philippines and had organized regular voyages between Manila and the port of Acapulco in Mexico. The ships carried not only spices, but also silks and porcelains from China.

In 1567, the Spanish Viceroy of Peru commissioned his nephew Alvaro de Mendaña de Neira to undertake "a search for the islands called Solomon." The Viceroy was no doubt aware of a Peruvian tradition according to which the Inca Tupac Yupanqui, had visited a ground of immensely rich islands in the Pacific. It was believed these islands lay not far off the Peruvian coast. In the course of his voyage, Mendaña discovered an archipelago that, predictably, he named the Solomons. He landed on the island of Isabela, and around Guadalcanal, Malaita, and San Cristóbal.

In 1595, Mendaña was commissioned to establish colonies on the rich islands that he had discovered; but, as luck would have it, he was unable to find them

The world at the beginning of the seventeenth century. This illustration appeared in a narrative of Le Maire and Schouten's voyage across the Pacific. Above the map are depictions of Magellan and Schouten. (Photograph Bibliothèque Nationale)

again. Instead, he discovered a new group, which he named the Marquesas, in homage to the Marquesa de Mendoza.

The phantom continent

In the interval between these two voyages, the English had been infected by the spirit of adventure and, in 1577, Sir Francis Drake rounded the Strait of Magellan and crossed the Pacific, reaching the Moluccas.

Pedro Fernández de Queirós, a Portuguese navigator who had served on Mendaña's second expedition, was convinced (as were most of the geographers of his time) that there was a *Tierra Firma,* a continent, awaiting discovery in the waters of the South Seas. In 1605, he sailed from Peru with three ships and three hundred men in search of this unknown land. All he discovered, however, was a single island—now known as Espíritu Santo, in the New Hebrides group. Nonetheless, believing that he had actually landed on the phantom continent, he named this bit of land *Australia del Espíritu Santo.* He found a river, and called it Jordan. He established a colony, and christened it ''New Jerusalem.'' And, finally, he founded a new order of knighthood, which he called ''the Knights of the Holy Spirit,'' the members of which were sworn to protect the natives of the new land. The knights, their New Jerusalem, and their good intentions did not flourish long. The Spaniards had the bad judgment to requisition a herd of swine that the natives had reserved for sacrifice when this sacrilege was discovered, the explorers were compelled to return to their ships in the greatest possible haste.

Queirós' small fleet continued its voyage across the Pacific—thus far without having proved the existence of a new continent—and there arose a storm. One of the ships, the *Almirante San Pedrico,* commanded by a Portuguese named Luis Vaez de Torres, was separated from the rest of the fleet. Torres, now on his own, decided to sail in a southwesterly direction and to continue the search for the elusive continent. He was the first to sail around the entire coast of New Guinea. In the course of this expedition, he thus discovered the strait on the northern tip of Australia that today is known as Torres Trait. He reached Ternate and the Philippines, and thus demonstrated that New Guinea is, in fact, an island—a discovery that was to remain secret for many years to come.

The Dutch

The Dutch appeared upon the Pacific scene at the end of the sixteenth and the beginning of the seventeenth centuries. In 1596, Cornelis de Houtman, commanding the first Dutch exploratory expedition, avoided the Strait of Malacca (which was controlled by Portugal) and passed through the Sunda Strait between Sumatra and Java. Thereafter, the Dutch had an easy access route to the Moluccas with their fabled ''Spice Islands.''

The Dutch, like the Spaniards and the Portuguese, believed in the existence of a mysterious southern continent, of which New Guinea and the Solomons were thought to be a part. In 1605, a small vessel, the *Duyfken,* was dispatched to explore the southern coast of New Guinea, which, it was said, was rich in gold.

The *Duyfken,* sailing southward, somehow overshot New Guinea and unwittingly skirted coasts of the Australian continent for a considerable distance, believing all the while that they were still in the waters of New Guinea.

In 1616, there occurred another voyage of some note. Two Dutchmen, Jakob Le Maire and Willem Schouten discovered the islands of Futuna and Alofi. There they were given some *kava* (a nonalcoholic beverage made from the root of the pepper plants). It is the first recorded mention of this product.

Australia

It was not until 1642 that the mystery surrounding the southern continent was, to some extent, dissipated. In that year, a Dutch navigator named Abel Janszoon Tasman discovered an island to the south of Australia that he called Van

Diemen's Land and that today is named Tasmania. In the course of the same voyage, he also landed at New Zealand, which he believed comprised a single island rather than two separate islands. Finally, he landed at Tonga, where he noted that the natives had the curious custom of cutting off the tips of their fingers, a practice still current today in New Guinea.

The most famous navigator of the Pacific at that time was William Dampier, an English privateer. Dampier's fame rested upon a spectacular series of raids that began on the western coast of the American continent and extended across the Pacific to Guam, Mindanao in the Philippines, and along the northwest coast of Australia (then known as New Holland).

Dampier was the first of a new generation of navigator-explorers who were also scientific researchers—geographers, naturalists, oceanographers. Like many of his contemporaries, he was firmly convinced of the exitence of the southern continent. When he was appointed head of an official voyage of exploration, however, his sole accomplishment was a more or less profitless exploration of New Britain and New Ireland—which he mistook for a single large island and re-named Nova Brittania. On the return ship, his ship sank in the Atlantic, at Ascension Island.

At the beginning of the 18th century, a Dutch mariner named Jacob Roggeveen crossed the South Pacific and discovered Easter Island. In the course of this voyage, he found new evidence of the existence of a southern continent: huge floating icebergs that, he surmised, "must have separated from a body of land that reaches to the South Pole."

In 1738, a Frenchman, Jean-Baptiste-Charles Bouvet de Lozier, sailed in search of a hypothetical "Gonneville land"[1], but, for his efforts, he discovered only a tiny island that was named after him.

Scientific exploration

The year 1756 marked a new beginning in the exploration of the South Seas. In that year, Charles de Brosses, president of the Parliament of Dijon, published a book entitled *Histoire des Navigations aux Terres australes* (*History of the Exploration of the Southern Lands*), in which he expressed his belief in the existence of a southern continent that's function it was to balance the continents of the northern hemisphere. The importance of the book, however, lay in its thesis: that, thenceforth, exploration should be undertaken for the sake of scientific inquiry rather than for that of immediate profit. The idea was revolutionary in its time.

It was, however, an idea that was not always applied in practice. In 1766, for example, an Englishman, Samuel Wallis, commanding the *Dolphin*, discovered the enchanted isle of Tahiti—and promptly bombarded the natives into submission. Thereupon, he landed and consorted amicably with his victims for the next five weeks.

---

[1] A mythical land that was supposed to have been discovered by the Sieur de Gonneville in 1503, and which his family was reputed to have kept secret.

Meanwhile, another Englishman, Philip Carteret, rediscovered the Solomon Islands. Carteret also established that Dampier's Nova Brittania was, in reality, three separate islands: New Britain, New Ireland, and New Hanover. He discovered the Admiralty Islands and reached the East Indies. On the return trip across the Pacific, he crossed a French frigate, the *Boudeuse*, captained by Louis-Antoine de Bougainville.

Bougainville

Louis-Antoine, Count de Bougainville, had sailed from France in December 1766 with two ships: the *Boudeuse* and the *Etoile.* He was relatively new to ships and seas, having spent his earlier life as an army officer. He was, however, an excellent mathematician and geographer. He had unbounded curiosity about exotic lands and peoples; and he was a passionate student of ethnography long before that word was ever invented. Bougainville shared President de Brosses' belief in an austral continent; and that conviction had inspired the voyage of the *Boudeuse* and the *Etoile.* With Bougainville were a small group of scholars: Verron, an astronomer who had perfected a new method of calculating longitude on the basis of stellar distances; Philibert de Commerson, a renowned physician and botanist; and de Commerson's faithful and equally enthusiastic servant, named Barré.

Bougainville and his companions landed at Tahiti several months after Samuel Wallis and christened the place *New Cythera.* Commerson and his servant chose to sleep on the island so as to facilitate their botanical research. Thus it was that the Tahitians—obviously more perceptive than the French seamen—discovered that Commerson's devoted manservant was, in fact, a woman-servant. Whereupon, it was decreed that Barré must thenceforth wear clothing appropriate to her sex. She was, however, allowed to retain her position as a member of the company of explorers.

Bougainville and his party left Tahiti and sailed westward, touched at Samoa, reconnoitered Futuna and Alofi, the islands discovered earlier by Jakob Le Maire, and reached a group of islands among which they recognized Australia del Espíritu Santo, discovered by Queirós. Bougainville, always haunted by his education in the classics, christened this group the Grand Cyclades Islands. Later, they would be re-named the New Hebrides.

The party continued westward, ignoring the danger that awaited them: the Great Barrier Reef of Australia, which stretches along the northeastern coast of the continent. It was not until the ships were already among the breakers that Bougainville became aware of their peril. With great difficulty, the ships put about and headed north—thereby missing the opportunity to chart the coastal lines of the Australian continent. They also bypassed the Torres Strait and ended up in the midst of a scattering of islands directly to the east of New Guinea, which they called the Louisiades. Further on, they found one island which they christened Choiseul Island; another, Bougainville—both at the northern tip of the Solomons.

The voyage of Bougainville and his companions was a watershed in the history of exploration. This was so not only because Bougainville was the first to or-

Upper: Louis-Antoine, Count de Bougainville.

Below: Bougainville's landing on Tahiti, which he called Nouvelle Cythère. (Photographs Bibliothèque Nationale)

ganize a team of scholars into an exploratory expedition and to gather scientific data of every kind, but also because his account of the voyage, written by himself, created a great stir in Europe. It seemed to confirm Rousseau's thesis concerning "the noble savage"; and from it Diderot drew the philosophical ideas of his *Supplement to Bougainville's Voyage*.

Captain Cook

Even before Samuel Wallis had reached England on his return trip from Tahiti, the Admiralty was busily organizing another expedition to Tahiti. The purpose of it was to observe the eclipse of June 3, 1769, when Venus was expected to pass between Earth and the sun. The command of this mission was assigned to Captain James Cook, a man 40 years of age, who was a superior seaman and, like Bougainville, a man of science. Also assigned to the mission was an astronomer, Charles Green; Joseph Banks, a naturalist; two botanists (one of whom was a student of the celebrated Linnaeus), and two artists. Cook's ship, the HMS *Endeavour*, was thus converted into a traveling laboratory.

Captain James Cook. (Photograph Bibliothèque Nationale)

Opposite: An engraving showing the pirogues of the Tahitians which so impressed Cook. (Récit des voyages de Cook)

The first voyage lasted three years. No ship before had ever remained at sea for so long without its crew falling victim to scurvy.

Unfortunately, the presence of an impenetrable fog at Tahiti made observation of the eclipse impossible. Nonetheless, the geographic data assembled by Cook, and the specimens of flora and fauna gathered by his team of scientists, were of more than sufficient value to have justified the voyage.

Cook's second, and secret, mission aboard the HMS *Endeavour* was to conduct yet another search for "the austral continent." Leaving Tahiti, the ship followed a southerly course, but without sighting land. Then it turned westward, with the intention of conducting a detailed study of the coasts of New Zealand. Passing through the strait separating the northern island from the southern island of New Zealand (a waterway known today as Cook Strait), Cook concluded, on the basis of careful observation, that the northern island was particularly suitable for colonization.

Continuing on a westerly course, the HMS *Endeavour* reached the Great Barrier Reef along the eastern coast of New Holland (Australia). It followed the reef for a thousand nautical miles—not without mishap, for the ship once foundered on the coral reefs. Somehow, the damage was repaired. Cook and his team of scientists took advantage of the delay to go ashore and establish contact with the natives. They also discovered the existence of a most peculiar type of fauna known as the kangaroo.

The journey home was by way of the Torres Strait; then, after a layover at Batavia (now Djakarta), the HMS *Endeavour* sailed westward and reached European waters without incident.

Cook was hardly ashore before his next venture was being organized. A year later, on July 13, 1772, he sailed again, this time with two ships: The *Resolution*, and the *Adventure*, the latter under the command of a Captain Furneaux.

Joseph Banks, the naturalist on the first voyage, refused to accompany Cook on this new expedition. He was replaced by Johann Reinhold Forster and his son, Georg, both of whom were naturalists. There were also two astronomers attached to the expedition. Cook took with him the new chronometers recently perfected by Harrison, which calculated longitude by comparing local time to Greenwich time.

Cook's team, in pursuit of the elusive southern continent, journeyed toward the glaciers of Antarctica and, without knowing it, actually came to within 75 nautical miles of the Antarctic continent. At that point, the two ships turned toward New Zealand, then toward Tahiti, and landed on the islands of Tonga—which the voyagers named "the Island of Friends." Finally, a course was set once more for Antarctica and the *Resolution* and the *Adventurer*, at the farthest point of this course, recorded a position of 71'10°.

Then, once again, the ships sailed northward and touched at Easter Island, with its mysterious statues already observed by the Dutch navigator, Jacob Roggeveen. Then, onward to the Marquesas—which no European had visited since the time of Queirós—and to Tahiti. The next stop was at Espíritu Santo, which Bougainville had visited only a short time before; on that occasion, he had given to the archipelago the name by which it was thenceforth to be known: the New Hebrides. Cook and his party also visited Malikolo, Erromango, and Tanna where a bay, known as Port Resolution, was named for Cook's ship.

Finally, Cook and his men discovered a major island, the existence of which had somehow escaped earlier explorers, and which we know as New Caledonia.

The *Resolution* and the *Adventure* returned to England in 1775, having covered a prodigious distance and having made a major contribution to the geographic knowledge of the Pacific.

In the following year, Cook set out once again aboard the *Resolution*. On this occasion, the second ship of the expedition was the *Discovery*, commanded by Captain Charles Clerke. The ships visited Tasmania, New Zealand, Tonga, and Tahiti. The expedition's real mission, however, was to search for another myth of the age: a passage between the Pacific and the Atlantic to the north of the American continent. Cook navigated the Bering Strait and sailed the glacial waters of the Arctic until, conquered by the ice and the advent of winter, he turned back to Hawaii to replenish his supplies.

It was there that Cook met a tragic death. Despite his constant efforts to ensure respect for natives and the care that he always used in attempting to win their friendship, he was killed by them on the beach at Kealakekua in February 1779.

Above: La Pérouse's ships at anchor: *Boussole* and *Astrolabe,* at Mowee Island.

Below: A depiction of the discoveries of La Pérouse and Cook. (Musée de la Marine, Photograph Flammarion)

A celebration in honor of d'Entrecasteaux, given by Toubau, king of Tonga. (From La Billardière's *Atlas pour servir à la relation du voyage à la recherche de La Pérouse*. Photograph Bibliothèque Nationale)

It has been said of Cook that he was the greatest mariner of all times. There is no reason why that verdict should not be allowed to stand.

La Pérouse

In February, 1786, the Count de La Pérouse sailed on an official mission of exploration under the auspices of the government of France. His ships, the *Boussole* and the *Astrolabe* rounded Cape Horn and dropped anchor first at Easter Island, then at Hawaii. From there, they sailed along the coasts of Asia to the Port of Petropavlovsk on the peninsula of Kamchatka. At that port, La Pérouse dispatched his first report, by land, to Paris. In return, he received orders to proceed to Botany Bay, on the eastern coast of Australia, to report of the development of the British colony established there. According to La Pérouse's report, the colony was in a sorry state, and the colonists lived in almost total privation.

From Australia, La Pérouse's party sailed to New Caledonia, Santa Cruz,

Dumont d'Urville's ships, *Astrolabe* and *Zélée,* arriving at Nuka Hiva. (Photo Bibliothèque Nationale)

and the Solomon Islands. His mission, on this leg of his journey, was to clear up a mystery. Four different persons, on four separate occasions, had "discovered" groups of islands (the Solomons) which, it appeared, may or may not have been the same islands. The first had been Mendaña, in 1568; he had been followed by a Frenchman, Captain L. de Surville, who had landed in 1769 and had christened the islands *Terre des Arsacides*—that is, Land of the Assassins. Finally, on two separate expeditions, there had come two Englishmen, Philip Carteret and Philip Shortland. It was not left to La Pérouse, however, to resolve this riddle. He and his two ships disappeared enroute to the Solomons, and were never heard of again.

In 1791, two French ships, the *Recherche* and the *Espérance,* were dispatched to learn the fate of La Pérouse's expedition. Under the command of Bruni d'Entrecasteaux, the party was also ordered to resolve, once and for all!, the riddle of the Solomons. The French expedition was manned by a brilliant group of scientists: Louis-Auguste Beautemps-Beaupré, a hydrographer; Iréné La Billardiére, a botanist; and a naturalist, Commander Hippolyte Rossel.

D'Entrecasteaux crossed the South Pacific to Tasmania, where Beautemps-Beaupré mapped the contours of the island. From there, the party sailed to New Caledonia, to the Solomons, and finally to the Admiralty Islands in search of La Pérouse. They found no trace of the latter or his ships. They did establish, however, that the Solomon Islands discovered by Mendaña, were indeed the same as the Land of the Assassins discovered by Captain de Surville, and rediscovered by Carteret and Shortland.

In the final phase of his exploratory mission, d'Entrecasteaux sailed among the treacherous maze of reefs and islets scattered off the southeastern tip of New Guinea, charting the area and naming the islands for his officers: Rossel, Renard, Trobriand, Bonvouloir, Lusançay—and giving to the archipelago his own name.

Finally, exhausted and afflicted with scurvy and dysentery, d'Entrecasteaux died on the return trip to France.

Nicolas Baudin

In the latter part of the 1800s, France dispatched still another scientific expedition, this one charged with charting the still relatively unknown coastline of the Australian continent. This mission, comprising two vessels, the *Géographe* and the *Naturaliste*, was commanded by Nicolas Baudin. Once in Australian waters, the French expedition met an English exploratory party, on an identical mission, commanded by Matthew Flinders. Although France and England were at war at that time, the two commanders freely exchanged information and the French were even given supplies and shelter at the flourishing English colony of Port Jackson.

Baudin died of tuberculosis before returning to France. The results of his research, however—the first exact map of Australia—were published in 1807. The English map did not appear until 1814, following delays caused by a series of mishaps among Flinders' party.

Dumont d'Urville

The last of the great French explorers of the Pacific was Dumont d'Urville. This was the same Dumont d'Urville who, at the beginning of his naval career, had won fame with his discovery of the *Venus de Milo*.

In 1825, d'Urville sailed in search of La Pérouse and, as an additional mission, to explore the islands of Polynesia. His two ships, the *Astrolabe* and the *Zélée*, succeeded in 1838 in accomplishing what the French Academy of Science had declared to be impossible: they crossed the barrier of ice that had, until then, blocked access to the Antarctic continent. There, d'Urville discovered a land to which he gave his wife's name, Adélie.

Sailing northward again, d'Urville, before heading homeward, passed through the Torres Strait.

D'Urville died in France in 1842, along with his wife and his son, in a train accident between Paris and Versailles.

Adieu misère, adieu bâteau

Perhaps the most striking fact in the history of maritime exploration is the incredibly high mortality rate of the explorers. In the eighteenth century, and even early in the nineteenth, the most common cause of death on the seas was not shipwreck, or slaughter by "savages," but disease and exhaustion. In 1763, for example, Philip Carteret's vessel, the *Swallow*, lost 27 men during a single crossing of the Pacific. Then, on the way home (a journey of six months), the *Swallow* lost seven more. At about the same time, Samuel Wallis, aboard the *Dolphin*, arrived at Tahiti with his entire crew stricken with scurvy.

In the waters off New Guinea, the Count de Bougainville found his crew in such a weakened condition that no one had sufficient strength to go ashore. They had already eaten a goat and the last of their dogs. "Tonight," Bougainville wrote, "the prince of Nassau and I had a rat for dinner. We thought it excellent; and we would be happy to dine so well more often."

In 1802, Nicolas Baudin's *Géographe* was unable to put into Port Jackson, so exhausted was the crew. It was necessary for a British vessel, the *Investigator*, to dispatch men to aid in the maneuver.

The sailing ships of the 19th century had undeniably attained a high degree of perfection. At the same time, however, one must bear in mind that the immensely complex apparatus of masts, sails, lines, and so forth, required a physical effort on the part of the crew that was virtually superhuman. Moreover, life aboard ship was primitive; hygiene, by modern standards, was nonexistent.

François Peron, a naturalist who sailed with Baudin, wrote enviously that, "As all the world knows, the English owe their superiority on the sea to the progress they have made in maritime hygiene."

Captain Cook gave the first impetus to this new science by his essay on *The Prevention and Treatment of Scurvy*. It is a matter of record that, on Cook's ships, scurvy was unknown. In the course of a four-year expedition, not a single instance of the disease was found—a near-miracle by 18th century standards.

In France, it was a cause of universal astonishment that Dumont d'Urville, in the course of an expedition that lasted almost three years, did not lose one crewman.

appendix II

MISSIONARY ACTIVITY IN THE PACIFIC

The first missionaries in the Pacific were English and Protestant, sent by the London Missionary Society. The first recorded instance of such activity occurred in 1797, when the first ship that took Protestant missionaries to Tahiti, the *Duff*, deposited eighteen missionaries. By 1801, one of this party, the Reverend Nott, was preaching to the natives in their own language. And, by 1819, Pomare II, king of Tahiti, was baptized a Christian.

One of the strongest personalities of this era was the Reverend John Williams, who preached successively at Raiatéa, the Cook Islands, and Samoa. Williams successively purchased two ships that enabled him to evangelize Polynesia and Melanesia. In 1839, he had a number of converts at Tanna. But his career ended when he was killed by the inhabitants of Erromango.

During the missionary period, the Australian port of Sydney served as the evangelical headquarters of the Pacific. It was there that the missionaries came to find wives for themselves.

Catholic missionary activity was initiated only in 1830, by the priests of the Society of Mary. It was not until the end of the nineteenth century that the New Hebrides received their first missionaries.

Among the most active of the Catholic missionaries was Msgr. Pierre Bataillon, who preached on Futuna and the Wallis Islands, Fiji, Samoa, and Tonga.

Another was Father Laval, who worked on Tahiti until the native ruler expelled him at the instigation of a Protestant missionary, Pastor George Pritchard. Laval, however, was restored—by force of arms—through the intervention of a squadron of French ships under the command of Captain Dupetit-Thouars.

Missionary efforts, both Protestant and Catholic, in Polynesia and Melanesia were directed toward the foundation of veritable theocracies. The missionaries, willing or not, were forced by circumstances to become involved in local politics. Also, since they were perennially afflicted by financial problems, they were not disinclined to finance their missionary endeavors by exploiting the limited resources of the islands. The most readily available of such resources was copra (a product of the coconut); for the sake of copra, it sometimes happened that the natives were robbed of their lands.

By granting the pastors far-reaching authority in local administrative matters and by allowing them to intervene in local political affairs, British policy during the missionary era in the Pacific actually made minor governors out of the missionaries. The French government followed the same policy, although to a less-pronounced degree, and not only supported Catholic missionary work in the Pacific, but also favored and, when necessary, defended the missionaries.

This theocratic approach to religious conversion sometimes was successful and sometimes was not. For example, the Presbyterian missionaries on Tanna, preaching austerity, strict observance of the Sabbath, and total abstinence from liquor and condemning nudity and "pagan" customs, made virtually no converts. The Wesleyeans, on the other hand, were eminently successful on Tonga. A Wesleyean pastor, Stirley Baker, was made prime minister of the island kingdom and united in himself supreme authority in all matters political as well as religious.

The 19th century—the heyday of missionary activity in the islands of the Pacific—saw the development of an intense rivalry among the various Christian sects to take advantage of the natural religious instincts of the natives. This unbecoming competition, however, eventually worked to the disadvantage of the missionaries. The Polynesians, Melanesians, and Papuans quickly learned to turn the situation to their own profit by playing the various sects one against the other.

The situation was further complicated by the arrival of new sects—Seventh-day Adventists and Latter-day Saints, chiefly—until the point was reached where the natives began to form their own sects from a mixture of pagan customs and Christian ritual. The "cargo cult," described in Chapter Three, is one such offshoot. In varying forms, it has spread from New Guinea to the Solomons; and the John Frum movement (Chapter Six) is little more than a political variant of the cargo cult.

In retrospect, missionary activity in the South Pacific had had considerable consequences—not all of them religious. Perhaps the most obvious achievement was to effect a relocation of the native population around the missionary stations along the coasts. The missionaries are largely responsible for whatever education exists on the islands and for modern notions of medical care and hygiene. The missionaries were also often responsible for the agricultural development of the islands.

Despite these benefits, it is obvious that the primary objective of the mission-

aries—religious conversion—met with limited success. In the interior of the islands, the inhabitants remain as attached as ever to their old ways and are reso-
lutely "pagan."

On some of the islands, the ministers and priests found people eager to believe and to pray. But these conversions have not always stood the test of time. It
is evident that the Melanesians, although willing to listen to preachers, are more
adept at piecing together religions of their own than at receiving them whole and
entire from others.

It should be noted that Protestant missionary activity was helped immeasura-
bly by the use of native assistances, who were called "teachers." The first missionaries made use of the more cultivated Samoans and Tongans to found new missions. These teachers were sent ahead of the foreign missionaries to prepare the
way for them. Occasionally, the converts were entrusted with the continuance of
the mission once the missionaries themselves had left. Usually, one finds these
teachers at the root of the various dissident sects that have flourished throughout
Melanesia and New Guinea.

PACIFIC

Torres Islands

Banks Islands Vanua Lava
Gaua

NEW

Espíritu
Santo
Island

Aoba Aurora

Pentecost
Island

Norsup

Malikolo 892 Ambrym

Lamap Epi

Mai

OCEAN

HEBRIDES

Efate

Port Vila

Erromango

Tanna Futuna

Aneityum

LOYALTY ISLANDS

Ouvéa

Wé

Lifou

Maré

1627

NEW
CALEDONIA

Nouméa Isle of Pines

0 250 km

Tropic of Capricorn

appendix III

WHALERS AND SANDALWOOD CUTTERS

There were two groups of adventurers who played major roles in the exploration of the South Seas: whalers and sandalwood cutters.

At the beginning of the nineteenth century, American whalers—sailing principally from the great Massachusetts whaling ports of New Bedford and Nantucket—became aware of the great abundance of sperm whales (cachalots) and other species of whales in the Pacific, from the Marquesas Islands and Tuamotu Archipelago to New Guinea and New Zealand. Not far behind the American ships were those of England, France, Holland, and Norway, all in search of the humpback whale (*Megaptera novaeangliae*), in the waters around Tonga and of the South Pacific whale (*Balaena antipodarum*). Along the length of the Equator, the sperm whale abounded throughout the year, around the Marquesas, and the Gilbert and Solomon Islands. (They are still found there, as witnessed by the presence of sperm whale teeth in the marketplaces of the islands, especially at Fiji.)

For decades, the whalers hunted without restriction or restraint, the slaughter of whales reaching its climax around 1840. Thereafter, beginning in 1850, the number of victims began to diminish. The market for whale oil lessened as the use of petroleum spread.

The memory of the whalers among the islanders is not always a happy one. The whaling ships often dropped anchor off the islands and sent parties ashore for water and food supplies, where they treated the natives with unbelievable violence.

It was not uncommon to find deserters from the whaling ships living among the islanders. A few of them "went native" and established themselves quite comfortably in their adopted homelands. In 1842, one American seaman who had jumped ship married the daughter of the chief of Maupiti.

Sandalwood

The craze for sandalwood was of no longer duration than that for whale oil, lasting only from 1825 to 1865.

For centuries, the Chinese had prized this perfumed wood for use in their religious ceremonies. Their chief source of supply was the Coromandel Coast, in southeastern India.

In the nineteenth century, the great tea plantations of Ceylon did not yet exist, and the English and the Australians imported tea in vast quantities from China. It did not take long for the shipping magnets of London and Sydney to realize that sandalwood would make an excellent cargo for their ships on the voyage to China. The cargo would be even more profitable, they reasoned, if it would be possible to discover a new source of supply in the South Pacific. As it happened, it was discovered that Fiji had sandalwood trees; and the traders made short work of them.

Of necessity, then, the sandalwood traders became explorers in the pursuit of more sandalwood trees. A particularly enterprising Australian trader from Sydney, Peter Dillon, discovered sandalwood growing wild on the island of Erromango. Then, more were found on Espíritu Santo, Tanna, Anatom, and the Isle of Pines.

As the cutters moved from island to island, they landed on beaches where no white man had ever trod before. Inevitably, there were conflicts between the natives and the cutters. The inhabitants of the New Hebrides acquired a particularly wide, well-deserved reputation for ferocity.

The relations of the sandalwood hunters with the missionaries were hardly better than those with the natives. The ministers and priests denounced the crimes of the sandalwood hunters to their faces and attempted to intervene so as to protect the natives from the white man's violence.

The cutters' sole contribution to the welfare of the islands was the introduction of iron objects: nails, axes, and knives. It should be added that they also gave the natives a few scraps of red cloth, some alcohol, and venereal diseases.

Sandalwood is an aromatic wood that derives its fragrance from an oil contained only within the trunk of the tree. The branches have no scent. The tree is of slow growth, and modest size. Even so, the tree must be at least 40 years old before it develops its characteristic aroma. Generally, the darker the wood the more oil it contains.

Above: A seaman prepares to harpoon a wounded whale. (Lithography Saint Aulaire. Photograph Bibliothèque Nationale)

Below: Whaling in the South Seas. (Lithography Lebreton. Photograph Bibliothèque Nationale)

appendix IV

THE SPICE ROUTE

The modern usage of the word *spice* was first recorded in the West in the twelfth century, in a manuscript entitled *Voyage de Charlemagne*, where it appeared in the French form from which the English is derived: *épice*. This is not to say, however, that spices were unknown until then. Herodotus, the Greek historian, mentions *kinnamon*—cinnamon; and the same word appears in the New Testament. In the first century A.D., clove was available to the Egyptians in the marketplaces of Alexandria, although that spice grew only in the Moluccas. The earliest known spice, however, was pepper.

When Rome ruled the world, oriental spices reached the West by the Silk Road and, by sea, from India to Egypt. The best known spices were black pepper, ginger, cinnamon, and clove.

By the Middle Ages, spices had become extremely rare and costly in Europe. The Venetians and the Genoese, enterprising seafaring peoples who imported very limited supplies from the East, called black pepper "the seed of paradise." The custom developed of offering a single grain to a presiding judge—no doubt in hope of obtaining a favorable verdict. The custom persisted in Europe until the end of the 18th century.

The Arabs, the Portuguese (after Vasco da Gama), and the Spaniards (after Magellan), imported black pepper from Malabar, cinnamon from Ceylon, nutmeg

I N D I A

Malabar Coast

Coromandel Coast

black pepper

Bay of Bengal

Sri Lanka (Ceylon)

cinnamon

Colombo

M A L A

Strait of Malacca

Sumatra

ginger

camphor sandalwood

S U N D A

Jav

Jakarta (Batavia)

I N D I A N

O C E A N

0   1 000 km

Taiwan

Tropic of Cancer

PHILIPPINES

P A C I F I C

O C E A N

Cebú

S I A

Borneo

Equator

black pepper

Moluccas

Celebes

Ceram

New Guinea

Ambon

nutmeg

ea

Ujung Pandang
(Macassar)

Banda Sea

curcuma

ava

clove

Port
Moresby

Timor

I S L A N D S

Timor Sea

Darwin

A U S T R A L I A

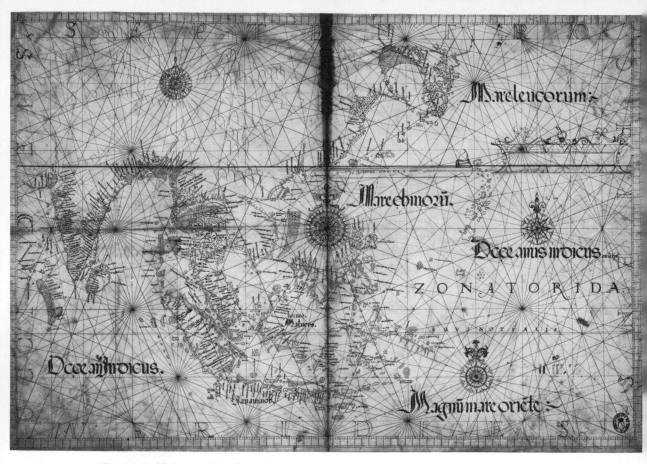

The Land of Spices and the Spice Route as depicted in a Portuguese atlas attributed to Diego Homem. India and Ceylon, of course, are to the left; then, moving to the right, one can distinguish the Malay peninsula, Sumatra, Java and the Moluccas. (Photo Bibliothèque Nationale)

from the Moluccas, curcuma from Java, cardamom from Cambodia, and sandalwood and camphor from Sumatra.

Until the sixteenth century, clove and nutmeg were available only from the Moluccas and the seafaring Portuguese periodically dispatched trading expeditions specifically for the sake of those spices. The Arabs, who provided these and other luxuries to Europe, jealously guarded the secret of their origin. It is known, however, that ginger (a Sanscrit word) came from Malasia and from India. The Banda Islands were known as the "spice islands."

The ascendency of the Portuguese in Far Eastern commerce lasted only eighty years. The Dutch, who already controlled the spice trade in European waters, now began to obtain their supplies directly from the Orient. They took Ceylon, the Sunda Islands, and the Moluccas. And, to supervise and control the traffic in spices, they created the East India Company, which held a monopoly in the trading of spices. Offices of the East India Company were established in the Spice Islands, at Malacca, on the Coromandel Coast, and at Malabar. The central office was at Batavia (now Djakarta), on the island of Java.

The history of the East India Company is the story of an unending struggle in defense of its monopoly and against smugglers. The Moluccas were guarded tightly to prevent illegal trading with the Philippines and Makasar. And the officers of the Company lived in constant dread that plants might be stolen and successfully cultivated on non-Company islands. To guard against such a possibility, all spice trees on the larger islands, which were more difficult to guard effectively, were cut down, and only the trees on the small islands were allowed to flourish and bear fruit. Under such a regime, it is not surprising that there were numerous revolts. These, though put down with severity, eventually brought about the downfall of the Company.

In order to maintain the market in spices, the Dutch resorted to artificial means. Harvests of spices were stockpiled rather than being released, sometimes for as long as sixteen years. In 1760, at Amsterdam, the stockpiles became so huge that it was necessary to burn an enormous quantity of clove and nutmeg.

Despite all the precautions of the East India Company, the French governor of Ile de France was able early in the 1770s to have several clove plants smuggled out of Ambon. As luck would have it, these contraband plants prospered on Ile de France, and the Dutch monopoly was rendered ineffective. Today, the chief supplier of clove (which is used to perfume cigarettes, as well as for cooking) is Zanzibar.

The Banda Islands in the Moluccas provide three-quarters of the world's supply of nutmeg (*Myristica fragrans*).

glossary

ATOLL

A ring-shaped coral formation, surrounding a central lagoon that connects with the open sea by means of one or more passages. The formative process of atolls around volcanic islands was clarified by Charles Darwin, who established that these islands gradually sink into the sea.

BANYAN (or BANIAN)

A fig tree of India, characterized by a root system that is largely above the surface of the ground. The word *banyan* originally was used to designate a Brahman sect. The tree is an object of particular veneration among Buddhists because it was Buddha's custom to teach while sitting under a banyan.

BEACHCOMBERS

This was a term applied to vagabonds—fugitives from justice, deserters, former whalers, and adventurers of all sorts—who were not uncommon in the South Seas in the nineteenth century. The most famous beachcombers escaped a tragic end of one kind or another. They were largely responsible for the introduction among the natives of venereal disease, alcohol, and firearms.

BENJAMIN (or BENZOIN)

An aromatic, resinous substance used in the manufacture of perfumes and certain medicines, obtained from the *Styrax benjoin.*

BETEL

The betel is a twining pepper bush. The term is also used to designate a product derived from the betel; that is a substance that has certain toxic and astringent qualities.

As a mild drug, betel was in much demand among the Indonesians and Chinese, and its use spread into the South Seas.

The betel leaf is customarily prepared as follows: a spatula is used to spread a layer of lime on the leaf, to which is added the areca nut (seed of the areca palm) and a few aromatic seeds. The leaf is then chewed. The immediate effects are acceleration of heartbeat, reddening of the saliva, and discoloration of the teeth.

BONITO

A fish of the *Scombridae* family. There is a blue bonito, and another species whose sides are marked by oblique bands.

BOUGAINVILLE, Louis-Antoine, Count de

Bougainville was born in Paris in 1729. Although his later fame rested upon his maritime adventures, he was first a lawyer, then served as a colonel on the staff of the Marquis de Montcalm in Canada.

He transferred to the navy at the age of 34 and, three years later, in 1766, he was sent on a mission of scientific exploration to the Pacific. After numerous adventures and many accomplishments, he returned to France in 1769, bringing with him a native of Tahiti who created a sensation in the salons of Paris.

He had promised the Tahitian, Aotourou, that he would return him to his native land. To redeem this promise, Bougainville spent a third of his fortune in outfitting a ship. Aotourou, unfortunately, died aboard ship before reaching Tahiti.

Bougainville's account of his voyage, *Voyage autour du monde* (*A Voyage Round the World*), was an enormous success in Europe, and Napoleon made him a Senator and a Peer of the Empire. The book served to awaken public interest in the South Seas generally, and in Tahiti in particular.

Bougainville died in Paris, in 1811.

It is worth noting that the concept of the "noble savage," preached in France by Rousseau and popularized by Bougainville's exploits among his own "noble savages" of the Pacific, was known in England long before either Rousseau or Bougainville. In 1668, almost a half century before Rousseau's birth and a full century before Bougainville's return to France, an Elizabethan novel, entitled *Oroonokao* and written by Mrs. Aphra Behn, told the story of a native of Surinam who lived in "a state of primal innocence." (I owe particular thanks to Jeanine Delpech for having called *Oroonokao* to my attention.)

CALAO

The *Calao* (a Malayan word), also known as the Hornbill, is a bird of the tropical forests. It has a long, curved beak crested by a horny substance. It is immediately known by its peculiar cry.

CASSOWARY

This is a large flightless bird whose head and neck are without feathers. It has a distinguishing horny appendage on its head (known as a "helmet"), which is very tough. A full-grown Cassowary stands almost five feet tall and may weigh as much as 50 kg. It is an aggressive bird, and its strong feet, armed with thick claws, are formidable weapons.

CAURI (or COWRIE)

A small snail found in tropical waters. The shell serves as both money and ornaments in certain parts of Africa and Asia. There are two varieties: *Cypraea moneta* and *Cypraea aurantium*. The characteristic form of the cauri has sometimes caused it to be regarded as a symbol of female sexuality.

CHINESE YAM

The Chinese yam (*Dioscorea batatas*) is a climbing plant, the starchy tuber of which is edible. The taste is not unlike that of the American yam or sweet potato. Uncooked, however, the Chinese yam is toxic. It does not grow wild.

COOK, James

James Cook was born at Marton, England on October 27, 1728. He was the ninth son of a farm worker. Before enlisting in the royal navy, he served as a cabin boy aboard a coal burner. After the Seven Years' War and the taking of Quebec by the English, he first came to the notice of his superiors by his work in the charting of the St. Lawrence River and the coasts of Newfoundland.

His reputation as a scientist led to his appointment as commander of an expedition to Tahiti, the purpose of which was to observe the eclipse of the sun on June 3, 1769. He remained in the Pacific for three years, studying the coasts of New Zealand and Australia. During this three-year expedition, not one case of scurvy occurred aboard his ship—a remarkable achievement for his time.

In 1772, Captain Cook undertook a second voyage to the South Pacific, this time with two ships, the *Resolution* and the *Adventure*. His ships, in search of the Antarctic continent, reached a position of 71°10′. In the course of the same voyage, in 1774, he landed on the island of Malikolo, at Port Sandwich, then at

Erromango—where he and his companions narrowly escaped being massacred. He also landed on Tanna and at the Banks and Shepherd Islands. He charted the archipelago to which he gave the name, New Hebrides.

Here is Cook's log entry, dated July 22, 1774, describing his landing at Malikolo, in the magnificent bay of Port Sandwich: "I decided to go ashore. We were soon face to face with four or five hundred natives, armed with spears and maces. . . . I went forward along, a green branch in my hand. One of the men, who seemed to be the chief of the natives, gave his weapons to a companion and took up a branch similar to the one that I carried. We exchanged the branches."

On Cook's third voyage, in 1776, his ship sailed northward to the Bering Strait in search of a sea passage from the Pacific to the Atlantic. In the course of the same expedition, he discovered the Sandwich Islands (today known as the Hawaiian Islands), where he was killed in February, 1779.

Dumont d'Urville's words on Cook are a fitting epitaph: "Never did a navigator plan an expedition with such talent, never did a man undertake an expedition with such dedication, or achieve it with such ingenuity and success. In him, nature realized the perfect prototype of the mariner."

CRICKET

The national sport of the British. It is played with wooden bats and a ball.

CUT FINGERS

The custom of cutting off the tips of one's fingers, common among the islands of the Pacific and reported by early navigators, is an ancient one. In the wall paintings of many Paleolithic caves, there are hundreds of depictions of the human hand. A large number of them (particularly paintings of the left hand), seem to show mutilation of one or more fingers. From the size and positioning of these hands on the cave walls, it is believed that these hands are those of females.

DAYAK (DYAK)

The Dayaks are a tribe native to Borneo where, until recent times, they followed the practice of headhunting. They practice a religion based upon ancestor worship, and their carved funeral barges are remarkable for their beauty.

The Dayak live in the jungle, in "long houses"—bamboo structures built on pilings that are sometimes two or three hundred feet long. It is not unusual for several dozen families to inhabit a single such structure. They raise chickens and ducks and hunt a species of small black bear native to the island.

D'ENTRECASTEAUX, Joseph Antoine Bruni

D'Entrecasteaux was born in 1739 at Aix-en-Provence in France, and joined the navy at the age of fifteen. In 1785, he became commanding officer of the East Indian Fleet. The following year, aboard the *Resolution*, he campaigned along the Chinese coast, sailed through the Sunda Strait (between the Sunda Islands and the Moluccas), and skirted the Marianas and the Philippines.

In 1791, he was given the mission of finding Jean François La Pérouse, who had vanished three years earlier. With two ships, the *Recherche* and the *Espérance*, he went first to Australia, where he learned that La Pérouse had been shipwrecked in the Admiralty Islands. D'Entrecasteaux was not able to find a trace of the missing explorer there, however. Thereafter, he explored the coasts of New Caledonia, Van Diemen's Land (now Tasmania), sailed among the New Hebrides and the Solomon Islands, and put ashore at the Tonga Islands. He died at sea, a victim of scurvy in 1793

Captain Cook lands on Tanna, in the New Hebrides, holding a green branch in his hand. (Engraving from *Récit des voyages de Cook*. Photograph Bibliothèque Nationale)

An archipelago, off the eastern coast of New Guinea, bears his name.

DRILL

The drill is a tool well known among ancient and primitive peoples. Among the latter, it usually consists of a verticle rod that is made to revolve rapidly by means of a cord and a horizontal rod. It is used to drill holes in hard materials, such as shells.

DUMONT D'URVILLE, Jules-Sébastien-César

In 1820, a young French naval ensign named Dumont d'Urville was assigned to the *Chevrette*. The mission of the *Chevrette* was to chart the waters of the Greek Islands; d'Urville, who was an excellent Hellenist and naturalist, was put in charge of botanical, entomological, and archeological research. Thus it was that the young ensign, while on the island of Melos, heard that a Greek peasant had uncovered a very old statue in his fields. D'Urville notified the French ambassador in Constantinople (now Istanbul), the Marquis de Rivière, who dispatched an emissary to purchase the statue. After a certain amount of haggling, the statue changed hands and was placed aboard the *Es-*

tafette and forthwith shipped to the Louvre in Paris.

The statue, of course, was the *Venus de Milo*—except that when d'Urville first saw it and made a drawing of it, Venus still had both of her arms. It appears that the latter were broken off and lost in the sea, when the statue was being loaded onto the *Estafette* in rough waters.

Subsequently, Dumont d'Urville was assigned to read the report of the *Chevrette*'s expedition before the Academy of Sciences. On that occasion, he devoted ample time to the statue, and described it as follows: "It represents a nude woman, whose left hand, unraised, held an apple. The right hand held a piece of draped cloth. . . . At this time, however, both hands are damaged and detached from the trunk of the body."

In 1821, d'Urville conceived an expedition across the Pacific to New Holland (Australia); but when the time came for the plan to be realized, another officer, Captain Duperrey, was appointed to head it. D'Urville, nonetheless, accompanied the expedition as botanist and entomologist aboard the *Coquille*. The voyage of the *Coquille* lasted thirty-two months. Among the conclusions reached was that New Guinea was a true continent, and that "we must not be put off by the terror inspired by the mention of Papuans; for the Papuans are weak and timid."

At once, d'Urville began planning a new expedition, which would take him back to the South Pacific in search of the fate of Jean François La Pérouse, whose disappearance 38 years earlier had never ceased to intrigue the public's imagination. On this occasion, it was d'Urville himself who was put in charge of the expedition, and, in memory of one of La Pérouse's lost ships, he changed the name of his own ship from *Coquille* to *Astrolabe*.

He visited Australia, New Zealand, the Louisiade Islands, New Britain, and New Ireland, and the northern coast of New Guinea. At Hobart, in Tasmania, d'Urville heard that a well-known British captain and merchant, Peter Dillon, had purchased the silver handle of a sword from a native of Tikopia—an island near Fiji. It was believed that La Pérouse had owned a sword with such a handle. The sword, it appeared, had been found on an unnamed island which, according to d'Urville's calculations, was Vanikoro.

Peter Dillon, in fact, went to Vanikoro in 1827 and there found various articles from La Pérouse's ships; among them, two clocks and four cannons.

D'Urville, learning of this, set sail at once for Tikonia and Vanikoro. In the latter place, he discovered, in shallow water, some anchors, cannons, and cannon balls, already encrusted with coral. The crewmen succeeded in raising a heavy anchor and a short cannon.

Finally, Dumont d'Urville, satisfied that this was indeed the scene of La Pérouse's death, went ashore and had the ship's carpenters construct a memorial to the lost explorer. It was made of stone and surmounted by an obelisk. La Pérouse's name and that of his ship, the *Astrolabe*, were engraved on a lead tablet.

Bruni d'Entrecasteaux, who had hunted throughout the South Seas for traces of La Pérouse in 1793, had passed only a few miles from Vanikoro. Ironically, he had named the island after his own ship: the *Recherche*. In 1832 during the first expedition, the *Coquille* commanded by Duperrey had passed even closer to Vanikoro. Duperrey, rather than Dillon, could have had credit for the discovery; d'Urville never forgave Duperrey for having missed the opportunity.

Dumont d'Urville returned to France by way of the Moluccas, Batavia (Tasmania), the Indian Ocean, and the Cape of Good Hope, after an expedition that had lasted three years. Not a single human life had been lost. The remains of La Pérouse's *Astrolabe* were turned over to the Marine Museum in Paris; and d'Urville's account of his voyage was published by the French government.

After the revolution of July 1830, d'Urville was given the mission of conducting the dethroned king, Charles X, and the royal family across the Channel to England. He accomplished this delicate task with a tact and deference that impressed the new French king, Louis-Philippe. d'Urville was duly rewarded for this singular service. A new Pacific expedition was conceived by the king himself, with d'Urville as the provisional commander of the mission. The idea was widely criticized as having political motivations, and Deputy Arago cruelly attacked d'Urville in the following terms: "Seamen tell us that he is a botanist; but the botanists assure us that he must be a seaman." (Deputy Arago, it should be said, was himself an astronomer with no qualifications for judging seamen, botanists, or hydrographers.)

With two ships, the *Zélée*[1] and the *Astrolabe* (the former *Coquille*, an old ship built in 1811) d'Urville finally sailed in 1837 on an expedition that was to last for three years. The vessels called at Tahiti, where the intrigues of the English missionary, George Pritchard, were just beginning; explored the New Hebrides and the Banks archipelago, "of which," d'Urville noted, "we do not even know the name"; and revisited Vanikoro, where d'Urville had the monument to La Pérouse refurbished.

On two occasions during the expedition, d'Urville, despite the poor condition of his ships and the exhaustion of his crewmen, sailed in search of the Antarctic continent. Finally, he discovered a large body of land, where he went ashore to collect geological specimens. Once there, he named this "block of ancient rock, a witness to distant ages," after his wife, Adélie. Then, good courtier that he was, d'Urville proceeded to name the surrounding rocks after members of the royal family of France: Louis-Philippe, Amélie, Joinville.

D'Urville returned to France in 1840. Two years later, he, his wife, and his son burned to death in a train accident between Versailles and Paris. In those days, it was customary to lock passengers in their compartments.

ECHIDNA (SPINY ANTEATER)

A primitive anteater found in Tasmania and New Guinea. The Echidna is quilled, and digs into the earth with its birdlike beak in search of insects. Its anatomical structure and its reproductive means are very primitive.

The Echidna has no teeth. It crushes its prey between the horny formations of its palate and the upper surface of its tongue. The Echidna bears a single egg, which is incubated for one week in a sort of temporary pouch. When the egg

[1] The *Zélée* was rebuilt at Toulon in 1853 and transformed into a steam vessel. She was still in service in 1885 as a storage ship for gunpowder. She was sold and demolished in 1887—after a career of 76 years.

Joseph Antoine Bruni d'Entrecasteaux. (Bibliothèque Nationale. Photograph Roger Viollet)

hatches, the young Echidna spends the first ten weeks of its life in the pouch. The movements of the newborn Echidna in the pouch cause the mother's milk to flow.

ENTREMONT

The location of an ancient Celto-Ligurian fort. The structure was destroyed by the Romans who, alongside the site, founded Aix-en-Provence in 122 B.C.

EPIPHYTE

A term applied to plants that live and grow while attached to another plant, but without taking their nourishment from the latter. The epiphyte is distinguished from the parasitic plant, which does take its nourishment from its host plant.

FILAO

A very large tree found in the South Sea islands and Australia. The filao, on the basis of its mode of reproduction, is classed somewhere between the gymnosperms and the angiosperms. Its branches are similar to those of the cattail. The wood of the tree lends itself to carpentry and to woodwork.

FIRE-WALKERS

The Polynesian ritual of fire-walking is of religious origin. Participants in the ceremony walk on hot stones and on burning embers, without apparent pain and without physical injury. Before the fire-walking begins, the walkers pray for assistance from their bird gods and from the goddess of lightning. (Concerning the latter deity, even the natives themselves have only very vague information.)

Today, on Raiatea (the Polynesian island where fire-walking originated) and on Mbau (one of the Fiji Islands), the ceremony is nothing more than a tourist attraction.

FISHHOOK

The fishing folk of the Solomon Islands are adept at making fishhooks from various materials. They use mother-of-pearl, ivory, and fish scales. I have a large hook fashioned entirely from a piece of scale. Generally, however, hooks are made in two pieces: a piece of mother-of-pearl or bone, to which a piece of scale is fastened by means of a cord. The piece of mother-of-pearl or bone is often carved in the image of a fish.

The most carefully worked hooks are those used in fishing for the bonito—the staple food of the islands.

HIBISCUS

A member of the mallow family, this genus of plants is native to tropical and temperate areas. The various species of hibiscus have many uses—as sources of fiber for lines and rigging, of wood for canoes, of amber seed, of an edible fruit used in gumbo, etc.

HURRICANE

The hurricane is a violent storm characterized by a gyrating movement of wind converging and ascending, accompanied by dense clouds and heavy rains. The hurricane season in the New Hebrides is from November to March.

IATMUL

Native population of the Sepik Valley in New Guinea, first studied by the American ethnographer, George Gateson.

KORWAR

The Korwar of western New Guinea is an ancestral statue fashioned in a manner peculiar to the natives of that region, who have a particular method of preserving the skulls of their forebears. Once the artist has sculpted the body of the ancestor—always shown holding his shield before him—the actual skull of the dead man is added as the statue's head. "It is a very lifelike representation," writes Maurice Leenhardt. "So much so that it is easy to understand why a New Guinean in trouble comes to take counsel with his ancestor."

LABYRINTH

The Labyrinth was an inextricable maze of corridors built on the island of Crete by Daedalus, as a place of confinement for the Minotaur. The term *labyrinth* is also applied to the meandering stone designs on the pavements of certain churches (for example, the cathedral of Chartres). The latter are also known as "Jerusalem roads," since the faithful follow them on their knees.

LAGOON

A body of water situated between land and a coral reef. Also used to designate the pool at the center of an atoll.

LAP-LAP

The traditional food of the New Hebrides natives, consisting of a base of Chinese yams and taro. The tubers are grated and then ground. The resulting paste is sprinkled with coconut milk and perfumed with aromatic plants, then wrapped in banana leaves and baked between layers of hot stones for several hours.

LA PÉROUSE, Jean François Galaup, Count de

Count de La Pérouse was born in 1741, near Albi, and entered the French navy at the age of fifteen. He fought alongside the Americans in the War of Independence.

After his tour of duty in the New World, he left in 1785 with two ships, the *Boussole* and the *Astrolabe*, on a voyage around the world. He had received instructions for this voyage from the king of France, Louis XVI, who had annotated these instructions in his own hand.

La Pérouse's ships rounded Cape Horn then dropped anchor at Easter Island. From there, they sailed to the Sandwich Islands (Hawaii) and, following a northwesterly course, toward Japan. On this leg of his voyage, La Pérouse discovered the strait to which he gave his name.

While visiting the Navigators Islands (the Samoa Islands), the captain of the *Astrolabe*, Fleuriot de Langle, and twenty of his crew were massacred by the natives.

La Perouse's last report to the king of France was dispatched from Botany Bay near Sydney, Australia, in July 1788. At some point after that date, he, his men, and his ships disappeared.

The position of the sunken ships was not discovered until 1827, when a South Seas adventurer named Peter Dillon found traces of the vessels near the island of Vanikoro. Relics from the *Astrolabe* were also discovered by Dumont d'Urville in 1827, on the barrier reef near the same island, which is one of the Santa Cruz Islands located between the New Hebrides and the Solomons.

In 1958, Pierre Anthonioz, French High Commissioner in the New Heb-

Jean François Galaup, Count de la Pérouse. (Bibliothèque Nationale)

rides, discovered traces of the sunken ship hidden among the coral. He raised a group of bronze cannons and anchors from the site. Then he invited Haroun Tazieff to continue the research. Tazieff explored the site for a month, using dynamite to remove the coral from the area of the ship. Among the items he uncovered was a silver ruble dated 1723 and bearing the image of Czar Peter I. This find established the identity of the vessel; for, in 1787, La Pérouse had paid long visits at the ports of Valdivostok in Siberia, and Petropavlovsk in Kamchatka.

In the course of the investigation, and thanks to information from one of the natives, Tazieff was able to locate the probable whereabouts of the second missing ship from La Pérouse's expedition, the *Boussole*. He did not have sufficient time, however, to verify this information. A local tradition has it that the *Boussole* was the first ship to skin off the southern coast of the island during a nocturnal storm.

Later one of Tazieff's associates, Reece Discombe, a New Zealander, investigated that site and found in a hundred feet of water what appears to be vestiges of the *Boussole:* a silver sword handle and a gold Spanish *real.*

LONDON MISSIONARY SOCIETY

An English religious association that in the nineteenth century inaugurated Protestant missionary in the South Pacific. The Society was first established on Tahiti, and from there spread as far as New Guinea.

MAGELLAN, Ferdinand

On September 20, 1519, a Spanish fleet comprising five ships sailed from the port of Sanlúcar de Barrameda in Spain. This small fleet was under the command of a crippled Portuguese navigator—aged fifty and named Fernão de Magalhães—whom we know as Ferdinand Magellan.

After many years in the East Indies, Magellan had taken service under the Emperor Charles V, and His Majesty had entrusted five ships—half-rotted as they were and manned by convicts—to his new subject.

Magellan sailed westward across the Atlantic and, following the South American coast, noticed many fires lighted by the natives. He therefore christened the land *Tierra del Fuego,* Land of Fire. Rounding the southern tip of the continent (through a strait now known as the Strait of Magellan), he entered unknown waters that he named "Pacific" because of their tranquility. He sailed as far west as the Philippines, where he was killed.

What remained of Magellan's flotilla continued westward to Borneo, then visited the Moluccas. It was not until September 6, 1522, that the sole surviving ship, the *Victoria,* captained by Juan Sebastián del Cano, limped into the port of Sanlúcar de Barrameda. Of the original crew, only 19 men remained. The *Victoria*'s incredibly rich cargo of spices, however, was worth twice the cost of Magellan's entire fleet.

It had now been established that the earth was indeed round, and that the New World was separated from Asia by a vast ocean.

MAHDI

The term used by the Chiites and the Ismaelians to designate their expected messiah.

MARSUPIAL

Marsupials are an order of mammals. They bear their young alive; however, the development of the embryo is not complete when the young is born, but is completed in the ventral pouch peculiar to marsupials. The mother's mammary glands are located in that pouch.

The kangaroo, koala, opossum, phalanger, dasyure and wombat are all marsupials.

MAUPITI

One of the Society Islands.

MENDAÑA DE NEIRA, Alvaro de

Mendaña was the nephew of Don Castro, who was Spanish Viceroy of Peru in the latter half of the 16th century. The viceroy, at the instigation of an adviser, formulated a plan to rediscover a group of islands from which, according to Peruvian tradition, the Inca Tupac Yupanqui had gained fabulous wealth. The mission of finding these legendary islands was entrusted in 1567 to Mendaña who, at the time, was 25 years of age.

Mendaña sailed from Peru with two ships, *Los Reyes* and *Todos Santos.* The ships were lightly provisioned, however, since it was believed that the islands were near the Peruvian coast. To Mendaña's astonishment, the ships sailed westward for 62 days before sighting land—the Ellice Islands. Finally, Mendaña's expedition discovered a group of islands that they called the Solomons. Mendaña explored Guadalcanal, Malaita, and San Cristóbal.

Their stay in the Solomons ended tragically. The Spaniards had taken hostages from among the natives and had destroyed several villages. When the natives ambushed and massacred a group of Mendaña's men, the Spaniards retaliated by murdering their hostages.

The return to Peru was a four-month nightmare, with a mutinous crew decimated by scurvy.

In 1595, Mendaña was commissioned by the king of Spain to colonize the islands he had discovered. With a Portuguese navigator, Pedro Fernandez de Queirós, Mendaña sailed westward once more, but never succeeded in relocating the Solomons.

During the expedition, the Spaniards discovered the Marquesas Islands (named for the Marquesa de Mendoze), where they conducted themselves with singular brutality, killing two hundred natives without provocation. In the Santa Cruz Islands, which they also discovered, they behaved with comparable savagery.

While at the Santa Cruz Islands, Mendaña was stricken with fever and died, along with 47 members of his expedition. It was left to Queirós to lead what remained of the expedition back to Peru.

MISSION DRESS

The classic "mission dress," distributed by the Christian pastors among the women of the South Sea islands, was a mumu: a long, loose garment designed to conceal the figure of the women and, presumably, to inhibit the libido of the menfolk. The women were required to wear these garments on mission property; converts were ordered to wear them elsewhere as well. At first, the women, who were accustomed to having their breasts bare, made themselves more comfortable by cutting holes in the front of the dress—a frivolous practice to which the stern pastors quickly put an end.

MORNE

Morne is a French Creole word, derived from the Spanish *morro*, meaning "little mountain." It is generally used to designate the small, rounded mountain that often dominates a tropical island.

MUNDUGUMOR

A tribe of New Guinea situated along the Yuat, a tributary of the Sepik. The tribe became famous as the result of a study published by Margaret Mead.

NAURU (officially NAOERO)

A Micronesian island, situated to the north of the Solomons and at the level of the Equator. Nauru became independent in 1968. Until then, it was under Australian control.

Since attaining autonomy, Nauru has enjoyed unprecedented prosperity by exporting phosphate without regard for the day when its resources will have

Reverend George Pritchard. (Bibliothèque Nationale)

Rear Admiral Dupetit-Thouars. (Bibliothèque Nationale)

been exhausted. The 3,600 citizens of the island republic share an annual income of some eighty million Australian dollars—one of the highest per capita incomes on earth.

The republic of Naoero, as it is officially known, comprises approximately 21 square kilometers of land, of which about half resembles a bare, lunar landscape.

The republic owns its own airline and shipping line—and the most impressive building in Melbourne. No citizen of Nauru works in the phosphate mines. The actual physical labor of mining is all done by foreign workers.

NEW GUINEA

The name *New Guinea* first appeared on a map (that of Geradus Mercator) in 1569. The island was so designated by a Spaniard, Ynigo Ortiz de Retez, in 1545.

POMARE and PRITCHARD

In 1797, at the time of the arrival of the first Protestant missionaries in Tahiti, the island was ruled by Chief Tu Pomare, who soon adopted the Christian religion.

Tu Pomare died in 1821, and was succeeded by his one-year-old son, Pomare III. Pomare III died in 1827, and was replaced by his sister, Amaita, who took the name of Pomare IV. She reigned for fifty years, until 1877.

Pomare IV signed a request, addressed to the French king, asking that France establish a protectorate over the island. However, the Reverend George Pritchard, who was British consul as well as a missionary, prevailed upon her to rescind the request. Whereupon, Admiral Dupetit Thouars landed French troops on Tahiti and took possession of the island in France's name.

Between 1844 and 1846, Pritchard incited several revolts, until he was finally imprisoned and deported to England. This action brought about a serious international crisis and there were a flurry of diplomatic exchanges between London and Paris. Finally, France expressed her regrets over the incident and agreed to pay Pritchard an indemnity, notwithstanding the fact that he had already been disavowed by the British government.

The Pritchard affair, as it was known, outraged public opinion in France and contributed to the unpopularity of King Louis-Philippe and to his eventual overthrow in the Revolution of 1848.

QUEIRÓS, Pedro Fernandez de

Queirós was a Portuguese seaman who had been a companion and pilot of Mendaña's. He was commissioned by the king of Spain in 1606 to head an expedition "as far as New Guinea and Greater Java." In the course of this mission, Queirós discovered an island that he believed to be the great "southern continent" that every navigator of the time dreamed of finding. He named it *Terra Australia del Espíritu Santo.* Today, it is known simply as Espíritu Santo and is the largest of the New Hebrides group.

In his dealings with the natives of the Pacific islands, Queirós, a devout man, made every attempt to curtail the violence of his men. On Espíritu Santo, he founded a city named New Jerusalem on the bank of a new River Jordan.

Queirós' companions, unfortunately, were not as high-minded as their chief. Defying Queirós' orders, they confiscated a herd of swine destined by the natives for a great feast. This theft provoked a revolt among the natives and, after many casualties, the Spaniards were forced to abandon New Jerusalem and flee the island.

Queirós reached Mexico, but a storm separated him from the *San Pedrico,* under the command of a Portuguese named Luis Vaez de Torres. Torres sailed between New Guinea and Australia, discovering the passageway that today is known as Torres Strait.

ROQUEPERTUSE

Roquepertuse is a Celto-Ligurian sanctuary comprising a porticle and a series of niched pillars. The Celts, who were headhunters, stored the skulls of their enemies there, as is attested by archeological relics found in the south of France dating to an age before Greek and Roman influence was felt in ancient Gaul. The sanctuary was destroyed by the Romans.

RĀMĀYANA

A Hindu epic poem written in Sanscrit approximately two thousand years ago. The legend of Rāma, the abduction of the beautiful Sítá, and the antics of Hanumán, chief of the monkeys, are the principal subjects of the work.

SAGO

The Papuan word for bread, *sago* also designates the starchy substance extracted from the sap of the sago tree (a species of palm), from which a kind of soup is made.

The sago tree (*Metroxylon rumphii*) grows in the damp equatorial soil of Amboina, Sumatra, etc. The sap, strained and mixed with water, produces *sago.* Other varieties of palm serve the same purpose and are also known popularly as "sago trees."

SPONDYLUS

A bivalve mollusk. The spondylus' pink shell is sometimes covered with nettles. It lives on rocky bottoms, in the shallow waters of tropical seas. The ancient Romans had a taste for spondylus flesh, and they ate these mollusks just as we eat oysters today.

TABOO

The word *taboo* first appeared in 1785, in Captain James Cook's account of his Pacific expedition. It is derived from the Polynesian word *tapu,* meaning "forbidden" or "impure." Generally, it refers to a religious system of interdictions applied to something that is considered sacred or impure.

TADJOURA

The Gulf of Tadjoura is located off the coast of Somaliland, north of Djibouti. It is known for its abundance of sharks.

TARO (or EDDO)

A generic name applied to various edible tuberous plants commonly grown in tropical regions and belonging to the Araceae family—*Colocasia, Alocasia,* and so forth. None of these grow wild.

TEA

Tea was a popular beverage among the Chinese as early as the 11th century A.D. In Europe, however, it was unknown, or at least was so rare that, in the 17th century, the English monarch Charles II regarded two pounds of tea as a munificent gift. Yet, by the following century, tea had become so popular in Britain that, in 1715, the English imported 120,000 pounds of it.

TELEFOLMIN

A tribe of cannibal pygmies living on the Upper Sepik in New Guinea. The word also designates a valley, and also the headquarters from which Australian authorities supervised this long-unexplored area. Even now there are no roads into this region. Jacques and Pauline Villeminot have made a particularly valuable study of the Telefolmin tribe.

TORRES, Luis Vaez de

Torres, a Portuguese navigator, served as Queirós' second-in-command during the expedition of 1606 when the New Hebrides were discovered. Upon leaving Espíritu Santo, Torres' ship, the *San Pedrico*, was separated by a storm from Queirós' flagship. Queirós continued across the Atlantic, while Torres, on his own, sailed westward in search of the austral continent—the quest for which had been the primary mission of the expedition. Unable to round the eastern tip of New Guinea, he followed the southern coast in a westerly direction, sailing among the islets, reefs, and currents that make the strait, now known as Torres Strait, so hazardous to navigation.

Eventually, Torres reached the Moluccas and the Philippines, thereby demonstrating that New Guinea is indeed an island. Thereafter, Torres, his ship, and his men all disappeared and were never heard from again. In 1760, English hydrographer Alexander Dalrymple discovered the documents bearing witness to Torres' discoveries. It was Dalrymple who named the strait after Torres.

TROBRIAND, Denis de

Trobriand was an officer aboard the *Espérance* when that ship, along with the *Recherche*, was sent in search of Jean François La Pérouse in 1791 under the command of Bruni d'Entrecasteaux. Contrary to what certain Australian publications have stated, Trobriand was not d'Entrecasteaux's second-in-command. The latter office was held by Hesmiwy d'Auribeau. The captain of the *Espérance* was Huon de Kermadec.

In the *Voyage of d'Entrecasteaux*, which appeared in 1808 under the direction of M. Rossel, we read: "Having rounded Gurnian Island, we sailed northwest, intending to visit the northern part of those newly discovered islands that we know as the Trobriand Islands."

In 1793, with the French Revolution in full swing, d'Entrecasteaux was no longer bound to the traditional practice of naming discoveries after kings and princes. Instead, as new islands were discovered, he gave them the names of his officers. Thus, the Huon Islands were named after Huon de Kermadec[1]; the Beaupré Islands, after Beautemps-Beaupré, the expedition's hydrographer; and Rossel Island after Flag-Captain Rossel.

Trobriand was killed by a bomb in 1809 at Martinique while in command of the frigate *Amphitrite*.[2]

TOTEMISM

The word *totem* is derived from an Algonquin word, *ototeman*, which means "it belongs to my tribe." At the end of the nineteenth century and at the beginning of the twentieth, the word came to designate an ensemble of beliefs or practices by virtue of which a group or an individual is identified with

---

[1] There is also a group of islands, north of New Zealand, known as the Kermadec Islands.

[2] I am particularly grateful to Ms. Gwenola de Carné. Musée de la Marine, for her kindness in making available to me data on the career of Denis de Trobriand.

a particular animal, plant, object, or natural phenomenon.

It does not appear that totemism, as a religious and sociological system, exists among the natives of New Guinea and Melanesia, although several animals are the objects of particular attention among these tribes: the pig, the frigate bird, and the cuscus.

TRIDENT

The trident is a three-pronged spear or harpoon, the tines of which are often barbed at their tips. It usually has a long wooden handle and is used by fishermen to spear fishes and squid. Neptune, the god of the sea, is usually depicted holding a trident.

bibliography

Aubert de la Rue, E. *L'Homme et les Iles*. Paris: Gallimard, 1935.

Bonnemaison, Joel. *Nouvelle-Hebrides*. Paris: Editions du Pacifique, 1975.

Doumenge, François. *L'Homme dans le Pacifique Sud*. Paris: Publication de la Société des Océanists, no. 19, 1966.

Drilhon, Freddy. *Le Peuple Inconnu*. Paris: Amiot-Durmont, 1955.

Dupeyrat, A. *21 Ans chez les Papous*. Paris: Arthème Fayard, 1953.

———. *La Bête le Papou*. Paris: Albin Michel, 1962.

Fortune, R. F. *Sorciers de Dobu*. Paris: Maspero, 1972.

Gaisseau, Pierre-Dominique. *Visa pour la Préhistoire*. Paris: Albin Michel, 1956.

Gourguechon, Charlène. *L'Archipel des Tabous*. Paris: Robert Laffont, 1975.

Guerillot-Vinet, Andrée, and Lucien Guyot. *Les Épices*. Paris: Presses Universitaires de France, 1963.

Guiart, Jean. *The Arts of the South Pacific*. New York: Brazillar, 1963.

———. *Un Siècle et demi de Contacts Culturels à Tanna*. Publication de la Société des Océanistes, no 5, Paris: Musée de l'Homme, 1956.

———. *Océanie*. Paris: Gallimard, 1963.

Lawrence, Peter. *Le Culte du Cargo*. Paris: Arthème Fayard, 1974.

———. *Road Belong Cargo: A Study of the Cargo Movement in the Southern Madang District New Guinea*. Humanities, 1967.

Leenhardt, Maurice. *Arts de l'Océanie*. Paris: Editions du Chêne, 1948.

Malinowski, Bronislaw. *Argonauts of the Western Pacific*. New York: Dutton, 1961.

———. *Les Jardins de Corail*. Paris: Maspero, 1974.

———. *Moeurs et Coutumes des Mélanésiens*. Paris: Payot, 1933.

———. *Trois Essais sur la Vie Sociale des Primitifs*. Paris: Payot, 1975.

Mead, Margaret. *Growing Up in New Guinea*. New York: Morrow, 1975.

———. *Male and Female*. New York: Morrow, 1975.

Neverman, H., E. A. Worms, and H. Petri. *Les Religions du Pacifique et d'Australie*. Paris: Payot, 1972.

Poignant, Roslyn. *Découvertes dans les Mers du Sud*. Paris: Flammarion, 1976.

Shineberg, Dorothy. *They Came for Sandalwood: A Study of the Sandalwood Trade in the Southwest Pacific*. Melbourne: Melbourne University Press, 1967.

Tazieff, Haroun. *Vingt Cinq Ans sur les Volcans du Globe*. Paris: Fernand Nathan, 1974.

Vergniol, Camille. *Dumont d'Urville*. Paris: La Renaissance du Livre, 1930.

Villeminot, J. and P. *La Nouvelle-Guinée*. Marabout, 1966.

photo credits

The color photographs in this book were taken by the author. The exceptions are two photographs by Bernard Sonneville of the paintings on a tree-bark cathedral. A number of the black and white photographs are courtesy of the Musée de l'Homme in Paris, and proper acknowledgement for these is made in the captions of those illustrations.

acknowledgements

Special thanks are due to the following:

Companie U.T.A.

M. Gauger, Resident Commissioner of France in the New Hebrides, and M. Massias, Director of Public Information.

M. Pouillet, Delegate of France on the Island of Tanna.

M. Datchary, Delegate of France on the island of Malikolo, and to M. Langlois, Départements et Territoires d'Outre Mer.

M. Herry.

All were most helpful and made my task much easier than it would otherwise have been.

Dépôt légal 4e trimestre 1976 - Flammarion, éditeur, N° 9684 - N° d'imp : 6360.
Imprimerie Déchaux, 93 Aulnay-sous-Bois - Printed in France.